C000163319

THE WORK OF WORLD LITERATURE

Cultural Inquiry

EDITED BY CHRISTOPH F. E. HOLZHEY AND MANUELE GRAGNOLATI

The series 'Cultural Inquiry' is dedicated to exploring how diverse cultures can be brought into fruitful rather than pernicious confrontation. Taking culture in a deliberately broad sense that also includes different discourses and disciplines, it aims to open up spaces of inquiry, experimentation, and intervention. Its emphasis lies in critical reflection and in identifying and highlighting contemporary issues and concerns, even in publications with a historical orientation. Following a decidedly cross-disciplinary approach, it seeks to enact and provoke transfers among the humanities, the natural and social sciences, and the arts. The series includes a plurality of methodologies and approaches, binding them through the tension of mutual confrontation and negotiation rather than through homogenization or exclusion.

Christoph F. E. Holzhey is the Founding Director of the ICI Berlin Institute for Cultural Inquiry. Manuele Gragnolati is Professor of Italian Literature at the Sorbonne Université in Paris and Associate Director of the ICI Berlin.

THE WORK OF WORLD LITERATURE

EDITED BY FRANCESCO GIUSTI
AND BENJAMIN LEWIS ROBINSON

ISBN (Paperback): 978-3-96558-011-4
ISBN (Hardcover): 978-3-96558-012-1
ISBN (PDF): 978-3-96558-013-8
ISBN (EPUB): 978-3-96558-022-0

Cultural Inquiry, 19
ISSN (Print): 2627-728X
ISSN (Online): 2627-731X

Bibliographical Information of the German National Library
The German National Library lists this publication in the Deutsche Nationalbibliografie (German National Bibliography); detailed bibliographic information is available online at http://dnb.d-nb.de.

Cover design: Studio Bens with an image by Claudia Peppel, collage detail, 2013

In Europe, the paperback edition is printed by Lightning Source UK Ltd., Milton Keynes, UK. See the final page for further details.

The digital edition can be downloaded freely at:
https://doi.org/10.37050/ci-19.

ICI Berlin Press is an imprint of
ICI gemeinnütziges Institut für Cultural Inquiry Berlin GmbH
Christinenstr. 18/19, Haus 8
D-10119 Berlin
publishing@ici-berlin.org
www.ici-berlin.org

Contents

The Work of World Literature

Introduction

FRANCESCO GIUSTI AND BENJAMIN LEWIS ROBINSON

> It's the most interesting thing
> in the world, maybe more
> interesting than the world.
>
> Jacques Derrida, 'This Strange
> Institution Called Literature'

The conception of this volume goes back to a conversation about the state of literary studies that the two of us had in a park adjacent to the ICI Berlin Institute for Cultural Inquiry in the summer of 2018. With the combination of elation and despair characteristic of such conversations, we were remarking on the sheer breadth of literary studies today and wondering what commonalities in the study of literature remained — between, for example, Francesco's work on the theory of the lyric and Ben's interest in post-colonial literature. Two literary scholars of disparate interests and areas of specialization — what of substance did we ultimately have to say to one another? It was in this context that Francesco mentioned the name, Derek Attridge. For Francesco, Attridge was first and foremost a literary theorist, while for Ben he was above all the author of an extraordinary book on the South African writer J. M. Coetzee, which is at once a work of postcolonial literary criticism, a theory of literature, and an ethics.

What is intriguing about the case of Attridge is that these two dimensions of his work are intimately and explicitly related. In *The Singularity of Literature* (2004), his influential intervention in literary theory, Attridge refers to *J. M. Coetzee and the Ethics of Reading*, published in the same year, as its 'companion book'.[1] It is as if the theory of literature, of literature in general, emerges out of a particular literary encounter, in this instance with a postcolonial writer preoccupied with geopolitical, historical, and ethical limits, not least the limits of literature itself. At a certain level of abstraction, one might say, the theorization of literature, of that which is specifically literary, emerges out of an encounter with 'world literature'. For, although Attridge studiously avoids the phrase — indeed, even the word 'world' is noticeably absent from the concepts he develops to explore the literary — by almost every metric Coetzee is taken as exemplary of the emergent disciplinary and discursive paradigm of 'world literature'. It was this constellation that drew into focus the concerns we had idly been seeking to express, namely, what is the place of the literary, of its theorization, of its appreciation, in the expanded field of literature studies that increasingly takes its bearings by the beacon of 'world literature'?

---

1 Derek Attridge, *The Singularity of Literature* (London: Routledge, 2004), p. 3; Derek Attridge, *J. M. Coetzee and the Ethics of Reading: Literature in the Event* (Chicago: University of Chicago Press, 2004).

Taking up the titular phrase of Attridge's more recent book *The Work of Literature* (2015), we proposed to insert 'world' into the title — *The Work of World Literature* — to see what this supplement might bring. We invited Attridge and a group of scholars to the ICI Berlin in June 2019 for a conversation from which the essays in this volume emerged. At first glance, the insertion of 'world' seemed to lend the well-worn phrase on which Attridge draws a distinctive kind of currency. Indeed, our gesture could be said to capitalize on the contemporary proliferation of the term as a normative aspiration or ideal, of which 'world literature' would be a particularly telling case. This topicality owing to the 'world' in world literature, or the topicality lent to literature on account of the modifier 'world', is profoundly ambivalent. On the one hand, world literature presents itself as the most significant expression of the necessary, urgent, and long overdue efforts in literary studies to reckon with and transcend the parochialism and Eurocentrism of its tradition by adopting transnational, transhistorical, and transcultural perspectives. On the other, advocates of world literature have to contend with the suspicion that the currency of world literature is related, as seems all too evident, to an altogether problematic entanglement in processes of 'globalization'.[2] Much of the debate around world literature in fact turns on the question of the relation of literature to the imperious progress, or rather the 'combined and uneven development'[3] of global capital: Is literature

2 See Eric Hayot, 'World Literature and Globalization', in *The Routledge Companion to World Literature*, ed. by Theo D'haen, David Damrosch, and Djelal Kadir (London: Routledge, 2012), pp. 223–31; he also provides a catalogue of the ways that 'world' operates normatively in contemporary discourse in Eric Hayot, 'On Literary Worlds', *Modern Language Quarterly*, 72.2 (2011), pp. 133–34.

3 Warwick Research Collective (WReC), *Combined and Uneven Development: Towards a New Theory of World-Literature* (Liverpool: Liverpool University Press, 2015).

world literature when it critically engages globalization in some capacity, or is world literature rather a function of the global propagation of a capitalist 'world-system' that it uncritically reflects, or even champions?

In any case, we did not mean by our title to capitalize cynically on the currency of world literature as the staging ground, in literary studies, of 'globalization and its discontents'. Rather the intention was to bring into focus the sometimes obscured dimension of the literary in world literature. For the study of world literature, in contrast with the approach Attridge advocates that foregrounds the literariness of literature, tends to be concerned rather with the worldly aspects of the literary enterprise. Its socio-political and cultural references, its contexts and conditions of production, its circulation, distribution, and translation, are taken to be decisive. Consequential for the study of world literature are for the most part criteria that are not in the first instance literary. But what then becomes of the 'work' of literature as distinct from the circuits of labour, production, and activity in which literature is taken up? Is the study of literature without attention to its literariness ultimately worth pursuing? Or does, as some fear, the rise of world literature register, or even solicit, the demise of the work of literature and along with it, as Gayatri Chakravorty Spivak succinctly puts it, 'the death of a discipline'?[4]

The abnegation of the literary in world literature studies is most conspicuous in the paradigmatic quantitative and sociological approaches of Franco Moretti and Pascale Casanova. But even in cases like David Damrosch, who insists on the intensiveness of particular literary experience, the decisive criteria for world literature relate not to

4 Gayatri Chakravorty Spivak, *Death of a Discipline* (New York: Columbia University Press, 2003).

its literary characteristics but to the ostensible relation to the world that it affords. For Damrosch, world literature circulates globally and offers 'a window on the world'.[5] As a rule, the question of world literature revolves around the uncertain status of the 'world' in the phrase. Even advocates who have vigorously defended the literary in the context of world literature, have done so by problematizing the implied understanding of the 'world'. World literature, these critics argue, is for the most part informed by a pre-understanding of what is meant by the world — one that often and too easily conflates the world with the globe of globalization. Spivak's conception of the 'planetary' as an inappropriable alterity led the way in unsettling what Emily Apter calls the 'oneworldedness' on which the discipline of world literature tacitly relies.[6] In a similar vein, Pheng Cheah has recently criticized 'spatial' or descriptive conceptions of world literature which treat literature as a worldly entity within a given world rather than appreciating the 'temporal' capacity of a properly world literature *to world*, that is to open up 'other possible worlds', in a manner that challenges and transforms the established world order.[7]

Cheah's engagement with the concept of world literature leads him to the question that is the title of his book: *What Is a World?* But it is not only the concept of world that threatens to remain uninterrogated in world literature, there is equally an implied assumption about literature.

5 David Damrosch, *What Is World Literature?* (Princeton, NJ: Princeton University Press, 2003), p. 15.

6 Spivak, *Death of a Discipline*, chap. 3; Emily Apter, *Against World Literature: On the Politics of Untranslatability* (London: Verso, 2013), pt. 1.

7 Pheng Cheah, *What Is a World? On Postcolonial Literature as World Literature* (Durham, NC: Duke University Press, 2016), p. 129.

For, like the world, literature too is often taken as given. World literature is a problematic category not only because of the tendentiousness or instability of the world but because of the troubled status of literature. Paradoxically, investigations in world literature, even those committed to socio-political critique, often take the transcultural validity or general applicability of the notion of 'literature' for granted, as if 'literature' as a cultural practice were fully transferable from one culture to another or translatable from one language to another. This scholarly practice is perhaps understandable, although not necessarily justified, when critics engage with contemporary literary production in a globalizing world. Yet it clearly reveals its flaws when deployed in or across different cultures and epochs. Even before the conundrums of *untranslatables* that Apter discusses in *Against World Literature*, the question of an implied translatability of the field called 'literature' poses itself.

In a seminar on 'The Concept of Comparative Literature and the Theoretical Problems of Translation' held at Yale in 1979–80, which Apter quotes in her study, Jacques Derrida observes: 'In order to compare literatures or literary phenomena, I must first know, at least by way of precomprehension, what the literary is, lacking which I risk comparing anything with anything in the name of comparative literature.'[8] The question arises: Do we need to have an idea of what the literary is — or what it does — in order even to conceive of world literature? Or inversely: What is the implied pre-conception of literature that informs world

8 Jacques Derrida, 'Who or What Is Compared? The Concept of Comparative Literature and the Theoretical Problems of Translation', trans. by Eric Prenowitz, in *'Who?' or 'What?' — Jacques Derrida*, ed. by Dragan Kujundžić (= *Discourse*, 30.1/2 (Winter/Spring 2008)), pp. 22–53 (pp. 29–30); quoted in Apter, *Against World Literature*, p. 237.

literature — and is it ultimately even literary? It is the sense of 'literature' in world literature that we propose to explore in this volume. From this perspective, the advent of world literature can be regarded as sign and symptom of a profound uncertainty about the literary, one that is expressed notably in a disparagement of literature that extends even to literature departments, where approaches are now advocated that dispense with the concern for the specifically literary. Attridge's attempt to reinvest or reinvigorate the meaning of the phrase 'the work of literature' in a manner that foregrounds the specificity of literary experience can be read as a counter-response to this contemporary anxiety.

As an intervention into the current state of literary studies, Attridge's work reminds us why we read literature in the first place. His gesture is to reduce the critical, literary-historical, and philological apparatus of literary studies in order to expose a peculiarly literary experience that arguably motivates all literary study, including the particular pleasure of simply reading literature. The work of literature, Attridge argues, is an event that is characterized by singularity, inventiveness, and otherness. For Attridge then, a text is not literary — or non-literary — by essence. It becomes literary when readers let it work as literature, when they do justice to it in a singular act of reading. Attridge thus shifts the question of the object of literary study to what he calls the 'act-event' of the literary encounter.

That 'world literature has to be made' is the point of departure that Ben Etherington and Jarad Zimbler take in their *Cambridge Companion to World Literature*. This approach acknowledges the open, diverse, and contingent character of world literature while also bringing into focus the 'material' of both literary practice and literary criticism in a manner that Zimbler elaborates in this volume.[9] In contrast, to take 'the work of world literature' as the point of departure is to ask instead: How does world literature *work*? What does literature do, perform, enact when it is world literature — and what sort of responses does it solicit in turn? This approach has the advantage of leaving suspended the definition of world literature as an object or field or orientation — indeed it does not even have to be decided whether such a thing as world literature exists. Instead, we will know world literature when it works — and perhaps, like the singular work of literature according to Attridge, each time differently. Each of the essays in this volume presents a response to a particular working of world literature. We neither seek to conceal nor reconcile the differences between the contributions, nor do we consider this volume simply to present a compilation of disparate and possibly incompatible perspectives. Instead we are interested in the way that, taken together, they cast a particular light on tensions inherent to the problematic of world literature. In the remainder of this introduction, we will sketch some of these tensions.

TRANSLATION

A quick look at the numerous monographs and edited volumes in the field attests to the extent to which the practice and problem of translation is central to the concept of world literature. Indeed, in an often-quoted statement by Damrosch — 'World literature is writing that gains in

9 Ben Etherington and Jarad Zimbler, 'Introduction', in *The Cambridge Companion to World Literature*, ed. by Ben Etherington and Jarad Zimbler, Cambridge Companions to Literature (Cambridge: Cambridge University Press, 2018), pp. 1–20 (p. 5).

translation'[10] — translation becomes definitive of world literature to the point of becoming almost coextensive with it. A curious paradoxical aspect, however, is inherent in every act of translation: the rendering of a text, literary or otherwise, in another language is meant to overcome those boundaries that it in fact helps to establish or at least reinforce. Translation seems often to rely on the assumption of the existence of discrete languages while, in turn, it contributes to their normalization and their respective positions of power. This could constitute quite a precarious ground for world literature, especially if, as Robert Young argues, the very idea of a language 'is altogether a Western construction'.[11]

The mutual implication of world literature and translation receives a different articulation in Rebecca L. Walkowitz's discussion of works that are 'born translated' in the context of the production and circulation of English-language novels in the current global world.[12] This peculiar condition undermines notions of authorship, uniqueness, and the original, by showing how such novels are inherently collective works crossing and mixing national and generic traditions, as well as readerships and languages. Yet, one could wonder to what extent such works of world literature are distinctively due to globalization, or whether their proliferation is simply accelerated and intensified by it. After all, literature is to some degree always born in translation. It has always crossed borders, languages, and traditions, as Wai Chee Dimock and Laurence Buell have shown with respect

10 Damrosch, *What Is World Literature?*, p. 288.

11 Robert J. C. Young, 'That Which Is Casually Called a Language', *PMLA*, 131.5 (2016), pp. 1207–21 (p. 1208).

12 Rebecca L. Walkowitz, *Born Translated: The Contemporary Novel in an Age of World Literature* (New York: Columbia University Press, 2015).

to 'American' literature and as Jahan Ramazani claims about poetry's transnationalism.[13] It could indeed be argued that the idea of national literatures — which world literature as a contemporary phenomenon and as an academic discipline is meant to overcome — does not rest on properly literary grounds. In any case, on account of the trans- or post-national literary currents that it brings into view, the acceleration and intensification of the globalization of literature is seen as a source of hope as well as anxiety.

In the space opened between the two axioms 'Nothing is translatable' and 'Everything is translatable', Apter points to the field of tensions that constitute what she calls the 'translation zone' and the challenging position that comparative literature occupies within it. Between the accusations levelled by Spivak in the name of autochthony and Djelal Kadir's denunciation of the dangers of incomparability,[14] Apter acknowledges a need for translation:

> The challenge of Comp Lit is to balance the singularity of untranslatable alterity against the need to translate *quand même*. For if translation failure is acceded to too readily, it becomes an all-purpose expedient for staying narrowly within one's own monolingual universe. A parochialism results, sanctioned by false pieties about not wanting to 'mistranslate' the other. This parochialism is the flip side of a globalism that theorizes place

13 *Shades of the Planet: American Literature as World Literature*, ed. by Wai Chee Dimock and Laurence Buell (Princeton, NJ: Princeton University Press, 2007); Jahan Ramazani, *A Transnational Poetics* (Chicago: University of Chicago Press, 2009).

14 Djelal Kadir, 'Comparative Literature in an Age of Terrorism', in *Comparative Literature in an Age of Globalization*, ed. by Haun Saussy (Baltimore, MD: Johns Hopkins University Press, 2006), pp. 68–77.

> and translates everything without ever traveling anywhere.[15]

Negotiating this treacherous passage between the Scylla of translation and the Charybdis of incomparability in her subsequent book *Against World Literature*, Apter explores the potentiality of *untranslatables* in order to reinstate the moments of difference that translation tends to erase, and thereby accentuate the tensions that traverse that field. The approach based on the philology of untranslatables seems to raise the question of the translatability of 'literature' itself. For the investigation of untranslatables in or as literature either implies a global idea of 'literature' or treats 'literature' as itself affected by the same untranslatability. Apter's challenge to 'world literature' thus destabilizes not only the assumed oneness of the world but also that of literature.

In a characteristic gesture, Attridge in his intervention in this volume shifts the inflection from the work in translation to the work of translation, from product to process. It is a matter of finding strategies that convey the work of literature, indeed in a certain sense take part in the work of literature, while 'acknowledging the unavoidable force of untranslatability'.[16] Focusing on the use of Kaaps in a poem by South African poet Nathan Trantraal, he challenges the idea of translation as a linear movement from *one* source language to *one* target language, as if they were two distinct unitary systems, by considering porous speech communities and variations within a linguistic continuum. Accordingly, translation for Attridge does not aim at do-

15 Emily Apter, *The Translation Zone: A New Comparative Literature* (Princeton, NJ: Princeton University Press, 2006), p. 91.

16 Derek Attridge, 'Untranslatability and the Challenge of World Literature: A South African Example', p. 48.

mesticating the otherness of the original, but rather at creating, 'by whatever means appropriate, an experience that corresponds in some measure to the experience of a reader who's able to enjoy the original directly.'[17] Rather than an equivalent text in another language, translation thus becomes a dynamic and responsive process of approaching the work that envelops a broad field of practices, 'including literal translation, explanation, and suggested equivalents, with the recognition that readers' differing idiolects will mean that different strategies have differing chances of success in different contexts'.[18]

By interrogating the political construction of languages as discrete entities, Attridge's approach resonates with Apter's project. In her Afterword, Apter picks up on Attridge's 'South African example' in order to sketch a genealogy of racialized structures that underpin standardized 'sovereign' languages and dominant forms of translation in a manner that, she argues, projects of 'World Literature' (capitalized) risk reproducing. In order to redress ingrained forms of linguistic violence, Apter explores the possibilities of a 'reparative translation' with radical theoretical and methodological implications for any approach to the work of world literature (without caps).

Translation emerges in Attridge's account as internal to the work of literature. After all, for Attridge, in the act-event of reading a literary work every reader brings their own *idioculture* — their own 'unique (indeed, singular) cluster of attributes, preferences, habits, and knowledges'[19] — to the encounter, regardless of the degree of

17 Ibid., p. 52.

18 Ibid., p. 49.

19 Derek Attridge, *The Work of Literature* (Oxford: Oxford University Press, 2015), p. 61.

familiarity with the language in which the text is written. The singularity of literature, for Attridge as for Derrida, has to do with its iterability which he presents as a play of translatability and untranslatability:

> If singularity names the translatability of both languages and literary works, it also names their untranslatability. That is to say, the process of translation is not a process of exhaustive replication; even exact repetition does not produce an exact equivalence because repetition always takes place in a new context and singularity, as I have said, is always open to context and changes in context.[20]

One could venture that a degree of translation as a process of familiarization and adaptation is always involved in any act of reading and in any singular experience of literature, even when the text being read is in the reader's so-called 'mother tongue'.

In the both active and passive encounter with a text and its singularity, as Jarad Zimbler makes clear in his essay in this volume, 'a dialectic of proximity and distance unfolds.'[21] In other words, the text must present itself to readers with a certain degree of familiarity — in terms of medium, language, form, genre, technique, subject matter — in order for them to be exposed to its otherness. To work as literature, a text must be first of all *legible*, and translation is what can make culturally distant texts relatively familiar and therefore *workable* in other contexts. Zimbler traces how Arvind Krishna Mehrotra's English translations of the

---

20 Derek Attridge, 'Contemporary Afrikaans Fiction and English Translation: Singularity and the Question of Minor Languages', in *Singularity and Transnational Poetics*, ed. by Birgit Mara Kaiser (New York: Routledge, 2014), pp. 61–78 (p. 70).

21 Jarad Zimbler, 'Working Conditions: World Literary Criticism and the Material of Arvind Krishna Mehrotra', in this volume, p. 172.

songs of the fifteenth-century *bhakti* poet Kabir exhibit this kind of domestication for contemporary American readers by offering an analogue to the Beat poetry of the Sixties. A reading that focuses on this transnational domestication, however, risks overlooking the relational literary dynamics that informed Mehrotra's translations and that only 'archaeological' criticism can bring to light. As Zimbler shows, translation across languages, traditions, and epochs plays a significant role in making received literary materials workable again. The 'work of world literary criticism' for which Zimbler argues should, therefore, reflect on 'our capacity for making texts work' and 'the resources that we activate in writing, and in reading, and in writing about reading'.[22]

Attending to transhistorical continuities in lyric poetry, Francesco Giusti in his essay proposes a shift away from the question of the linguistic translatability (or untranslatability) of contextual meaning in world literature in order to think about the transferability of gestures. Literature makes these gestures available for re-enactment in different contexts and it is in the context of each re-enactment that they acquire a specific meaning. Within the discursive mode of the lyric, the notion of gesture — which Giusti develops from Walter Benjamin, Bertolt Brecht, and Giorgio Agamben — could be helpful to account for the transferability of texts across diverse contexts and for an approach to world literature which takes into consideration both the literariness of that world and the fact that texts can perform different functions in different situations. While reading (or 'translating') a poem, even one 'originated' in a culture distant in time or space, or both, readers find themselves sharing those gestures — and thereby participating in a

22 Ibid., p. 177.

peculiar form of transcultural community. It is at the level of gesture that the ethical ground of lyric poetry is to be found.

ETHICS, POLITICS

Although it markets itself as a 'good', world literature is often reproached for downplaying political or ethical considerations. Young, for example, argues that an ethical impetus decisively distinguishes postcolonial from world literature. While world literature presents itself as universal, postcolonial literature, which insists on its partiality and particularity, is engaged in a genuinely universal project that he calls an 'ethics of humanity'.[23] The ostensible neutrality of world literature arguably betrays a more invidious and profoundly political operation, in fact suppressing the cosmopolitan diversity it is supposed to celebrate. In a public discussion with Damrosch in 2011, Spivak expressed the concern that the unproblematic propagation of world literature risked becoming a process in which 'the politics of identity' overcomes 'the ethics of alterity'.[24]

A number of the essays in this volume approach the question of the ethics of alterity in relation to the particular alterity exhibited by literature. Taking up Young's distinction between postcolonial and world literature, Lorna Burns explores the possibility of a 'postcolonialism after world literature', to cite the title of her recent book, that retains 'the dissident spirit'

23 Robert J. C. Young, 'World Literature and Postcolonialism', in *The Routledge Companion to World Literature*, pp. 213–22 (p. 218).

24 David Damrosch and Gayatri Chakravorty Spivak, 'Comparative Literature/World Literature: A Discussion', *Comparative Literature Studies*, 48.4 (2011), pp. 455–85 (p. 467).

of postcolonial thought.[25] Burns criticizes approaches ranging from Pascale Casanova's field-theory to the world-system analysis propounded by the Warwick Research Collective (WReC) for presupposing a priori structures that condition world literature. Drawing on the work of Bruno Latour, Gilles Deleuze, and Jacques Rancière, she argues in contrast for the significance of modalities of 'absolute otherness' in literary works that produce instances of 'dissensus'. Rather than departing from a supposition of 'inequality' or 'difference', Burns deploys Rancière's thought in order to argue for a critical approach that sets out 'to assemble and verify moments of dissensus insofar as they enact an assumed fundamental equality between actors'.[26]

In her essay on extractivism and indigenous form Rashmi Varma is, in contrast, circumspect about the insistence on 'otherness'. If the 'other' is supposed to be outside of or to present an alternative to the capitalist system, then the task of literary criticism is rather to show the ways in which such ostensible alterity is in fact profoundly implicated in and even integral to the system. Rather than reading Hansda Sowvendra Shekhar's collection of short stories *The Adivasi Will Not Dance* as performing an ethics of alterity, Varma reads it as contouring forms of extractivism that make visible otherwise obscured processes of capitalist extraction of adivasi peoples, lands, and cultures in neo-liberal India. Varma, a member of the WReC, shows how treating world literature as '*the literature of the world-*

25 Lorna Burns, *Postcolonialism After World Literature: Relation, Equality, Dissent* (London: Bloomsbury, 2019).

26 Lorna Burns, 'World Literature and the Problem of Postcolonialism: Aesthetics and Dissent', in this volume, p. 73.

system'[27] does not involve immediately reaching for the abstractions of the system as the explanatory instance, but requires rather the finely calibrated work of articulating the uneven development of modernity in the concrete.

In Attridge's theory the work of literature is defined by its 'otherness', an otherness that ultimately resists total assimilation by means of interpretation, translation, or analysis. Benjamin Lewis Robinson's essay approaches the question of the particular alterity of the work in a time of world literature by considering J. M. Coetzee's *The Childhood of Jesus*, in which two kinds of otherness are explicitly played off against each other. The first, which might be called 'other-world literature', belongs to a tradition of literary theology discussed by Derrida in his reading of Kierkegaard's reading of the story of Abraham where the 'secret' of literature lies in the absolute otherness it harbours, as if literature were ultimately not of this world — or as if it presented the promise of another one. The second, exemplary of 'this-world literature', approaches otherness as absolute 'likeness' elaborating differences within the world. The ethical question of world literature in Coetzee's novel depends on the extent to which readers are ready and willing to leave the 'other-world literature' behind.

Attridge sees the work of literature to be inherently ethical precisely because it opens onto and negotiates with otherness. Drawing a provisional distinction between politics as being concerned with the universal and the programmatic, and ethics as addressing the concrete and the singular, Attridge opposes readings of literature that too quickly translate the literary into the political. Dirk Wiemann's essay interrogates this attachment to the eth-

27 Warwick Research Collective (WReC), *Combined and Uneven Development: Towards a New Theory of World-Literature*, p. 8.

ical in the name of a more robust account of the potential politics of world literature. While the ethical account certainly corresponds to a characteristic experience of literature as the encounter between an individual reader and a singular work, Wiemann argues that what is needed is a form of literary reception and critical analysis that brings the collective dimensions of literary experience into focus and ultimately solicits an 'ethics of commitment'. Attridge's concept of 'idioculture', understood as the particular worldly context that the reader brings to the work of literature, ought to be expanded or developed with an eye to the ways in which it intersects with a broader *sensus communis*.

Led by a similar interest in how literature can put us in common or solicit community, but moving away from the level of meaning, Giusti focuses on the movement of individuation and dis-individuation that characterizes the 'act-event' of the encounter of a reader (and potential future writer) with a lyric poem. In the process of re-enacting a poem, readers are brought together as a 'we' in a 'gestural community' that is not based on a pre-existing identity — on systems of knowledge, beliefs, and behaviours — but rather on the shareability of certain transcontextual gestures.

In *The Singularity of Literature* Attridge observes, 'Literature — when it is responded to as literature — is not a political instrument, yet it is deeply implicated in the political.'[28] In different ways, the contributions in this volume have explored this *implication* of the literary and the political. But there is also the question of the relation of literature, especially when it is supposed to be 'world literature', to what is *external* to it. A number of the con-

28 Attridge, *The Singularity of Literature*, p. 120.

tributions in this volume point in this direction by taking up the problematic translation *into* literature of histories and positions that perhaps have nothing or want nothing to do with literature, understood as a particular, historically Western institution. In Robinson's reading, Coetzee's novel radicalizes the question of such indifference to literature by presenting a world without literature; its inhabitants exhibit no interest in, no passion for literature, and the absence of the literary is not even felt as a loss. More concretely, Wiemann's contribution focuses on *Refugee Tales*, a project of translation of (unnamed) refugees' oral histories into literature by well-known British writers, while Varma's essay reflects on the ambivalences of writing about the expropriation of indigenous culture in literary form. Responding to a similar constellation of concerns with particular attention to questions of racial justice, Apter advocates in the Afterword for a 'reparative translation' that seeks to redress the wounds inflicted by violent forms of translation that perpetuate 'white sovereignty on historicized language worlds'.[29]

Within the Rancièrian framework which Burns brings into the discussion, the question can be phrased as the degree to which works of literature that seek to account for the 'unaccounted-for' reinforce or disrupt the 'distribution of the sensible'.[30] Perhaps then world literature is literature that acknowledges what lies outside of the world of literature and resists being inscribed into it. Decisive would be the ways in which the literary exhibits modalities of hos-

---

29 Emily Apter, 'Afterword: Towrads a Theory of Reparative Translation', in this volume, p. 225.

30 Jacques Rancière, *The Politics of Aesthetics: The Distribution of the Sensible*, trans. by Gabriel Rockhill (London: Continuum, 2004); see also Jacques Rancière, 'Ten Theses on Politics', trans. by Rachel Bowlby and Davide Panagia, *Theory & Event*, 5.3 (2001).

pitality, however partial and precarious, to the 'preliterate' or 'preliterary' external body, which is thereby rendered visible or audible and, in any case, available for particular forms of care.

SCALE, PRESENTISM

Wiemann's title 'Being Taught Something World-Sized' brings into focus the question of scale. While the phrase 'world-scale' is often evoked in discussion of world literature, the essays in this volume tend rather to trace the ways in which world literature operates between scales. It is as if the work of literature consists precisely in scaling, in providing passage between otherwise incommensurable experiential and analytic dimensions of the world. Varma, for example, develops the notion of allegory, in Fredric Jameson's sense as 'profoundly discontinuous, a matter of breaks and heterogeneities', as a means of registering the multiple levels on which extractivism operates.[31] Precisely on account of its fragmentary and disjunctive quality, allegory in this way presents a way of mapping ecological imperialism. In contrast, Attridge's essay, which presents a conception of language as differing by degree, indicates how one may approach the translation of literary works, especially of works in 'minor languages', by being attentive to the specific calibre of language used. Treating language as a continuum, rather than emphasizing the ostensible boundaries between (national) languages, presents an alternative way of thinking about how literature articulates the world.

---

31 Fredric Jameson, 'Third-World Literature in the Era of Multinational Capitalism' (1986), reprinted in *Allegory and Ideology* (London: Verso, 2019), pp. 159–86 (p. 170).

So far in this introduction we have avoided the habitual references to the historical precedent for world literature, notably Goethe and Marx.[32] Without denying the value of historical and genealogical investigations of the concept — Aamir Mufti's study of the co-relation between Orientalism and world literature presents one of the most provocative of such approaches[33] — we have sought to insist on world literature as a largely distinct contemporary phenomenon, one that is defined by its presentism. Indeed, the popularity and proliferation of world literature can arguably be considered a symptom of an epoch that is presentist.[34] Giusti shows how world literature risks not only conflating objects of study to include works that cannot straightforwardly be categorized under the contemporary term 'literature', but also the adoption of critical approaches which import contemporary questions — that of translation for instance — into contexts where they do not necessarily apply. At the same time, the presentist disposition tends to occlude the specific temporality of works of literature, such as the transhistorical lyric gestures Giusti traces. A different conception of 'nonsynchroneity' is at the centre also of Varma's reflections on 'combined and uneven development' in adivasi literature. Wiemann's recovery of the 'anagogic' moment of medieval hermeneutics may be read as part of a project to expand the present understanding of literature and reconfigure what literature can do. While in an archeological manner, Zimbler shows with the example of Mehrotra's translations of the songs of Kabir

32 For an expansive take on the historical dimension, see *The Routledge Companion to World Literature*.

33 Aamir R. Mufti, *Forget English! Orientalisms and World Literatures* (Cambridge, MA: Harvard University Press, 2016).

34 François Hartog, *Regimes of Historicity: Presentism and Experiences of Time*, trans. by Saskia Brown (New York: Columbia University Press, 2015).

that the fascination with the actuality or the actualization of world literature, which in this case meant its ostensible Americanization, obscures transnational and transhistorical dynamics responding to local exigencies that are essential to a thoroughgoing understanding of the work as world literature.

In a 1989 interview that Attridge conducted with Derrida and published in *Acts of Literature* under the title 'This Strange Institution Called Literature', Derrida remarks: 'It's the most interesting thing in the world, maybe more interesting than the world.'[35] It's a joke of course but one that is revealing of the present conundrums of literary studies. For if the peculiar fascination of literature that we, following Attridge, have called the work of literature, owes indeed to its being more interesting than the world, then it presents the risk of disparaging the world and discounting its concerns. And this would in turn explain the widespread distrust of literature in the face of more urgent if ultimately less interesting worldly concerns. Within literary studies, the turn to 'world literature' evinces such distrust by deliberately shifting away from what is most interesting about literature in order to attend to more mundane concerns. But 'interest' comes from *inter-esse,* to be among, to be in the midst of, even to participate, to take part in — and for that reason to matter. Perhaps there is then another possible inflection of the phrase: Literature is more 'worldly' than the world. If literature is 'more interesting than the world' it is not because it transports beyond the world but rather because it engages in the world — it is an intensification of the world.

35 Derek Attridge, '"This Strange Institution Called Literature": An Interview with Jacques Derrida', trans. by Geoffrey Bennington and Rachel Bowlby, in Jacques Derrida, *Acts of Literature,* ed. by Derek Attridge (London: Routledge, 1993), pp, 33–75 (p. 47).

ACKNOWLEDGMENTS

We would like to thank the ICI Berlin for making both the workshop and this publication possible. Christoph F. E. Holzhey and Manuele Gragnolati showed enthusiasm for the project from the start and we are particularly pleased that this volume will join the *Cultural Inquiry* series and the new venture of the ICI Press. Claudia Peppel was a tireless source of support and inspiration, and we have her to thank for the cover image. Arnd Wedemeyer's comments were most helpful. We would like to extend our thanks to all the contributors to this volume as well as to the interlocutors who joined us for the workshop in the summer of 2018, especially Refqa Abu-Remaileh, who led the concluding discussion.

Untranslatability and the Challenge of World Literature

A South African Example

DEREK ATTRIDGE

WHAT IS A LANGUAGE?

Serbo-Croatian no longer exists. Having been acknowledged by this name for well over a century and spoken by some sixteen or seventeen million people, the language disappeared without trace when the state of Yugoslavia disappeared. It was replaced by four separate languages, Serbian, Croatian, Bosnian, and, more recently, Montenegrin. Of course, the inhabitants of these four countries didn't start speaking differently at this moment in history, and they continue to understand one another without difficulty, but

* Research carried out at the Stellenbosch Institute for Advanced Study (STIAS), Wallenberg Research Centre at Stellenbosch University, Stellenbosch 7600, South Africa.

nationalist sentiment prohibits the idea of a single language with four (or more) dialects — or, more accurately, a continuum of language use over the entire geopolitical area, and to some degree across its borders, permitting mutual intelligibility. Thus a comment on a BBC website can claim, in defiance of linguistic history, that these new languages 'have separate histories, developments, origins and most importantly identities. Even though they can be mutually understood by its speakers, they are not and cannot be one language [...] The term "Serbo-Croatian" is a communistic fantasy language which existed only on paper.'[1]

This example makes the *political* basis of what we call 'natural languages' strikingly evident, and a similar picture could be drawn by looking at actual language use in many parts of the globe.[2] Whatever the origin — and it's disputed — of the saying 'A language is a dialect with an army and a navy', it captures nicely the political and hegemonic determination of those systems of speech we unthinkingly call 'languages'. Enshrined in the doxa, and operative in many scientific spheres, is the view that the domain of

---

1 Marjina, '"Serb-Croation" is a Communistic Fantasy Language', in 'Your Say — Language and Identity', BBC <http://www.bbc.co.uk/languages/yoursay/language_and_identity/serbiancroatianbosnian/serbocroatian_is_a_communistic_fantasy_language.shtml> [accessed 27 August 2019].

2 A good example is the co-existence of languages called 'Urdu' and 'Hindi': Aamir Mufti observes that '[p]art of the difficulty of making this argument about Hindi-Urdu as a spectrum, which is instinctually evident at various levels to native speakers, is that there is no name for this more encompassing and contradictory linguistic formation — whether Hindi, Urdu, or Hindustani — that is not subject to the terms of the conflict itself: Indian and Pakistani speakers, for instance, routinely use 'Hindi' and 'Urdu' respectively, to refer to exactly the same common speech forms', in Aamir R. Mufti, *Forget English! Orientalisms and World Literatures* (Cambridge, MA: Harvard University Press, 2016), p. 120.

language — *le langage* in Saussure's classification — consists of distinct, named, languages — *les langues* — as the unmarked, 'natural', entities, and that there are subsidiary, and often less prestigious, variants that can't be classified in this way and are marked as 'dialects'. Samuel Weber describes the reality with his customary perspicacity:

> Usually, the linguistic systems between which translations move are designated as 'natural' or 'national' languages. However, these terms are anything but precise or satisfactory. 'Portuguese,' for instance, although named for a specific nation, is no more a 'national' language than is 'English,' 'French,' 'German' or 'Spanish.' Yet, to call these languages 'natural' is perhaps even more unsatisfactory than to designate them as 'national.' The imprecision of such terms is in direct proportion to the linguistic diversity they seek to subsume.[3]

A more accurate account, then, would be that the domain of natural language — which we may think of as the global totality of the psychological mechanisms and internalized lexicons enabling speech — is a multidimensional continuum, and that it is the distinct, named, languages that are artificial and marked.[4]

---

3 Samuel Weber, 'A Touch of Translation: On Walter Benjamin's "Task of the Translator"', in *Nation, Language, and the Ethics of Translation*, ed. by Sandra Bermann and Michael Wood (Princeton, NJ: Princeton University Press, 2005), pp. 65–78 (p. 66). Emily Apter, also quoting from Weber's essay and building on the work of Edouard Glissant, argues that Creole, understood as a loose umbrella term for language varieties that don't sit easily under standard language names, 'denaturalizes monolingualization, showing it to be an artificial arrest of language transit and exchange' (*The Translation Zone: A New Comparative Literature* (Princeton, NJ: Princeton University Press, 2006), p. 245).

4 Naoki Sakai makes the interesting suggestion that languages are not empirically verifiable but operate like Kantian regulative ideas, in 'How Do We Count a Language? Translation and Discontinuity', *Translation Studies*, 2 (2009), pp. 71–88.

Each of these named languages has a singular history, usually with a political dimension, arising from the domination of one group over others and often part of a nationalistic endeavour.[5] (The affirmation of a named language can contribute to a movement of resistance against a hegemonic power, such as the promotion of Irish in the early twentieth century and the current campaign on behalf of Catalan; though if a resistance movement of this type is victorious it inevitably continues to champion the language as a unifying nationalist instrument.) The establishment of a written form of the language with an agreed orthography is frequently part of the process, as is the creation of dictionaries and grammars; writers of literary works, too, can play an important role in the promotion and stabilization of a language, a well-known example being Dante's choice of the Tuscan dialect for the *Commedia*.

If we think not in terms of discrete languages but in terms of speech communities, we can reconceptualize global linguistic variation as a matter of groups of individuals each of whose use of language is intelligible within the group. Such communities are porous, overlap with one another, and are subject to continual change as a result of movement and interaction. They can also be seen to exist at various levels: members of a small group may be able

---

5 George Steiner follows Herder in advancing a strong version of the commonplace idea that languages themselves possess an identity: 'I am suggesting that the outwardly communicative, extrovert thrust of language is secondary. [...] The primary drive is inward and domestic. Each tongue hoards the resources of consciousness, the world-pictures of the clan. [...] [A] language builds a wall around the "middle kingdom" of the group's identity. It is secret towards the outsider and inventive of its own world', in *After Babel: Aspects of Language and Translation*, 3rd edn (Oxford: Oxford University Press, 1998), p. 243. A less naïve view is reflected in Benedict Anderson's discussion of the role of 'languages-of-state' in nineteenth-century European nationalisms in *Imagined Communities*, 2nd edn (London: Verso, 1991), ch. 5.

to communicate with one another in a thoroughgoing and detailed way but with members of a larger group in a more limited manner — this might be the case for a speaker of Swedish in the context of Scandinavia, say. Even the family can operate in this way, achieving an intimacy of communication impossible in wider groups. The speech practices of a particular individual constitute a unique *idiolect*, that is to say, a singular combination of the elements conventionally regarded as belonging to specific languages or dialects.[6] An individual's idiolect is the product of a unique personal history, usually involving exposure to several kinds of speech practice; one can think of it as an aspect of what I've called the individual's *idioculture*, the particular constellation of knowledge, memories, presuppositions, habits, abilities, prejudices, tastes, affective tendencies, and so on operative at any one time to constitute the subject. (An idiolect is not the same as a 'private language'; every element in an idiolect is shared, though not necessarily all elements are shared with the same group of speakers, and the same is true of an idioculture, which is a way of looking at subjectivity as an open, cultural process rather than the closed entity suggested by terms like 'self' or 'individual' — or, for that matter, 'subject'.) A spontaneous utterance will usually reflect its author's idiolect, though certain types of written text are designed to minimize idiolectal features.[7]

---

6 The term is not always understood by literary critics. Rebecca Walkowitz's use of it, for instance, is hard to distinguish from 'dialect'; thus the work of Chang and Voge is said to be 'full of idiolect', in *Born Translated: The Contemporary Novel in an Age of World Literature* (New York: Columbia University Press, 2015), p. 220.

7 Some interpretations of idiolect continue to rely on a conventional notion of language: an idiolect is regarded as the version of a language spoken by an individual. I am using it to designate the totality of an individual's language knowledge and habits, which may include the ability to speak one or more languages in the conventional sense.

Though the idea that languages do not exist except as constructions that are artificial, after the fact, and often political in origin goes against common assumptions, it's not news to linguists who study language variation. In the standard textbook on dialectology, Chambers and Trudgill explain that 'a "language" is not a particularly linguistic notion at all':[8] they speak instead of 'dialect continua' linked by a chain of mutual intelligibility between neighbouring areas. Examples are the West Germanic continuum, including what we call German, Dutch, and Flemish, and the Scandinavian continuum, comprising Norwegian, Swedish, and Danish, itself part of the North Germanic continuum. The languages that were once subsumed under the label Serbo-Croatian are all part of the South Slavic continuum, which also includes Macedonian and Bulgarian. A similar picture emerges in most parts of the world, with social distinctions playing a part in addition to geographical spread in producing continua. The stronger the nationalist agenda of the state power, the more likely there will exist something like a language, enshrined in grammars and dictionaries and often policed by an academy.

My example today is the South African language — or the particular section of the West Germanic continuum — we know as 'Afrikaans' (which simply means 'African', and derives from the older term 'Afrikaans-Hollands', that is, 'African Dutch', to distinguish it from the Dutch of the Netherlands). But first I want to give some attention to the consequences for literary study, and, more particularly literary translation, of acknowledging the reality of language use as I have described it.

8 J. K. Chambers and Peter Trudgill, *Dialectology*, 2nd edn (Cambridge: Cambridge University Press, 1998), p. 4.

'WORLD LITERATURE' AND TRANSLATION

Robert Young, in an important article titled 'That Which Is Casually Called a Language', argues that

> the idea of a language, and of languages in a socio-cultural sense, is altogether a Western construction, part of the same process whereby Europeans produced indigenous law from custom, races and castes from ethnological or anthropological semiotics, or cultures from varieties of social institutions and human behaviour.[9]

Young points out that even the well-intentioned promotion of 'multilingualism' relies on a notion of 'separate, classifiable, and classified single languages, each of which by definition is marked by a border that ensures unity, like the boundary of a nation', and argues that '[i]n considering the idea of world literature, we need to reflect on the history of the construction of languages and to question any assumption of an intrinsic relation between languages and geographic location or ethnic, indigenous, or other identity'.[10]

Central to any conception of 'world literature' is translation. One of the most influential definitions, that of David Damrosch, includes the statement, 'World literature is writing that gains in translation', and Damrosch insists that 'the study of world literature should embrace translation far more actively than it has usually done to date'.[11]

---

9 Robert Young, 'That Which Is Casually Called a Language', *PMLA*, 131.5 (2016), pp. 1207–21 (p. 1208). Young gives examples of theorists — e.g. Trubetzkoy and de Courtenay — who resist the usual model.

10 Ibid., p. 1209.

11 David Damrosch, *What Is World Literature?* (Princeton, NJ: Princeton University Press, 2003), pp. 288–89. Nicholas Harrison presents a telling critique of this claim in 'World Literature: What Gets Lost in Translation?', *Journal of Commonwealth Literature*, 29 (2014), pp. 411–26.

An alternative view would be that translation is something like a necessary evil in avoiding the conception of 'world literature' as simply the totality of non-communicating literary traditions. In either case, the work of translators is unavoidable in making up for the inevitable limitations of readers. Young perhaps overstates the case in suggesting that the practice of translation only emerged when the idea of separate languages became established, and that 'the whole point of translation is to keep languages apart. [...] Not to carry meaning across languages but to confirm the presumption of the division between them',[12] but it's surely correct that the current dominant conception of translation relies on, and helps to entrench, the notion that languages are discrete and self-contained. A text in source language *a* is translated into a text in target language *b*, and the translated text is roughly the same length as the original text. Saussure's highly influential positing of *langue*, the autonomous system held at any given time in the minds of a language community, as the proper object of linguistic study, does nothing to dispel this idea, and, through his positing of the science of semiotics, extends it to other cultural sign-systems.

The question I wish to address is this: How does our conception of translation, and therefore of world literature, change if we revise our understanding of language so as to give full weight to the spectrum of human linguistic activity and to acknowledge the historical and politically-influenced character of named languages? I want to tie this question to the issue of literary experience, which includes the pleasure we take in literary works, the responsibility we are under as readers to do justice to the work's singularity, and the ontological status of the work as event.

12 Young, 'That Which Is Casually Called a Language', p. 1217.

One way of approaching these questions is to ask how the procedures of translation have to change when the source text is not in a named language but occupies a place in the continuum at which the resources of more than one of those languages are drawn on. The challenge of translating a text in which two or more languages are used has often been discussed; long passages of *War and Peace*, for instance, are in French — does the translator leave them in French, assuming the reader will cope in the same way that Tolstoy assumed the Russian reader would cope, or translate them into the target language, resulting in the disappearance of their linguistic distinctiveness? One reason for the impossibility of translating *Finnegans Wake* is the multiplicity of tongues in which it's written: it can be seen, in fact, as Joyce's full-blown attack on the idea of separate languages. Jacques Derrida selected a phrase of two words from the *Wake* — 'he war' — to spell out the difficulties that arise for translation, stressing that what the translator is dealing with is an *event*:

> To translate 'he war' into the system of a single language — as has just been tried in French ('et il en fut ainsi') — is to erase the event of the mark, not only what is said in it but its very saying and writing, the mark of its law and the law of its mark. The current concept of translation is still regulated according to the twice one, the operation of passing from one language into another, each of them forming an organism or a system the rigorous integrity of which remains at the level of supposition, like that of a body proper.[13]

Finnegans Wake may be a limit-text but, as I've argued in another context, it may also be seen as an extreme that reveals

13 Jacques Derrida, 'Two Words for Joyce', in *Post-structuralist Joyce: Essays from the French*, ed. by Derek Attridge and Daniel Ferrer (Cambridge: Cambridge University Press, 1984), pp. 145–59 (p. 156).

the nature of the centre: any literary text, in so far as it is literary in the fullest sense, challenges the constraints that arise from a conception of a language as an autonomous body.[14] My question can be generalized further, then: what would the consequences be of taking non-standard languages and cultures (what would conventionally be called 'mixed' languages and cultures) as the norm of speech practice rather than the standard, named, languages?

AFRIKAANS, ENGLISH, AND KAAPS: A POETIC EXAMPLE

The Afrikaans language is one of the world's youngest. It descends from the Dutch of the original colonial power in South Africa — the first ships arrived at the Cape of Good Hope in 1652 — but bears the traces of a number of other languages into which its speakers came into contact, including indigenous languages and those of slaves imported from the East. Beginning in the eighteenth century, a relatively stable version of the linguistic mixture gradually emerged, derived at least in part from the simplified version of Dutch used by the slaves and by their masters in speaking to them.[15] (The earliest written documents in what is recognizably Afrikaans were in Arabic script.) The establishment and recognition of Afrikaans became a polit-

---

14 Derek Attridge, 'Deconstructing Digression: The Backbone of *Finnegans Wake* and the Margins of Culture', chapter 8 of *Peculiar Language: Literature as Difference from the Renaissance to James Joyce* (Ithaca, NY: Cornell University Press, 1988).

15 The origin and history of Afrikaans remains subject to debate; Wannie A. M. Carstens and Edith H. Raidt, in *Die Storie van Afrikaans: Uit Europa en van Afrika* (Pretoria: Protea Boekhuis, 2017), provide a table showing 19 different theories (pp. 428–30). One reason for the many different accounts is that the myth of the 'pure' language requires an appropriate origin story, which may not correspond to the factual evidence.

ical project in the nineteenth century: the 'Genootskap van Regte Afrikaners' (or Fellowship of True Afrikaners) was formed in 1875, and set to work creating the dictionaries and grammars needed to constitute the new way of speaking and writing as a language in its own right, clearly distinguishable from Dutch. Formal recognition (but only as a 'variety of Dutch') was achieved with the passing of the Official Languages of the Union Act of 1925. Of the types of Afrikaans that existed at that time, preference was given to 'Oosgrensafrikaans' (Eastern border Afrikaans), the language of the Boer republics, in preference to 'Kaapse Afrikaans' (Cape Afrikaans, to which I'll return) and 'Oranjerivierafrikaans' (Orange River Afrikaans, influenced more strongly by the indigenous Khoi languages). Eventually, the 1961 Constitution of the newly-declared Republic of South Africa demoted Dutch and made Afrikaans one of the two official languages with English. (As a footnote: the arrival of democracy in 1994 meant the recognition of eleven official languages.)

Part of the unacknowledged rationale for the project of establishing a 'true' Afrikaans was the fact that the language spoken by the white descendants of European immigrants was worryingly close to the language spoken by the people known as 'Coloureds' — many of them the descendants of slave-women impregnated by their Dutch-speaking masters. So Afrikaans had to be instituted and safeguarded as a pure language spoken by white people, and differentiated from the similar language spoken by those who were not white. One way of doing this was to exclude 'anglicisms', thus establishing a clear difference between white Afrikaans and the version spoken by the Coloured community (largely in the area around Cape Town and on the West Coast), which did not operate any such exclusion. Members of this community frequently drew, and continue to draw, on English vocabulary in their speech, giving it a distinctive lexical character in combination with a distinctive pronunciation. The white version of Afrikaans was promoted and regulated by the Afrikaner Nationalist government that came to power in 1948, and Afrikaans writers did much to create the norms of the language and give it richness and prestige. The speech of the Cape Coloured community, lacking an army and a navy, could then be safely classified as a mere 'dialect' of Afrikaans.[16]

One might think, and many in South Africa did and perhaps still do think, that this so-called 'dialect' is the first language of fewer speakers than Afrikaans 'proper', but the reverse is the case. Afrikaans — in all its varieties — is spoken as a first language by around seven million people, and some 60% of these Afrikaans speakers would have been classified as 'non-white' under apartheid.[17] In the light of what I have been saying, it's of course a simplification to assert that there are just two types of Afrikaans, sharply distinct from one another; continua exist among both white and non-white speakers as well as between the two groups. But thanks to the efforts of the Afrikaans Taalkommissie (Language Commission) of the Akademie vir Wetenskap en Kuns (Academy for Science and Arts) the historically white version of the language has relatively

---

16 For a useful account of the history of Afrikaans that stresses the role played by non-white speakers, see Menán van Heerden, 'Afrikaans: The Language of Black and Coloured Dissent', *South African History Online* <https://www.sahistory.org.za/article/afrikaans-language-black-and-coloured-dissent> [accessed 27 August 2019].

17 See the figures from the 2011 census (the most recent) at <http://www.statssa.gov.za/census/census_2011/census_products/Census_2011_Census_in_brief.pdf>, p. 26 [accessed 27 August 2019]. For a comprehensive account of South Africa's languages, see *Language in South Africa*, ed. by Rajend Mesthrie (Cambridge: Cambridge University Press, 2002).

well-defined boundaries. It's often referred to as 'standard Afrikaans' ('Standaardafrikaans'), but to give it this name is to perpetuate the implication that it's the unmarked form and all other varieties are dialects. The Afrikaans spoken in the Coloured community of the Cape, often referred to as 'Kaapse Afrikaans', 'Afrikaaps', or simply 'Kaaps' (though its speakers mostly just think of it as Afrikaans) lacks a governing academy and is not enshrined in scholarly publications such as dictionaries.[18] Few literary works have employed it (though the picture is changing).[19]

Though there is no standard form of Kaaps — different speakers will use more or less English, for example, and do so for different purposes and in different situations — and no fixed orthography, the positing of a distinct language with its own name is an important weapon in the struggle to acknowledge the speech habits of this section of the population as equal to those of white Afrikaners — which is, of course, also a struggle to gain respect for the culture of this community. I shall therefore follow suit in referring to Kaaps as a language, in spite of my reservations about the identification of separate languages. As was the case with 'white' Afrikaans, writers using Kaaps — which is primarily a spoken language — have played and will continue to play a crucial role in securing for Kaaps the prestige and stability it needs. As Rebecca Walkowitz, summarizing what she calls 'the celebration of the untranslatable', puts it, 'By using nonstandard versions of a national language, a work opposes political and cultural homogenization, both

18 Coloured children are taught 'standard Afrikaans' at school, however, though some literature in Kaaps may be studied.

19 The most significant writer using Kaaps during the apartheid years was Adam Small (1936–2016), whose plays and poems in the language revealed the rich resources it offered. See <https://www.litnet.co.za/adam-small-1936/> [accessed 27 August 2019].

the kind imposed by other speakers of that language and the kind imposed by translators and publishers.'[20]

One of the newer writers to make use of Kaaps is Nathan Trantraal. Born in Cape Town, he is the author of three collections of poems and a graphic novel. I have selected one of the poems that appeared in 2013 in his debut collection, *Chokers en survivors*,[21] in which Trantraal developed an orthography to reflect the pronunciation of Kaaps and captured the manner in which English words and phrases pepper the primary use of Afrikaans.[22] (Linguists call this process 'code-switching', a term which, of course, perpetuates the idea that languages are completely separate, existing as distinct systems in the brain.) Notice, by the way, that speakers of Kaaps operate two phonological systems: English words are pronounced as English, Afrikaans words as Afrikaans, both in a distinctive accent.

Woensdag, sestien Februarie neëntien-ag-en-tagtig

Ek is nog klein.
Ek staan allien innie agtejaat
by my ouma-hulle hys en ek voel sad
omdat ek wiet vandag isse boring, unimportant dag.
Ek wiet die dag het niks gedoen
wattit worthy maak om onthou te wôtie.
Ek voel sad omdat ek wiet daa was al dysende dae
soes dié wat ek al kla vegiet et.
'n Mens kyk trug op jou liewe ennie goed wat ytstaan,
dai is vi jou jou liewe.

---

20 Walkowitz, *Born Translated*, p. 32.

21 Nathan Trantraal, *Chokers en survivors* (Cape Town: Kwela Books, 2013). Trantraal has published two further collection of poems, *Alles het niet kom wôd* and *Oolog* (Cape Town: Kwela Books, 2017 and 2020). He is also the author of a collection of stories written in Kaaps, *Wit issie 'n colour nie* (Cape Town: Kwela Books, 2018).

22 Brian Lennon discusses such 'plurilinguistic texts' in *In Babel's Shadow: Multilingual Literatures, Monolingual States* (Minneapolis: University of Minnesota Press, 2010).

Maa dai issie die liewe nie.
Dai issie highlights reel.
Jou liewe isse klom dae wat niks gebee nie.

Ek stap narrie wasgoed wat oppie lyn hang,
ek sit my hand tien 'n nat handdoek
en ek dink ek gaan nooit die dag vegietie.

To provide some sense of how far the language of the poem deviates from 'correct' Afrikaans, here's a version in which I've ironed out the 'irregularities' as well as the instances of English.[23] Most of these irregularities are there to reflect the typical pronunciation of a speaker of Kaaps. For instance, a distinctive feature of Afrikaans syntax is its handling of negatives: all negative words, such as 'niks' and 'nooit' — 'nothing' and 'never' — are followed at the end of the sentence by 'nie'; in the Kaaps represented in Trantraal's poetry, this is reduced to '-ie' at the end of the word, as in 'wôtie' and 'vegietie'. In this version, I've restored 'nie' where appropriate.

Woensdag, sestien Februarie neëntien-ag-en-tagtig

Ek is nog klein.
Ek staan alleen in die agterplaas
by my ouma-hulle se huis en ek voel hartseer
omdat ek weet vandag is 'n vervelige, onbelangrike dag.
Ek weet die dag het niks gedoen
wat dit die moeite werd maak om onthou te word nie.
Ek voel hartseer omdat ek weet daar was al duisende dae
soos dié wat ek reeds klaar vergeet het.
'n Mens kyk terug op jou lewe en die goed wat uitstaan,
daardie is vir jou jou lewe.
Maar daardie is nie die lewe nie.
Daardie is die hoogtepunte spoel.
Jou lewe is 'n klomp dae waarin niks gebeur nie.

---

23 My thanks to Imke van Heerden, Heinrich Gerwel, and Andrew van der Vlies for their assistance in this process.

Ek stap na die wasgoed wat op die lyn hang,
ek sit my hand teen 'n nat handdoek
en ek dink ek gaan nooit die dag vergeet nie.

If poetry like this is going to be appreciated beyond a very narrow circle, and its political importance registered, it needs to be translated. How are we going to translate this poem for an Anglophone readership? There is no version of English that I know of that could capture a similar use of the words of a different language, and no way the difference in cultural prestige between the principal language and the secondary language could be replicated. (I suspect it would be difficult in any language.) In the following version, I've simply translated the non-English words into English, and left the English words as they are.

Wednesday, 16 February 1988

I am still little.
I am standing alone in the back yard
at my grandma and them's house and I feel sad
because I know today is a boring, unimportant day.
I know the day has done nothing
that makes it worth remembering.
I feel sad because I know there have already been thousands of days
like those I have already completely forgotten.
A person looks back on your life and the things that stand out:
That, for you, is your life.
But that isn't life.
That is the highlights reel.
Your life is a bunch of days when nothing happens.

I walk to the washing hanging on the line,
I put my hand against a wet towel
and I think I am never going to forget this day.

I think it works fairly well as a poem in English, conveying the thoughts of a child grappling with the sense of a past made up of unmemorable days leading up to yet another unmemorable day — and then finding that this day has turned into a memorable day precisely through the thinking of those thoughts. The hints of an impoverished childhood (which are much stronger in many of Trantraal's other poems) — the boredom, the lack of stimulation as he hangs about in his grandmother's back yard, and the washing on the line — contribute to the value of the discovery at the end of the poem. And the sensory vividness of the wet towel, the arbitrariness of which contributes to the poem's realism at this point, is part of the child's experience of unexpected significance.

But the losses are great in this version: there's none of the colloquial tang that suggests a particular environment, social class, and — this being South Africa — racial community. Part of the reason for Trantraal's success is his challenge to the pieties of Afrikaner linguistic purism: for white Capetonians to see the language they hear on the street every day given the status of print in a poetry collection constitutes, for many, a surprise (pleasant or unpleasant), and for Coloured readers of poetry, it's an affirmation of the value of their discourse and culture. Trantraal is on record as complaining that Adam Small used the language largely for comic purposes,[24] and although he himself does the same in many of his poems, this example shows how it can participate in something that may be light in tone but has real depth.[25] And, of course, the translation loses

24 Small in fact played an important role in promoting the dignity and standing of Kaaps. 'Kaaps is nie 'n grappigheid of snaaksigheid nie, maar 'n taal' (Kaaps is not a joke or a comedy, but a language), he insists in the Introduction to the revised edition of his poetry collection *Kitaar my Kruis* (Cape Town: Hollandsche Afrikaansche Uitgewers Maatschappij, 1973), p. 9.

25 The use of Kaaps for non-comic purposes is illustrated by Olivia M. Coetzee's project of Bible translations published on Litnet

entirely the sense of an inbetween way of speaking, neither fully Afrikaans nor English, and it can't avail itself of the resource constituted by the availability of two vocabularies, with different connotations, to draw from.

How, then, could we bring to the translation some of the qualities imparted by the use of Kaaps? An attempt to replicate in English the 'nonstandard' features of the original has been made by Alice Inggs:[26]

Wednesday, 16 February 1988

I am still small.
I stand alone inna backyard
at my granma-and-them's house and I feel sad
becos I no today issa boring, unimportant day.
I no the day has done nothing
that make it worthy of remembering.
I feel sad becos I no there were alredy thousands of days

<https://www.litnet.co.za/category/nuwe-skryfwerk-new-writing/bybelinkaaps/> [accessed 27 August 2019]. It is noticeable, however, that Coetzee very rarely draws on the tendency of Kaaps-speakers to use English words. (In her own account of her project, she does so more freely: 'Waarom die Bybel in Kaaps?' (Why the Bible in Kaaps?) <https://www.litnet.co.za/waarom-die-bybel-kaaps/> [accessed 27 August 2019].) The free use of English in a largely Afrikaans context is evidenced in Marlene van Niekerk's hard-hitting play, *Die Kortstondige raklewe van Anastasia W* (The brief shelf-life of Anastasia W) (Script published with CD, issued by Teaterteater, 2010); my thanks to Hannes van Zyl for providing me with a copy of this work.

26 Nathan Trantraal, 'Wednesday, 16 February 1988', trans. by Alice Inggs, *Asymptote* <https://www.asymptotejournal.com/poetry/nathan-trantraal-chokers-en-survivors/> [accessed 27 August 2019]. Another poet who uses Kaaps is Trantraal's wife, Ronelda Kamfer; her first collection, *Noudat slapende honde* (Now that sleeping dogs), appeared in 2008, her second, *Hammie*, in 2106; both published by Kwela Books in Cape Town. Several of her poems appear in the bilingual anthology, *In a Burning Sea*, ed. by Marlise Joubert (Pretoria: Protea House, 2014) with translations by Charl J. F. Cilliers. Cilliers does not attempt to find an equivalent for Kamfer's 'non-standard' Afrikaans, but uses straightforward English with a couple of untranslated slang words, one of which is explained in a footnote.

lyk this that I have alredy fo'gotten.
A person looks back on your life anna things that stand
    owt,
fo you that is your life
But that isn't living,
That's the highlights reel.
Your life issa stack of days when nothing happened.

I walk to the washing hanging onna line,
I put my hand gainst a wet towel
and I think I am neva gonna fo'get this day.

There are a number of problems with this worthy attempt. For instance, Inggs makes the mistake of confusing spelling mistakes with variant pronunciation. Trantraal spells 'weet' — 'know' — as 'wiet' because this is an accurate representation, using the phonetic rules of Afrikaans, of a Kaaps pronunciation; but Inggs's 'becos' for 'because', 'no' for 'know', and 'alredy' for 'already' (to mention only three examples) produce no difference in pronunciation unless one already knows the Kaaps accent — in which case the spelling change is redundant. Trantraal's poem captures the voice of a distinct and distinctive community; but it's hard to know what kind of English Inggs's version is meant to represent.

What is to be done, then, to convey to a non-Afrikaans speaking reader or listener the power and subtlety of this poem and the pleasures it has to offer? I hope I have done a little of this already, in providing several versions and commenting on them; every individual will have been able to appreciate some aspects of the poem, depending on their own idiolect and idioculture. A further strategy would be to go through the original poem with further comments. If, as I have argued elsewhere, the literary is constituted by the experience of readers, a translation that succeeded only in conveying the semantic dimension of a text would be failing to treat it as a literary work, so this process is not simply one of clarifying meaning but also of looking for ways of conveying that experience.[27]

We may look at the first few lines.

> Ek is nog klein.

- 'I am still little' — the historic present plunges us directly into the mind of a child;
- 'klein' — I have suggested 'little' rather than 'small', since the former is more associated with age than the latter, and 'klein' is common in references to children;
- 'nog' — still: in other words, I have not yet grown up, and am aware of this fact.

> Ek staan allien innie agtejaat

- 'I am standing alone in the back yard'. Now we hear the distinctive voice of the Coloured speaker: the diphthong in 'alleen' disappears in 'allien'; the two words 'in die' become one in 'innie';
- 'agtejaat' is not as correct as 'agterplaas' — this suggests the influence of the English 'yard'.[28]

> by my ouma-hulle hys en ek voel sad

- 'at my grandma and them's house and I feel sad' — 'x-hulle' is common colloquialism in Afrikaans, only partially captured in the English 'and them';

---

27 See Derek Attridge, *The Singularity of Literature* (London: Routledge, 2004) and *The Work of Literature* (Oxford: Oxford University Press, 2015), *passim*.

28 The massive *Reader's Digest Afrikaans-Engels Woordeboek/English-Afrikaans Dictionary* reflects the authority of the *Taalcommissie*: '*jaard, jaards, jaardjie:* these English borrowings are not standard Afrikaans, although many unsophisticated speakers use them. Since the *Suid-Afrikaanse Akademie* has not approved them, they are unacceptable', ed. by Peter Grobbelaar (Cape Town: Reader's Digest Association, 1987), p. 230.

- ‘hys’ for ‘huis’ indicates the Kaaps pronunciation;
- the syntax is characteristic in its omission of the possessive: ‘huis’ rather than ‘se huis’;
- ‘sad’ — a blunt English word; the Afrikaans words are more refined: hartseer, treurig, droewig, swaarmoedig…

omdat ek wiet vandag isse boring, unimportant dag.

- ‘because I know today is a boring, unimportant day’. The English words ‘boring, unimportant’ emphasize those adjectives, conveying the mood with more power than the Afrikaans: their stressed syllables rhyme and can be elongated.

Ek wiet die dag het niks gedoen
wattit worthy maak om onthou te wôtie.

- ‘I know the day has done nothing | that makes it worth remembering’ (literally, ‘to be remembered’)
- the day becomes the subject of the sentence: it hasn’t made itself memorable.
- ‘wôtie’ combines ‘word’ and ‘nie’, the passive ‘be’ and the second negative required by Afrikaans syntax — with a circumflex to indicate the pronunciation.
- ‘worthy’: the English word where we might expect ‘waardig’, or a phrase like ‘die moeite werd’, perhaps emphasizes the worthiness in question by drawing on the more prestigious language.

The most striking use of an English word in the rest of the poem is ‘highlights’; I’ve suggested ‘hoogtepunte’ as an Afrikaans alternative, but ‘highlights’ would be the word made familiar by television and recordings, especially in the phrase 'highlights reel', which has outlived the use of tape spools in recording vision and sound. The final section of the poem, whose climactic function is emphasized by the extra space before it, is entirely in Afrikaans; perhaps this is a way of resisting any potential comic qualities of the interpolation of English.

My hope would be that going through the poem like this with a willing auditor would make it possible for such a person to engage with the poem in its original form with understanding and enjoyment. Clearly, the degree to which this could happen would depend in part on the linguistic competence of the individual — someone who knows Dutch would find it quite easy to enjoy the poem, someone with German less so, and someone with only, say, French or Italian, would find it more difficult. This mode of translation is less easy to achieve in print, as my limited comments show; it's not unthinkable, however. For such purposes, the poem would be given in the original as well as in straightforward translation, but with notes and alternatives, all geared to making it possible for the reader to attempt the real thing. The danger would be that the poem might disappear under the commentary, as could be said of Nabokov's translation of Pushkin's *Eugene Onegin*, in which the notes take up six times the space of the poem; clearly, a balance between helpfulness and overwhelmingness needs to be created.

It will be obvious that part of the challenge for the reader who is not a member of the Cape Coloured community — and I include myself, as a white South African who emigrated fifty years ago — is to understand and appreciate the cultural implications of this use of language, and information about this aspect of the poem would also be useful in any edition for readers unfamiliar with Kaaps. Trantraal's primary audience in South Africa is white Afrikaans speakers; given the relative poverty in which the majority of Coloureds live, poetry-reading is not widespread among the community whose language and experiences the poems capture. Trantraal therefore runs the risk of presenting the portraits of his own family and friends, and the anecdotes he relates about life in the Cape Town Coloured township of Bishop Lavis,[29] as curiosities for the entertainment of those whose lives are very different. The unusual appearance of the language on the page, the mixture of English and Afrikaans, and the colourful lives of the characters portrayed can all too easily be enjoyed as quaint and exotic features of this poetry; a responsible engagement, on the other hand, would be one that registers the real deprivation and suffering the poems chart and appreciates the linguistic complexity not as a comic device but as a reflection of local speech patterns, used as much for the gravest subjects as for light-hearted ones. I see the attempt to understand the disparity between the conditions registered in the poetry and those of most of its consumers as one aspect of the responsibility of the reader.[30] For those few readers who do share Trantraal's background, the reading experience must be a very different one — including justifiable pride that their way of speaking, so often denigrated, has been given the prestige of poetry on the page.

29 Wikipedia describes Bishop Lavis as follows: 'It had, as of 2001, a population of 44,419 people, of whom 97% described themselves as Coloured, and 90% spoke Afrikaans while 9% spoke English' <https://en.wikipedia.org/wiki/Bishop_Lavis> [accessed 27 August 2019].

30 Trantraal has reflected on these disparities in 'Cash for Gold', which begins, 'Ek wonne of ekkie ienagste | prize-winning poet is | wat copper wire | vie kosgeld moet strip' (I wonder if I am the only prize-winning poet who has to strip copper wire for money for food), in *Alles het niet kom wôd*, p. 42.

UNTRANSLATABILITY AND THE EXPERIENCE OF TRANSLATION

I chose this poem, and Trantraal's work more generally, because it foregrounds the question of untranslatability: the conventional model of translation simply does not work in this case. I've written elsewhere about Afrikaans literature that employs forms of the language that are somewhat less resistant to translation (though not without many challenges),[31] and noted that such works rely on translation to achieve a readership beyond the very small number of Afrikaans readers in South Africa. But in choosing to write in Kaaps, Trantraal and others even more obviously deny themselves a wider readership. This clearly has consequences for any notion of 'world literature' that relies on translation, such as David Damrosch's. Are we to consign all those works written according to linguistic protocols that fall between standard languages to oblivion, as far as any conception of the 'world' is concerned? My preference would be to expand the notion of translation so that it includes a variety of ways of conveying the experience of the original, wherever possible allowing the reader to engage, at least to some degree, with that original — and acknowledging the unavoidable force of untranslatability.[32]

31 See Derek Attridge, 'Contemporary Afrikaans Fiction and English Translation: Singularity and the Question of Minor Languages', in *Singularity and Transnational Poetics*, ed. by Birgit Mara Kaiser (New York: Routledge, 2014), pp. 61–78, and 'Contemporary Afrikaans Fiction in the World: The Englishing of Marlene van Niekerk', *Journal of Commonwealth Studies*, 49.3 (2014), pp. 395–409.

32 For a study that harnesses the notion of untranslatability in opposing expansionist versions of 'world literature', see Emily Apter, *Against World Literature: On the Politics of Untranslatabilty* (London: Verso, 2013).

Translation, instead of being conceived of as the simulation, for the reader competent in *one* language, of the experience of a reader competent in a *different* language, would become an open field of varied practices including literal translation, explanation, and suggested equivalents, with the recognition that readers' differing idiolects will mean that different strategies have differing chances of success in different contexts. Stefan Helgesson suggests that the process of retranslation 'contributes to establish not "a" text, but an expandable, multilingual *textual zone*, issuing from multiple subjectivities, produced in discrete systems of publication, and constituting thereby the effective world-literary existence of a poem or a novel'.[33] This approach would mean dropping the implicit requirement that the translation be roughly the same length as the original and exploiting to the full whatever elements of the original are available to the reader of the translated version.[34] Derrida has argued that '[n]othing is untranslatable, if only one gives oneself the time necessary for the expenditure or expansion of a competent discourse measuring up to the power of the original'. He urges the

33 Stefan Helgesson, 'Translation and the Circuits of World Literature', in *The Cambridge Companion to World Literature*, ed. by Ben Etherington and Jarad Zimbler (Cambridge: Cambridge University Press, 2018), pp. 85–99 (p. 97).

34 Damrosch discusses three translations of Murakami Shikibu's *Book of Genji*, pointing out that the increasing number of notes in successive translations significantly enriches the reading experience (*What Is World Literature?*, pp. 296–97). He quotes André Lefevere: 'When we no longer translate Chinese T'ang poetry "as if" it were Imagist blank verse, which it manifestly is not, we shall be able to begin to understand T'ang poetry on its own terms. This means, however, that we shall have to tell the readers of our translations what T'ang poetry is really like, by means of introductions, the detailed analysis of selected texts, and such', Lefevere, 'Composing the Other', in *Postcolonial Translation: Theory and Practice*, ed. by Susan Bassnett and Harish Trivedi (London: Routledge, 1999), pp. 79–94 (pp. 77–78).

renunciation of the ideal of an 'economic equivalence', that is, the traditional demand that the translated work be close to the original in length.[35] We now have relatively new tools at our disposal in getting to grips with writing in a language with which we're not familiar, including online translation tools such as Google Translate, cloud-based dictionaries, easily accessible background information, and text-to-speech and speech-to-text applications. When J. M. Coetzee published his novel *The Death of Jesus* first in Spanish translation I was able to read it by using these tools to complement my rudimentary Spanish, alternating between using my phone's camera for instantaneous translation, reading the Spanish aloud to Google, and taking advantage of the handwriting facility.

Translation in this guise would be seen less as a matter of producing an equivalent text in another language and more as working with the original to find ways of enabling access to it. The virtues of partial comprehension of the original, in contrast to complete comprehension of a translation, would be acknowledged. Translation in this sense would be understood as an unending process (and in this respect is akin to Barbara Cassin's untranslatables, which in other respects present a rather different understanding of the working of discrete languages).[36] If I may be autobiographical again, I recently completed a book on the experience of poetry from Ancient Greece to the Renaissance. This meant working on poems in a number of languages, including Ancient Greek, Latin, Old English, Old French, Occitan, and Medieval Italian as well as

35 Jacques Derrida, *Le Monolinguisme de l'autre* (Paris: Galilée, 1996), p. 56 (my translation).

36 Barbara Cassin, ed., *Dictionary of Untranslatables: A Philosophical Lexicon*, trans. by Steven Rendall and others (Princeton, NJ: Princeton University Press, 2014).

Middle and Early Modern English. My expertise in these languages varies from none to a little to reasonable competence, and I had to rely heavily in places on translations. I found that having more than one translation was very helpful, as were translators' notes, as I could combine the translators' suggestions with my own, often limited, understanding to come up with what I hope was a reasonable grasp of the poem in question — but I have no illusions about the finality or exhaustiveness of that comprehension. (Though this is true of any poem worth reading.)

Such an expansion of the notion of translation shouldn't be confined to works in 'non-standard' languages; if we recognize the artificiality of the standard languages and think in terms of the experience of literature, we're free to experiment across traditional boundaries in seeking to create an experience for new readers that has some degree of resemblance to that of the original readers. Most literary works draw on a range of linguistic usages, implying, for those familiar with them, differences in class, age, location, profession, and so on, and a sense of that range is an important part of the experience of the reader. Finding an equivalent for that range in another linguistic habitat by means of traditional translation is sometimes impossible; other techniques are required. Moreover, different genres require different strategies: the line-by-line commentary I suggested for a short poem isn't going to work for a novel. There is also merit in translations written for those who *are* at home in the language of the original; Clive Scott has published several books exploring this possibility.[37]

---

37 See, for instance, Clive Scott, *Translating the Perception of Text: Translation and Phenomenology* (Oxford: Legenda, 2012); *Literary Translation and the Rediscovery of Reading* (Cambridge: Cambridge Univer-

This question of the cultural implications of the original is one that is posed by all translation; the more distant the culture of the writer, the more the reader has to intuit or research in order to appreciate the writing.[38] Here again, translation may work best if it's not thought of as the transfer of a set of meanings encoded in the words of one language into the words of another, but as an attempt to create, by whatever means appropriate, an experience that corresponds in some measure to the experience of a reader who's able to enjoy the original directly. We can go further: reading virtually any literary work involves some cultural distance, and perhaps some linguistic distance as well, even if it's in a language one knows well — hence the value of annotations of various kinds, including modern 'translations' of words that have changed their meaning over time. There will always be variations in the needs of different readers: every reader brings a singular idioculture to the practice of reading a literary work, whether in a familiar or an unfamiliar language. Over time, this idioculture changes as a result of further experiences, including further reading; to misquote Heraclitus, you can never read the same poem twice. Reading cultures more broadly change too; André Lefevere, presenting the argument that translations *refract* rather than *reflect* the original, wrote in 1982: 'Standards have changed so often in the history of Western literature that it must be obvious by now that translations are "good"' only with respect to a certain place and a certain time, in certain circumstances.'[39]

---

sity Press, 2012); and *The Work of Literary Translation* (Cambridge: Cambridge University Press, 2018).

38 See Attridge, *Work of Literature*, pp. 204–18.

39 André Lefevere, 'Literary Theory and Translated Literature', *Dispositio*, 7.19/21 (1982), pp. 3–22 (p. 9).

The experience of reading a work in translation is different only in degree from the reading of works in a language in which one is competent. Most accounts of the practice of reading — I'm thinking, for instance, of the studies that go under the name of 'reader-response theory' as well as the phenomenological tradition — underestimate, to my mind, the complexity of response of which the average literary reader is capable. To read well is to bring to bear on a text as much of one's idioculture as is relevant, which, since relevance can't be known in advance, involves a constant process of testing; it's to keep in play one's awareness that the work one is engaging with is the product of an individual's creative labour; it's to allow a role to whatever knowledge one possesses about the original context within which the work was written; it's to recall where appropriate other works by this author, or works from the same period, or works in the same genre; and it's to relate all this to the needs and values of one's own time. To read a translated work is not substantially different. It is true that one is aware of the creative labour of two individuals — but then many works in their original language bear the traces of more than one author. As Kate Briggs puts it in *This Little Art*, her superb meditation on the art of translation from the point of view of a practitioner, in reading a translation as a translation, we establish a relationship with two creative projects: 'Not either/or, but holding and maintaining a relation with both writers, a sense of both writing practices, in their shared project and in all the important ways those projects differ, in the head, and somehow together.'[40] (Of course, if one is unaware that one is reading a translation, the experience is no different from reading an original work — and there are commercial reasons for the attempt to

40 Kate Briggs, *This Little Art* (London: Fitzcarraldo Editions, 2017), p. 49.

create this illusion for readers.) It's worth emphasizing that translation, like all forms of commentary, quotation, or reinscription, is one element in the ongoing process that keeps literary works alive.[41] The singularity of the work is not *threatened* but *constituted* by translation — into the idiolectal and idiocultural frameworks of readers, into the words of commentators, and into other linguistic forms.

***

What, then, are the consequences of this approach to translation for the concept, and the associated scholarly and pedagogic programme, of 'world literature'? It's a concept that has been found wanting by several commentators, among them Aamir Mufti, Gayatri Spivak, and Emily Apter,[42] and to my mind these critiques contain much that is cogent and convincing. However, there's no denying the prominence of the idea of world literature in literary studies today, at least in the Anglosphere. Without a commitment to the notion of separate languages, there might be less emphasis on discrete literary traditions and more attention to the fluidity of linguistic and literary practices around the globe. The privileging of standard languages and the communities they are associated with would be challenged by increased attention to so-called 'dialects' and 'multilingual' communities. There might be a greater willingness on the part of writers to employ their own non-standard speech practices if they could expect a global read-

41 Stefan Helgesson, 'Clarice Lispector, J. M. Coetzee and the Seriality of Translation', uses Sartre's term 'serial collective' to describe the many contributors to a work's continuing vitality, in *Translation Studies*, 3 (2010), pp. 318–33.

42 See Mufti, *Forget English!*; Gayatri Chakravorty Spivak, *Death of a Discipline* (New York: Columbia University Press, 2003); Emily Apter, *Against World Literature*.

ership. The pedagogic consequences in courses of 'world literature' might include a greater use of original texts and an awareness of the provisionality of any effort of translation. This is not to take sides in the old 'domestication' versus 'foreignization' debate: there's room for both kinds of translation in this picture.[43]

In *The Singularity of Literature* and *The Work of Literature* I proposed an account of literary experience as an encounter with alterity, inventiveness, and singularity, treating these as three aspects of the same event, an event and experience whereby the reader is taken into a space of unfamiliarity that effects a change — which may be mental, emotional, or even physiological. Literary cultures other than that in which I am at home hold out enormous promise for this experience; and rather than seeing translation as a way of remoulding the strange into the familiar, I want to see it as a way of maximizing exposure to the singularity, inventiveness, and alterity of the original. In this way, world literature may be appreciated as the rich and diverse body of creative artefacts that it really is.

43 I also like Briggs's idea that translating challenging texts 'might put new pressures on the English language, forcing the discovery of new, or tapping into old and neglected, resources', *This Little Art*, p. 30.

World Literature and the Problem of Postcolonialism

Aesthetics and Dissent

LORNA BURNS

Despite their shared ambition to expand the canon beyond narrowly nationalist boundaries, the critical fields of postcolonial and world literary criticism, Robert Young argues, pull in different directions when it comes to their political ambitions. For Young, while world literature must always make at least some claim to the attainment of universal standards of aesthetic value, 'postcolonial literature makes no such assertion, and indeed insofar as it involves resistance, [it] will always in some sense be partial, locked into a particular problematic of power.'[1] Furthermore, he continues, aspiring 'to expose and challenge imbalances of power,

* This essay is taken from passages in the Introduction, Chapter One, and Chapter Four of Lorna Burns, *Postcolonialism After World Literature: Relation, Equality, Dissent* (London: Bloomsbury, 2019). Thanks are due to Ben Doyle and Bloomsbury for their permission to use material previously published in that work here.

1 Robert J. C. Young, 'World Literature and Postcolonialism', in *The Routledge Companion to World Literature*, ed. by Theo D'haen, David Damrosch, Djelal Kadir (London: Routledge, 2012), pp. 213–22 (p. 216).

and the different forms of injustice that follow from such factors [...] postcolonial literature will always seek to go beyond itself to impact upon the world which it represents'.[2] Evident in Young's claims is a view of postcolonial literature that identifies it primarily as a literature of resistance — literature that will aim to make a discernible impact on situations of injustice, exploitation, and oppression within the world that it represents. By this token, postcolonial literature, Young argues, is specific and particular, and thus opposed to the universal values of world literature; postcolonial literature often moves 'beyond itself' to make an engagement with the actual world behind mere representation, whereas world literature can conceive of an aesthetic realm apart. This view, however, obscures one of the most prominent debates in the field of postcolonialism: one which Graham Huggan has referred to as 'the overdrawn, often tedious debate between (post-)Marxists and poststructuralists [...] that continues to some extent to split the postcolonial field today'.[3] By raising the problem of literature in relation to representation, political action, and dissent, Young's initial foray into the 'virtually unmarked territory' of postcolonialism and world literature reanimates this debate.[4]

What is known as second-wave or Marxist postcolonial critique was a sharp criticism of the poststructuralist theories of Homi Bhabha, Gayatri Chakravorty Spivak, and, to a lesser extent, Edward Said. And we can see in Young's assumption that postcolonial literature must, necessarily, go beyond itself to impact on the world that

2 Ibid., p. 217.

3 Graham Huggan, *Interdisciplinary Measures: Literature and the Future of Postcolonial Studies* (Liverpool: Liverpool University Press, 2008), p. 11.

4 Young, 'World Literature and Postcolonialism', p. 213.

it represents an echo of Benita Parry's second-wave critique of Bhabha and Spivak for their disinterest in social praxis and their elevation of discourse.[5] At issue remains the question of the relationship between literature and the world: the degree to which a text represents a more fundamental reality or structure and how far its influence upon that world can be measured. World literature scholarship, to some extent, has overlooked the poststructuralist/Marxist division within the field of postcolonialism: Pascale Casanova, for example, argues that postcolonialism in all its forms 'posits a direct link between literature and history, one that is exclusively political',[6] while Franco Moretti observes that with postcolonialism 'a whole generation began to concentrate directly on historical materials, shifting the critical focus from the analysis of form to that of content'.[7] This elision, I argue, obscures the divisions within the field of postcolonialism between Marxists and poststructuralists, but it also serves to mask the extent to which world literature theory itself has reproduced aspects of this debate, most notably in the ideal of an autonomous world republic of letters as argued for in the work of Pascale Casanova.

In tension with this conceptualization of an autonomous literary realm, recent interventions into the field of world literature (including that of Casanova) have pursued a strongly materialist approach which views the text primarily as a product of the various factors that condition the literary field. For David Damrosch, literature becomes

---

5 Benita Parry, *Postcolonial Studies: A Materialist Critique* (London: Routledge, 2004).

6 Pascale Casanova, 'Literature as a World', *New Left Review*, 31 (2005), pp. 71–90 (p. 71).

7 Franco Moretti, *The Way of the World: The Bildungsroman in European Culture* (London: Verso, 2000), p. xiii.

world literature only when it circulates beyond its originating national borders;[8] for Casanova, it is part of a world literary field unequal in its distribution of capital;[9] for Rebecca Walkowitz, it betrays its global internationalism through its translatability.[10] Literature by this account, as Ben Etherington has argued, is studied 'as a special encoder of those conditions' which structure the global literary field and, in turn, the objective of critique is to uncover 'the material base through the superstructure of literature'.[11] World literature, following postcolonialism in its materialist, second wave articulation, can be read as a manifestation of the more fundamental modern global capitalist and imperialist world-system.

This is an approach that finds its clearest articulation to date in the recent manifesto by the Warwick Research Collective (WReC), *Combined and Uneven Development: Towards a New Theory of World-Literature*, in which it is argued that the world-literary text will 'register' the capitalist world-system.[12] The influence of Franco Moretti can be traced in this latest development in world-literary critical theory, for it is his structural premise of a world literary system that is '[o]ne, and unequal' that, alongside Casanova's contemporaneous *The World Republic of Letters*, underpins

---

8 David Damrosch, *What Is World Literature?* (Princeton, NJ: Princeton University Press, 2003).

9 Pascale Casanova, *The World Republic of Letters*, trans. by Malcolm B. DeBevoise (Cambridge, MA: Harvard University Press, 2004).

10 Rebecca L. Walkowitz, *Born Translated: The Contemporary Novel in an Age of World Literature* (New York: Columbia University Press, 2015).

11 Ben Etherington, 'What Is Materialism's Material? Thoughts toward (Actually against) a Materialism for "World Literature"', *Journal of Postcolonial Writing*, 48.5 (2012), pp. 539–51 (p. 539).

12 Warwick Research Collective (WReC), *Combined and Uneven Development: Towards a New Theory of World-Literature* (Liverpool: Liverpool University Press, 2015).

WReC's case for the literary registration of inequality.[13] And yet, at the same time, both Casanova and Moretti continue to make the case for the specific work of language and discourse, an aesthetic sphere that cannot be reduced to its material conditions. And so the poststructuralist–Marxist debate rages on.

I do not seek to finally resolve this debate, but rather to highlight that both tend to begin with a structural premise (language or an aesthetic sphere, for one faction; capitalism, for the other) that will explain not only the production and circulation of a text, but also the workings of plot, character, genre, and style, and, crucially, it will prefigure our interpretation of such elements. Indeed, Damrosch acknowledges as much when he notes the tendency in world literature scholarship to focus on 'deep structures' at the expense of particularity and individual literary effects, and, as such, 'systemic approaches need to be counter-balanced with close attention to particular languages, specific texts: we need to see both the forest and the trees'.[14] I would add, however, that the systemic approach has generated another set of conceptual problems, one that can be summarized by WReC's definition of 'world-literature' as 'the literature of the world-system', 'as the literary registration of modernity under the sign of combined and uneven development'.[15] World literature and its critical analysis, by this definition, will register the signs of globalized capitalism but, crucially, WReC adds, such an endeavour 'does not (necessarily) involve criticality or dissent'.[16] My counterargument to this claim is not that, by contrast, a text

13 Franco Moretti, *Distant Reading* (London: Verso, 2013), p. 46.

14 Damrosch, *What Is World Literature?*, p. 26.

15 Warwick Research Collective (WReC), *Combined and Uneven Development*, pp. 8 and 17.

16 Ibid., p. 20.

must (necessarily) be defined by its resistance but, rather, to suggest that just as there is no ontologically valid position to argue that a text will involve criticality or dissent (the assumption WReC resists), the reverse position is also true: there is no validity to the claim that it will not involve criticality or dissent. As this essay will go on to discuss with brief reference to the work of three philosophers — Bruno Latour, Gilles Deleuze and Jacques Rancière — the departure from a priori structures as the guiding principle of interpretation results in an ontology in which the world is understood as an assemblage of forces and actors, none of which can be said to be either reducible or irreducible to anything other.[17] In turn, world literature is reframed as an assemblage of actors (world, text, and reader together) by which we might trace the processes by which structures of dominance or inequality can emerge but never as the a priori conditions or teleological ends to which all actors are fated to be governed by. This processual philosophy holds that we cannot predict in advance what form an assemblage of world, text, and reader might take; or, in Latour's words, '[w]e cannot say that an actant follows rules, laws, or structures, but neither can we say that it acts without these'.[18] It

---

17 These three philosophers inform the argument throughout *Postcolonialism After World Literature*, shaping my approach to the materialist critique of WReC, Casanova and Moretti, and informing my approach to dissent and equality, most notably drawing on the ways in which each philosopher employs a concept of otherness (the virtual for Deleuze; plasma for Latour; and for Rancière the hitherto obscured actors made visible through the work of dissensus) in their conceptualization of the destabilizing force of newness. For a more detailed account of this argument, see Burns, *Postcolonialism After World Literature* — the Introduction and Chapter One (a response to the materialist critique of WReC, Casanova and Moretti), Chapter 2 (on Latour), Chapter 3 (on Deleuze and minor literature), and Chapter 4 (on Rancière's concept of equality).

18 Bruno Latour, *The Pasteurization of France*, trans. by Alan Sheridan and John Law (Cambridge, MA: Harvard University Press 1993), p. 160.

is in this sense, then, that I challenge WReC's shift away from the registration of criticality or dissent. While we cannot determine in advance what a text is capable of we equally cannot rule out what it is incapable of as it forms a new assemblage with the reader and world. In other words, although each text is, in line with both WReC and Moretti, potentially a rhetoric of innocence that sustains the inequalities of the world system, so too is it potentially a source of resistance. The question then becomes one which asks us to consider what we as readers and critics can do with a text, how it provokes us to think, and, in turn, what opportunities are lost if we choose only to trace the registration, and thus efficacy, of the capitalist world-system without finding in the text an ally in the ongoing contestation and (re)assemblage of the world.[19]

The 'structural' aspect of this problem of contemporary world literary theory is underscored, I suggest, by the arguments advanced by post-critical scholars like Bruno Latour and Rita Felski, for whom the Marxist readings of Fredric Jameson (and by extension, I suggest, the materialism of WReC) seek to uncover unconscious structures that underlie a text and therefore tend to confirm the critic's predetermined expectations.[20] From this perspective, the problem with a world-systems approach to world literature is its tendency to situate a primary reality as the unconscious ground of the text: literature as epiphenomenon of the capitalist world economy. Rather than preserving the notion that it is the work of the critic to reveal the hidden structures of economy, society, or history to which the text

19 For a further exploration of the role that dissent plays in world literary criticism, see the essays collected in *World Literature and Dissent*, ed. by Lorna Burns and Katie Muth (London: Routledge 2019).

20 Rita Felski, *The Limits of Critique* (Chicago: University of Chicago Press, 2015).

is blind, post-criticism asks us to 'place ourselves in front of the text' and reflect 'on what it unfurls, calls forth, makes possible'.[21] And, of course, what it 'makes possible' can be resistance to the hierarchies that dominate our world as much as those that anesthetize us to their acceptance (a nod to Moretti's rhetoric of innocence, explored in *Modern Epic*).[22]

World literature, I maintain, must be more than a reflection of its contemporary worldly contexts, and while texts need not necessarily, by definition, express 'criticality or dissent', they must always be considered as offering the potential to do so. This is not merely a question addressed to the text, but to how we read it. As Graham Harman notes, 'such questions restore the proper scale of evaluation for intellectual work: demoting the pushy careerist sandbagger who remains within the bounds of the currently plausible and prudent, and promoting the gambler who uncovers new worlds'.[23] This move beyond the status quo is the dissident force of critique in an era of world literature: finding in the literary text not confirmation of the structural permanence of capitalism and related forms of cultural and economic imperialism but, rather, the means to imagine a new society that functions without the opposition of self and other, oppressor and oppressed. Thus, for Harman, the effectiveness of the literary text is not simply a measure of the widest possible circulation or of its literary capital: 'The books that stir us most are not those containing the fewest errors, but those that throw most light on unknown portions of the map'.[24]

---

21 Ibid., p. 12.

22 Franco Moretti, *Modern Epic: The World-System from Goethe to García Márquez* (London: Verso, 1996).

23 Graham Harman, *Prince of Networks: Bruno Latour and Metaphysics* (Melbourne: re:press, 2009), p. 120.

24 Ibid.

These sentiments are at the core of my work, and specifically the recently published book from which this essay is drawn, *Postcolonialism After World Literature: Relation, Equality, Dissent.*[25] In this essay, I will sketch the argument made in detail in the book that the work of Gilles Deleuze, Jacques Rancière, and Bruno Latour can be turned toward an interrogation of current world literary criticism. Speaking directly to a concern that he shares with Deleuze and Rancière, Latour articulates a fundamental sense of the world as an assemblage of forces and actors, none of which can be said to be either reducible or irreducible to anything other. It is upon such grounds that Latour has opposed the sociology of Pierre Bourdieu (the doctoral supervisor of and clear inspiration to Pascale Casanova and, in particular, her modification of field theory in *The World Republic of Letters*).[26] Where Latour's critique of Bourdieu draws attention to the philosophical problem of a priori structures — a primary social field — in the work of his fellow sociologist, Casanova (and, indeed, Franco Moretti) follows suit by providing an account of literature that relies upon a fixed structural premise. For Moretti, world literature is not an object but the workings of an a priori system subject to analysis and interrogation; a single system structured by 'a relationship of growing inequality' between the core, periphery and semi-periphery.[27] In Casanova's work, we encounter a relatively autonomous field of literary production, structured by the uneven spread of literary capital that

---

25 Burns, *Postcolonialism After World Literature.*

26 My critique of Pascale Casanova's theory of world literature can be found in Chapter One of Burns, *Postcolonialism After World Literature.* See also Christian Thorne, 'The Sea Is Not a Place: or, Putting the World Back into World Literature', *boundary2*, 40.2 (2013), pp. 53–79.

27 For further discussion of Moretti's approach to world literature theory, see Burns, *Postcolonialism After World Literature.*

cannot be wholly reduced to the power relations which structure the 'real' world.

Like Deleuze before him, Latour is profoundly suspicious of the transcendentalism of philosophical arguments which posit a priori foundations and teleological processes. But the critique of field theory in Latour runs deeper, since the problem of Bourdieu's a priori social field is not only the 'a priori' nature of that framework, but also its privileging of one, determining factor apart. Modern thinking, Latour argues, has been characterized by the separation of spheres — nature and culture, science and arts, reality and its representation, or to signal its Kantian foundations, noumenon and phenomenon. Bourdieu is as guilty of this as Derrida, Latour argues, as each privileges one structure or sphere within their ontology (society or language) and ignores the fact that 'all of culture and all of nature get churned up again every day'; we cling to the belief that we must 'not mix up heaven and earth, the global stage and the local scene, the human and the nonhuman'.[28] Modern thinkers have sought to separate 'knowledge of things', on the one hand, from 'power and human politics', on the other.[29] To return to literature, for Latour and post-critical scholars like Rita Felski, the implications of this rejection of separate spheres is to render moot the question of whether or not literature can be political: there is no autonomous 'republic of letters', no grounds upon which the work of literature could be extracted from the workings of the world. And this is something which Latour shares with the other thinkers that I use in my work: Deleuze and Rancière. For Latour, as for Deleuze, there is no cogito

28 Bruno Latour, *We Have Never Been Modern*, trans. by Catherine Porter (Cambridge, MA: Harvard University Press, 1993), pp. 2–3.

29 Ibid., p. 3.

or transcendental subject that exists first and then enters into relations with others; nor is there any teleological framework or a priori system within which a subject's being unfolds. In this respect, the literary text, understood as one actor among many others, is not simply a material object to be encountered but something continually produced and reproduced through the translations and mediations of other actors in the network.

This snapshot of Latour's understanding of literature is worth pausing over because of its evocation of singularity or newness: each reading of the text produces something new. That in itself is not a surprising conclusion, but it raises an awareness of what is perhaps underplayed in Latour's work: to put it in Deleuzian terms, the role of the virtual. Indeed, some readers of Latour view these two philosophers as antagonistic because of Latour's seeming resistance to virtuality or otherness in his work (a point I find hard to agree with if one looks at Latour's definition of 'plasma').[30] But more broadly, I see this as a problem with post-criticism. Of concern in the post-critical turn is the repudiation of a form of literary theory in which the practitioner is engaged, like the spirit of perpetual negation, in undermining the text — by revealing what it has excluded

30 See Harman, *Prince of Networks*; and Mitchum Huehls, *After Critique: Twenty-First Century Fiction in a Neoliberal Age* (Oxford: Oxford University Press, 2016). In *Reassembling the Social*, plasma is introduced as a placeholder for that which remains unconnected as a society-network forms. Inspired by Gabriel Tarde's monad, plasma is 'the background necessary for every activity to emerge'; the 'not yet formatted, not yet measured, not yet socialized'; that which is 'in between and not made of social stuff. It is not hidden, simply unknown. It resembles a vast hinterland providing the resources for every single course of action to be fulfilled', Bruno Latour, *Reassembling the Social: An Introduction to Actor-Network Theory* (Oxford: Oxford University Press, 2007), pp. 243–44. This 'not yet' cannot be reduced to 'the possible' and, as such, it echoes Deleuze's own hesitancy in equating his virtual with the possible.

— or in undermining the reader — by exposing what they are blind to. In its place, Latour proposes a new critical approach in which the object of study is instead treated as an assemblage of actors and forces. For Latour, every state of affairs is an assemblage of translations and connections produced via their relation to other actors within the network, and the work of the analyst becomes one of tracing these connections, mapping the network as it registers them, without, however, attempting to trace them back to a single, systemic cause. What is missing from this picture, and what I am suggesting that post-criticism and indeed world-literary criticism needs, is a term which accounts for that which is in excess of our everyday, empirical reality. We need a concept that gestures towards an immanent alterity to account for how newness enters the world. And we see this in the philosophers I mention: each, when accounting for creativity and newness, finds it necessary to introduce an aspect of otherness into their thought, an otherness that is understood not as an inaccessible sphere apart (as it would be for Kant, according to Latour), but as one side of a dual reality. Each philosopher uses this 'other' as the basis for theorizing the emergence of newness, creativity, and dissident alternatives to the existing hegemony. When viewed from this perspective, the work of literature and, indeed, literary criticism, postcolonial or otherwise, can become a process of creating new associations, new alliances between actors, imagining new forms of belonging and of a society freed from current forms of oppression as a co-production between the reader and the text.

The dissident capacity immanent to all works of world literature, then, lies in a reading which brings to light those hidden dimensions which, for Deleuze, is the work of 'minor literature' or, for Rancière, 'dissensus'.[31] I want, in this final part, to turn more directly to Rancière, for through his work we can gain a further refinement of a world literary critique that retains the dissident impetus of postcolonial thought. Above, we encountered arguments which will provoke a world literary criticism that, while rejecting separate spheres and a priori structures, will be sensitive to that which escapes comprehension: deterritorializations and dissensus as the immanent capacity of the literary text. But I want to add to this discussion a further element drawn from contemporary world literary theory: the question of inequality. Because if we agree with Robert Young's characterization of postcolonial literature as literature of resistance — in other words, as literature that will aim to make a discernible impact on situations of injustice, exploitation, and oppression in the world — then we should be encouraged by recent world literary criticism and its focus on global capitalism and its attendant forms of inequality. In the hands of WReC, this critical shift offers an alternative to traditional forms of postcolonial critique which have been restricted by a focus on difference and diversity. Thus, for WReC, the work of Moretti promises to offer an alternative, promoting world-literature as a 'system [that] is structured not on difference but on inequality'.[32] Postcolonialism, thus, can learn from contemporary world literature theory to focus on inequality rather than difference, and in doing so address potentialities for comparison and cosmopolitan commonalities rather than divergence

31 See, for instance Gilles Deleuze and Félix Guattari, *Kafka: Toward a Minor Literature*, trans. by Dana Polan (Minneapolis: University of Minnesota Press, 1986), or Jacques Rancière, *Dissensus: On Politics and Aesthetics*, trans. by Steven Corcoran (London: Continuum, 2010).

32 Warwick Research Collective (WReC), *Combined and Uneven Development*, p. 7.

and diversity. But I want to push this enquiry further and, following Rancière, ask what if rather than starting from the premise of inequality we assume first the equality of all actors? What if, rather than posing a theory that hopes to explain inequality, that, in the words of Moretti, focuses on 'examples [which] confirm the inequality of the world literary system' that is '*internal* to the unequal system' of global, economic capitalism,[33] we instead turn our attention to that which stages the primary equality of actors within the world-literary assemblage? This is precisely the challenge that Rancière posed to philosophy, aesthetics, and political thought, and furthermore it is the basis of his contention that the work of politics and literature alike is a form of resistance he dubs 'dissensus'.

Rancière's philosophy, like that of Latour and Deleuze, is a rejection of a priori structures as the foundation of being. Just as inequality has no transcendental justification, so equality is not treated as a natural given or essential quality, but simply as 'a mere assumption that needs to be discerned within the practices implementing it'.[34] He prioritizes, crucially, an assumed equality as the baseline of his thinking, and he does so because of the contingency of inequality: 'In the final analysis, inequality is only possible through equality' because experience tells us that

> there is order in society because some people command and others obey, but in order to obey [...] you must understand the order and you must understand that you must obey it. And to do that, you must already be the equal of the person who is ordering you. It is this equality that gnaws away at any natural order.[35]

33 Moretti, *Distant Reading*, p. 115.

34 Jacques Rancière, *Disagreement: Politics and Philosophy*, trans. by Julie Rose (Minneapolis: University of Minnesota Press, 1999), p. 33.

35 Ibid., pp. 17 and 16.

Here we see, as one might with Latour and Deleuze, that the philosopher is not denying that order, hierarchies, or structures can exist within society, but he asks us to approach them as constructed via relational processes rather than fixed a priori foundations. And, as with Latour and Deleuze, because they are constructed, they are open to change — they might make a future, cosmopolitan society possible by confronting an unequal society with its equality.

For Rancière, this is the activity of politics. Order and hierarchy are created through mechanisms he names the police. Politics is the confrontation of that order or world with an alternative account:

> Politics exists because those who have no right to be counted as speaking beings make themselves of some account, [...] the contradiction of two worlds in a single world: the world where they are and the world where they are not, the world where there is something 'between' them and those who do not acknowledge them as speaking beings who count [a difference, an inequality, or imbalance of qualities] and the world where there is nothing.[36]

As such, a social world ordered by difference or inequality is always the site of a possible contestation or dispute by those who seek to demonstrate the equality that must first be assumed by any enactment of inequality.

Politics takes the form of 'dissensus' for Rancière in that its opposite, the police, is concerned with 'the distribution of places and roles, and of the systems for legitimizing this distribution'.[37] Politics, then, is that which breaks, disrupts and dissembles that sensible order by 'mak[ing]

36 Ibid., p. 27.

37 Ibid., p. 28.

visible what had no business being seen, and mak[ing] heard a discourse where once there was only place for noise'.[38] The affinities with Spivak's subaltern are striking for the postcolonial scholar: Spivak's contention that the racial, gendered subaltern figure 'cannot speak' insofar as the historical colonial archive affords them no space within which they can make their voices heard or their agency visible finds its counterpart in Rancière's philosophy of politics as dissensus.[39] The work of the intellectual, then, concerns not representation as Spivak's original essay argued, but rather an activity of tracing moments of dissensus in which previously silenced or hidden subaltern actors are registered. Such acts, we can add after Rancière, are not an expression of the subaltern's difference but of their equality. Dissensus is the act of staging one's equality, of demonstrating that the definition of the common good extends to those who were not 'counted' as equals by the police order. Rancière's example is the Parisian tailors' strike of 1833 in which better working conditions and pay were sought by means of a demonstration of the universal applicability of the 1830 Charter which claimed all French citizens to be equal under the law.[40] From a postcolonial perspective, the Haitian Revolution repeats this dissensus: the black slaves of Saint-Domingue looked to the 1789 Declaration of the Rights of Man and of the Citizen which pronounced all men free and equal, and demonstrated that they too belonged to the category of man. On both counts

---

38 Ibid., p. 30.

39 Gayatri Chakravorty Spivak, 'Can the Subaltern Speak?', in *Can the Subaltern Speak? Reflections on the History of an Idea*, ed. by Rosalind C. Morris (New York: Columbia University Press, 2010), pp. 21–78 (p. 41).

40 Jacques Rancière, *On the Shores of Politics*, trans. by Liz Heron (London: Verso, 2007), pp. 45–72.

the 'lie' of democracy is laid bare: a claim to freedom and of a common good is pronounced as if it extends to all citizens, and those who find themselves discounted and excluded by the practice of that common good demonstrate their equal share in it.

The assumption of this enactment is, as I have noted, equality rather than difference, but that does not make of Rancière a philosopher for whom the 'otherness' I've suggested is prominent in Deleuze (the virtual) and necessary in Latour's post-criticism is redundant. Indeed, as far as dissensus marks a rupture in the police order it involves a supplement or difference that cannot be measured. Moreover, it is because of the presence of this 'otherness' that what returns from this rupturing is not the same but a newly configured space with new possibilities for 'what is to be done, to be seen and to be named in it'.[41] Call it what you will, a concept of absolute otherness is vital to any philosophical account of newness, creativity, and radical dissent as the reimagining of a community. In other words, with Rancière we can find a means to rethink postcolonialism after world literature not as an articulation of difference but as an enactment of equality. This affords an approach to world literature that does not abandon but rather invigorates the dissident, future-orientated work of postcolonial literature and literary critique. Freed from a priori structures or unconscious motives and desires, Rancière's philosophy asks us to assemble and verify moments of dissensus insofar as they enact an assumed fundamental equality between actors. Hierarchical structures can, of course, emerge, but if they do so they are produced through the relational network that is the actual world, rather than

41 Jacques Rancière, *Dissensus: On Politics and Aesthetics*, trans. by Steven Corcoran (London: Continuum, 2010), p. 37.

structural givens that prefigure its contents. As a process, any structure is open to change and reconfiguration: this is a basic premise that unites the philosophies of Latour, Deleuze, and Rancière, and which reveals their potential for a postcolonial world literature scholarship concerned with the ongoing challenge to the neocolonial present as well as the possibilities of a postcolonial future yet-to-come.

Transcontextual Gestures

A Lyric Approach to the World of Literature

FRANCESCO GIUSTI

TRANSLATABILITY *VS* TRANSFERABILITY

As a starting point, it would be helpful to distinguish between at least two notions of 'world literature'. The first concerns a contemporary phenomenon, namely, the intense globalization of the production, circulation, and reception of literary texts across languages, cultures, and nations. The second is a methodological turn that intends to renew critical approaches and open up university curricula by giving them a much larger geographical frame going beyond national borders and ideally extending to the entire globe. If the former addresses mainly literature of the current era, the latter could also involve literary works of the distant past. Within these two different notions of world literature, the issue of translation acquires quite different contours. The translation of contemporary literary works from one language into another raises the problem of 'untranslatability', which is the conceptual instrument that Emily Apter, for instance, deploys *against* a 'secure' idea of world literature, and with good reason.[1] In the second field, untranslatability as usually conceived does not always hold. If one looks at the long history of Western literatures, translation becomes a widespread phenomenon that has less to do with respecting as much as possible the cultural context of the 'original' and its language than with transferring 'something' of a certain literary work from one context to another. Many pre-modern instances of literary translation had little to do with efforts at maintaining the contextual meaning of the 'original', let alone its original letter.

I am interested here in what gets 'translated' in the sense of 'transferred' from the previous literary work into the new one, and above all in what makes that transference possible. Therefore, more than on translatability or untranslatability, I will focus on questions of transcultural and, more specifically, transcontextual transferability. The idea is that the *transcontextual* — by which I mean both the diachronically transhistorical and the synchronically transcultural — could be grounded in pre-semantic or beyond-semantic recurrent features.[2] Transferability could

1 Emily Apter, *Against World Literature: On the Politics of Untranslatability* (London: Verso, 2013).

2 I prefer the term *transcontextual* to *transnational*, *transregional*, and *translocal* for several reasons. It is not bound to the modern notion of 'nation state' and therefore can be deployed transhistorically; it is not based on geographical spatiality, but can account also for cultural, socio-economic, physical, and temporal differences; and it may help engage with micro-variations, in fact the more flexible notion of context can span from the pole of one's own *idioculture* to the opposite pole of the global world as a macro-context, and potentially beyond. At least two contexts always interact in the act of reading, the one brought by the literary work, however underdetermined and mediated, and the one

be seen as a characteristic proper to literature, but not necessarily to one's world. For the approach I intend to pursue here, taking Derek Attridge's theory of the literary as a point of departure, the problem with world literature would not so much be that there is not one 'literature' as that there is not one 'world'. As long as there are singular readers, the world can hardly be one. However, when they put texts to work as literature, their experiences of reading may have something *in common*.

Each reader's *idioculture*, to use Attridge's term, combines global and local elements to form a singular arrangement of knowledge, experiences, and feelings.[3] Theory can describe features of literary texts spread all over the globe, but 'world' is an abstraction deployed by a relatively small community of interpreters. The notion of 'world' is indeed quite problematic even in the current age of the Anthropocene: not all the individual inhabitants of this globe would easily ascribe themselves to the general category of actors on a planetary scale, whatever the action might be. In other words, when 'I' read a novel or a poem, 'I' may be ready to expose myself to the experience of a generalizable use of language, but 'I' do not necessarily identify with a global, or globalized, reader. 'I' do not immediately transcend my *self* to become a representative member of a cosmopolitan reading community. Similar considerations may hold for writers too. What if, then, one thinks not in

---

brought by the reader, and several contexts may intersect in each of them.

3 Derek Attridge, *The Work of Literature* (Oxford: Oxford University Press, 2015), pp. 60–62. See also Derek Attridge, *The Singularity of Literature* (London: Routledge, 2004), pp. 21–22 and Francesco Giusti, 'Literature at Work: A Conversation with Derek Attridge', *Los Angeles Review of Books*, 11 June 2018 <https://lareviewofbooks.org/article/literature-at-work-a-conversation-with-derek-attridge/> [accessed 23 May 2020].

terms of shared meanings or feelings, but rather in terms of re-enacted *gestures* in order to conceive of a translingual world of literature?[4]

I will not engage here with the first notion of world literature as a set of phenomena in contemporary literary production, but will engage rather with a consequence of the second notion, namely, that there might be describable features recurring across different literary traditions. I intend to focus on gestures that come before the production of in-context meaning and are active at two different levels and at two different removes from it: *transcultural gestures* and a more basic *linguistic gesture*.[5] Therefore, my approach coincides neither with the ideal 'security' of full translatability denounced by Apter nor with the 'radical philology' advocated by John T. Hamilton in opposition to that 'security'.[6] To be clear, I do not want to argue for a sort of anthropological polygenesis (i.e., the same gestures appearing autonomously in different cultures), but rather want to query how and why literary texts work as vehicles for certain gestures (i.e., the ways in which those

---

4 This approach to world literature distinguishes itself from approaches based on the global circulation and impact of particular literary works: the Epic of Gilgamesh, Dante's *Divina Commedia*, Shakespeare's plays, Cervantes' *Don Quixote*, etc. See David Damrosch, *What Is World Literature?* (Princeton, NJ: Princeton University Press, 2003) and Martin Puchner, *The Written World: The Power of Stories to Shape People, History, and Civilization* (New York: Random House, 2017).

5 *Gesture* can be defined in opposition to *action* as the 'pattern' of an action that has no ends and no meaning in itself, but acquires these when performed in a particular context. Similar notions of gesture associated with a form of community and with literature can be found in Bertolt Brecht, Walter Benjamin, Giorgio Agamben (discussed in the last section), and in Roland Barthes, *How to Live Together: Novelistic Simulations of Some Everyday Experience*, trans. by Kate Briggs (New York: Columbia University Press, 2012), pp. 133–34.

6 Apter, *Against World Literature*, pp. 129–130. John T. Hamilton, *Security: Politics, Humanity, and the Philology of Care* (Princeton, NJ: Princeton University Press, 2013).

gestures travel along with actual texts). My aim is to explore, within the discursive mode of the lyric, whether these two types of gesture could be more helpful than notions of meaning-based linguistic translation to account for the transferability of literary texts across different contexts and for a conceptualization of world literature.[7] To do so, I will look at how the *act-event* described by Attridge — the both active and passive encounter in which readers put a text to work as literature — is processed in the transference of previous poems into new ones.[8] This approach may also be helpful to minimize the distorting effects of the historicity of the very idea of literature, especially when looking at texts composed before European modernity.

UNNECESSARY TRANSLATIONS

Let us have a look at the 'birth' of Italian poetry and to the richest manuscript of the so-called Italian 'poetry of the origins', the *canzoniere* Vaticano Latino 3793, which dates from the end of the thirteenth century, beginning of the fourteenth. The collection is divided into two parts according to metrical genres: the first consists of *canzoni*, the second of sonnets. In the ordering of the authors, several critics have detected the historiographic intent to trace the 'evolution' of Italian vernacular lyric of the thirteenth century: from the Sicilian School, through the Sicilian-Tuscan poets, up to Dante and the poet known as Dante's Friend.[9]

7 For an approach to the lyric based on classical poetics, see Boris Maslov, 'Lyric Universality', in *The Cambridge Companion to World Literature*, ed. by Ben Etherington and Jarad Zimbler (Cambridge: Cambridge University Press, 2018), pp. 133–48.

8 Attridge, *The Singularity of Literature*, p. 26 and note 16; *The Work of Literature*, pp. 59–60.

9 *I canzonieri della lirica italiana delle origini*, ed. by Lino Leonardi, 4 vols (Florence: SISMEL-Edizioni del Galluzzo, 2000), I: *Il Canzoniere*

The poem that opens the manuscript — and therefore to which a degree of precedence, if not origination, is attributed — is Giacomo da Lentini's (c. 1210–1260) *Madonna, dir vo voglio*.[10] Yet, the first two stanzas of this inaugural poem in the chronological order of the *canzoniere* are actually a 'translation' of an earlier poem, *A vos, midontç*, written by the Occitan troubadour Folquet de Marselha (c.1155–1231). The first stanza of Folquet's poem reads:

> A vos, midontç, voill retrair'en cantan
> cosi·m destreign Amor[s] e men'a fre
> vas l'arguog*ll* gran, e no m'aguda re,
> qe·m mostras on plu merce vos deman;
> mas tan mi son li consir e l'afan
> qe viu qant mu*e*r per am*a*r finamen.
> Donc mor e viu? non, mas mos cors cocios
> mor e reviu de cosir amoros
> a vos, dompna, c[e] am tan coralmen;
> sufretç ab gioi sa vid'al mort cuisen,
> per qe mal vi la gran beutat de vos.[11]

Vaticano; Roberto Antonelli, 'Canzoniere Vaticano latino 3793', in *Letteratura italiana: Le Opere*, ed. by Alberto Asor Rosa, 4 vols (Turin: Einaudi, 1992–96), I: *Dalle Origini al Cinquecento* (1992), pp. 27–44; Roberto Antonelli, *I poeti della scuola siciliana*, 3 vols (Milan: Arnoldo Mondadori Editore, 2008), I: *Giacomo da Lentini*, pp. xxvi–xxx.

10 The Sicilian poems are mostly transmitted in three manuscripts produced in Tuscany, a very different context form the court of Frederick II in which they were composed. They underwent a linguistic Tuscanization: 'a sort of translation, of phonic and thus graphic transcoding from the original Sicilian to Tuscan, more or less homogeneous, through which only slight traces of the previous formulation show themselves', Fulvio Delle Donne, *La porta del sapere: Cultura alla corte di Federico II di Svevia* (Rome: Carocci, 2019), p. 109. As Delle Donne makes clear, this is an 'absolutely common phenomenon' in textual transmission: 'in the Middle Ages, but to a different extent also in the preceding and subsequent epochs, any copyist, while transcribing a text, adapted it to his linguistic code of reference; in other words, he read and automatically "translated" it, adapting its parlance to the orthographic rules [...]' (p. 109; translation is mine).

11 Folchetto di Marsiglia, *Le poesie di Folchetto di Marsiglia*, ed. by Paolo Squillacioti (Pisa: Pacini, 1999), p. 414. Trans. by David Murray: 'To

Giacomo's version of the first stanza reads and looks quite different:

> Madonna, dir vo voglio
> como l'amor m' à priso,
> inver' lo grande orgoglio
> che voi, bella, mostrate, e no m'aita.
> Oi lasso, lo meo core,
> che 'n tante pene è miso
> che vive quando more
> per bene amare, e teneselo a vita!
> Dunque mor'e viv'eo?
> No, ma lo core meo
> more più spesso e forte
> che non faria di morte   naturale,
> per voi, donna, cui ama,
> più che se stesso brama,
> e voi pur lo sdegnate:
> Amor, vostr'amistate   vidi male.[12]

The two poems are not only in different languages, but also have different line-lengths, metrical structures, and rhyme patterns, not to mention Giacomo's adding three

---

you, madam, I want to relate in song | How Love torments me and directs me | To great pride (and it does not help me) | That you show me there where I ask you for greater mercy, | But so great are my worry and travails | That I live as I die, from loving exquisitely. | So I live and die? No, but my eager heart | Dies and lives again from love's worry | About you, lady, whom I love so deeply; | Accept with joy his life on painful death, | For I ill saw your great beauty', in David Murray, 'Telling the Difference: Linguistic Differentiation and Identity in Guillem de Berguedà, Giacomo da Lentini and Bonifacio Calvo', *Zeitschrift für romanische Philologie*, 134.2 (2018), pp. 381–403 (p. 389).

12 Roberto Antonelli, *I poeti della Scuola siciliana*, I, *Giacomo da Lentini*, pp. 10–14. Trans. by David Murray: 'My lady, I want to say to you | How love has taken me | Towards the great pride | That you, beauty, show, and do not help me, | Alas, my heart, | Which is placed in such pain | That it lives as it dies | From loving well, and keeps itself alive. | So do I live and die? | No, but my heart | Dies more often and more forcefully | Than it would from natural death | From you, lady, whom it loves | And craves more than itself, | And you just disdain it; | Love, I did not see well your friendship', in Murray, 'Telling the Difference', p. 390.

stanzas to Folquet's two (the only surviving ones for us). They were produced in rather different sociocultural contexts and possibly delivered through diverse media. The troubadour *canso* was probably performed orally with musical accompaniment in the feudal courts of Provence. The Sicilian *canzone* was most likely read and circulated among the lettered functionaries of the itinerant imperial court of Frederick II in Southern Italy, where its author worked as an administrative officer (*notaro*) trained in rhetoric and jurisprudence.[13] Both lament the pain of unrequited love, but they have quite different meanings in their respective contexts: the former might reflect the conditions and concerns of a feudal society, the latter seems to meditate, with a rather intellectual interest, on the effects of the fire of love on the individual and his language. So, what is it that the two poems share? What allows for this transcontextual re-enactment? Is it only the foundational value ascribed to Provençal poetry by the learned Sicilian poet decades later? Giacomo translates Folquet and appropriates his words.[14] In this way, not only does he acknowledge the troubadour poet as a predecessor and thus inscribe his own writing in a tradition he himself is tracing, but he also confirms the validity of that speech for an audience that knows the 'original' by introducing contextual differences. There is something in that speech act that is considered still prac-

---

13 Delle Donne, *La porta del sapere*, pp. 83–98.

14 Discussing Giacomo's operation, for which he 'was rewarded [...] by the compiler of the Vatican *canzoniere* with his position at the "start" of the Italian lyric tradition', Murray writes: 'More importantly, Lentini's lexical choices and those of his transmitters gesture at both stages toward the "old" language of poetry, be that Occitan or Sicilian, while simultaneously demonstrating what can be done with the new. Linguistic traits are used to triangulate relationships between connected traditions, and to construct a new literary identity, proving ownership of this new language, counter-intuitively, by drawing attention to its lineage', in Murray, 'Telling the Difference', pp. 392–93.

ticable in the new context and within the retrospectively traced 'genre'.

Emphasizing the innovations of *Madonna, dir vo voglio* in comparison to its model, Michelangelo Picone speaks of *translatio poesis* as a creative operation and concludes his analysis of the changes introduced by Giacomo with these words: 'A simple grammatical change is sufficient to generate a complex cultural transformation. Therefore, it is in the folds of linguistic translation that the seed of the nascent literary tradition hides itself.'[15] According to Picone, in Folquet, the 'I' is both alive and dead; in Giacomo, only the heart suffers that paradoxical condition, not the 'I' in his entirety. In any case, among other revelatory variations (including the Sicilian's reduction of emphasis on physical presence and on the request for mercy as a direct exchange), one could simply note that in Folquet the heart dies and comes back to life ('mos cors cocios | mor e reviu'; my eager heart | dies and lives again; ll. 7–8), in Giacomo it dies repeatedly ('lo core meo | more più spesso'; my heart dies more often; ll. 10–11). Deep down, it is not the 'biography' that is interchangeable, but a certain code, a set of signs that do not yet convey any contextual meaning. They perform an action when enacted in a certain context, but make themselves available for re-enactment and for the production of various meanings in different contexts. The

15 Michelangelo Picone, 'Aspetti della tradizione/traduzione nei poeti siciliani', in *Percorsi della lirica duecentesca. Dai siciliani alla 'Vita nova'* (Fiesole: Cadmo, 2003), pp. 17–31 (p. 31). Delle Donne speaks of an 'artistic translation' that follows a tradition that 'goes back to the origins of Latin literature, which begins with the translation of the Homeric *Odyssey* provided by Livius Andronicus', in *La porta del sapere*, p. 97; translation is mine. See also Roberto Antonelli, 'L'"invenzione" del sonetto', *Cultura neolatina*, 47 (1987), pp. 19–59 (p. 25); Furio Brugnolo, 'I siciliani e l'arte dell'imitazione: Giacomo da Lentini, Rinaldo d'Aquino e Iacopo Mostacci 'traduttori' dal provenzale', *La parola del testo*, 3 (1999), pp. 45–74 (pp. 45–53).

code's range of possibilities can be modified in a negotiation between conservation and innovation, but it is not radically alterable, otherwise the enunciation would be unrecognizable for the reader and the enunciated discarded as incomprehensible. The viability of a model is not predicated on biographical identity, but on the recognizability and shareability of the model itself.

The 'origins' of the Italian lyric tradition take place and are made possible by a validation, through re-enactment, of a model offered by troubadour poetry. It is a transfer that shows continuity across languages, time, and space. A similar case is Catullus' translation of Sappho's fragment 31 in his carmen 51: at the 'origins' of Latin love lyric lies the 'translation' with variations of a poem written by a woman in another land more than five centuries earlier. The subject of enunciation inscribes himself, even mentioning his own name and the name of his beloved Lesbia, into the re-enactment of the model. The previous poem functions as an offering of potentialities. The re-actualization does not need to be a 'faithful' rendering in another language, that is to say, a translation in the modern sense of the word. Those potentialities can be passed on through the re-enactment of the gesture that opens them up.

From a purely linguistic perspective, Giacomo's translation was probably unnecessary. One can in fact assume that the well-educated poet-officers at the court of Frederick II were perfectly able to understand the Occitan of the original. If such a translation was meant to enlarge the audience, one is compelled to ask: What audience? Whose audience? It may be hard to believe that this translation would have reached a much wider audience outside of the court, but it is the second question that interests me here. The audience supposedly to be enlarged does not seem to be Folquet's audience, but rather Giacomo's. More than a linguistic translation in the modern sense of the word, aimed at expanding the readership of Folquet's poem while maintaining as much as possible its 'original' meaning, this operation aims at creating both a new poem and a new poet, and in this way a new poetic tradition, by retrieving the gesture performed and valued in the earlier poem.

If the cultural gesture performable in both contexts is evidently the lament for unrequited love in association with the praise of the beloved, which is the linguistic gesture that can be repeated in diverse contexts and thus allow for this re-enactment? Which linguistic gesture needs a context for each of its performances in order to acquire a meaning, but at the same time is not bound to any historically fixed context? I would suggest that the linguistic gesture that makes such an iterability possible is *deixis*. In fact, the direct address to the beloved woman (*midontç/Madonna, vos/vo*) establishes from the outset an open referentiality that leaves the position of the addressee and object of the speech, as much as the position of the speaking 'I', open enough to be fulfilled in different speech contexts. My hypothesis, therefore, is that deixis may be the basic linguistic gesture that characterizes the lyric as a discursive mode.

EACH 'NOW'

Let us turn to another pair of poems — this time separated by a much longer temporal distance — or rather to one poem caught as it travels from the heart of an ancient empire to the periphery of a modern one: 'Anything Can Happen' by the Irish poet Seamus Heaney and the poem by the Latin poet Horace it re-actualizes (*Odes*, I, 34).

These two poems are at the centre of Jahan Ramazani's investigation of the relations between poetry and the news in *Poetry and its Others* (2013) and they are also mentioned in his illustration of the *translocal* character of Heaney's poetry in *A Transnational Poetics* (2009).[16] Horace's ode I, 34 reads:

> Parcus deorum cultor et infrequens,
> insanientis dum sapientiae
> consultus erro, nunc retrorsum
> vela dare atque iterare cursus
>
> cogor relictos. Namque Diespiter
> igni corusco nubila dividens
> plerumque, per purum tonantis
> egit equos volucremque currum,
>
> quo bruta tellus et vaga flumina,
> quo Styx et invisi horrida Taenari
> sedes Atlanteusque finis
> concutitur. Valet ima summis
>
> mutare et insignem attenuat deus
> obscura promens: hinc apicem rapax
> Fortuna cum stridore acuto
> sustulit, hic posuisse gaudet.[17]

---

16 Jahan Ramazani, *A Transnational Poetics* (Chicago: University of Chicago Press, 2009), p. 40. 'Neither localist nor universalist, neither nationalist nor vacantly globalist, a *translocal poetics* highlights the dialogic intersections — sometimes tense and resistant, sometimes openly assimilative — of specific discourses, genres, techniques, and forms of diverse origins. Located in translocation, transnational and cross-ethnic literary history thus differs from "postnational" or "postethnic" history, in which writers are viewed, when these terms are used most broadly, as floating free in an ambient universe of denationalized, deracialized forms and discourses' (p. 43).

17 'I was a stingy and infrequent worshipper of the gods all the time that I went astray, expert that I was in a mad philosophy. Now I am forced to sail back and repeat my course in the reverse direction. For Jupiter, who normally splits the clouds with his flashing fire, drove his thundering horses and flying chariot across a clear sky. At that the heavy earth and wandering rivers, at that the Styx, and the dreaded abode of hated

In this ode, Horace allegedly tells of how his certainties as a skeptical Epicurean rationalist were profoundly unsettled by the abrupt occurrence of an unexpected event: a lightning bolt hurled by Jupiter into the clear sky. This is precisely the phenomenon the absence of which had been used by Lucretius to question the general belief that thunderbolts are divine instruments in *De rerum natura* ('Again, why does he never hurl a bolt upon the earth and sound his thunder from a sky that is completely clear?', VI, 400–01).[18] Now, instead, this exceptional event that shakes the entire world induces the 'I' to ponder, astonished, on the omnipotence of the god and the unpredictable whims of Fortune. It is difficult to say whether this can be considered as a truly autobiographical episode, and it is equally problematic to specify to what extent Horace the poet is really distancing himself from his adherence to Epicurean philosophy. The general sense of the poem, however, is fairly clear: a dismay in the face of incomprehensible forces that humans are unable to explain.

Two thousand years later, Heaney rewrites Horace's ode into a poem first published in the *Irish Times* on 17 November 2001, under the title 'Horace and the Thunder', and then collected in *District and Circle* in 2006, under the new title 'Anything Can Happen'. The direct reference to the Latin predecessor is effaced in the collected

Taenarus, and the boundaries marked by Mount Atlas, were shaken. God has the power to cause the highest and the lowest to change places; he makes the illustrious dim and brings the obscure to light. With a piercing scream rapacious Fortune snatches the crown from one head and likes to place it on another', in Horace, *Odes and Epodes*, ed. and trans. by Niall Rudd (Cambridge, MA: Harvard University Press, 2004), pp. 84–87.

18 Lucretius, *On the Nature of Things*, trans., with introduction and notes by Martin Ferguson Smith (Indianapolis, IN: Hackett Publishing Company, 2001), p. 189.

poem: the title, which repeats the opening half-line and the beginning of line eight, is a general statement that summarizes the poem's 'message', perhaps even increasing the distance from the particular event to which the poem 'refers'.[19] Heaney's poem drops Horace's first strophe about the personal turnaround, and the 'now' (nunc; l. 3) of the change of mind, which follows the weather phenomenon in Horace, becomes the 'now' (l. 3) in which the event takes place. Heaney takes up the contrast between the usual phenomenon of lightning and the exceptional event that Jupiter makes happen, the unpredictable reversals that the god and Fortune bring about, and Mount Atlas, which marks the limits of the known Western world, becomes 'the Atlantic shore itself' (l. 7). Yet Heaney superimposes an intensely visual memory of the attack on the Twin Towers of 11 September 2001 on Horace's poem, especially in the catastrophic imagery of the added final strophe:

> Ground gives. The heaven's weight
> Lifts up off Atlas like a kettle-lid.
> Capstones shift, nothing resettles right.
> Telluric ash and fire-spores boil away.

Even though linked to an event very far from the 'original' one, this rewriting appears surprisingly close to Horace's words (particularly striking is the retention of Roman divinities in a context so charged with religious tension). An easy projection of the Epicurean vulgate on a materialistic West in pursuance of secularization is probably to be resisted, but the two poems undoubtedly evoke a similar reaction, that is, an unexpected dismay that overwhelms the experiencing subject and reveals the vanity of the convictions cultivated up to that point. The 'I' has to face the

19 Seamus Heaney, *District and Circle* (London: Faber, 2006), p. 13.

shocking irruption of unfathomable forces in their private life as well as on the stage of History. Heaney repeats with some variations the expressions pronounced two millennia earlier by his predecessor, letting their significance resonate with the new context. The words from the past return to be re-enacted in different circumstances, as if themselves independent of any temporal situation, establishing a kind of present outside of chronological time that speaks to every present as a discourse addressing itself specifically to it.

I am not interested here in the possible proximity of the abrupt fall of Horace's Epicurean illusions to the historical breakpoint Heaney is facing. What interests me is how those very words can be re-enacted in different cultural contexts. Heaney turns Horace's more I-centered meditative speech into a piece of wisdom — 'anything can happen' — addressed to a 'you' which, by mentioning ancient gods, seems to allude to its transhistorical validity. What in Horace is a personal crisis in the subject's belief becomes, in Heaney's poem, a sudden realization of a shared condition in the face of a historical catastrophe. The 'content-message' of Horace's ode may be suitable to the new context; yet, what is it that allows for the repetition of those words and figures?

Commenting on this pair of poems and comparing the durability of poetry with the rapid obsolescence of the news, Ramazani writes:

> The 'just now' of Horace's poem ('*nunc*') is renewed, doubling as the now of the ancient past and the now of the immediate present, unlike the once-only 'now' of the news. To reiterate and adapt Benjamin, poetry 'does not expend itself. It preserves and concentrates its strength and is capable of releasing it even after a long time.' [...] One part of our experience of Heaney's poem is the power of its compact and eerie evocation of

> the 9/11 attacks; another is our wonder at poetry's transhistorical durability and transnational adaptability [...]. Poet and reader encounter the 'news event' through a cross-historical and cross-cultural detour into literary antiquity, responding simultaneously to an ancient text and to current reality.[20]

For Ramazani, in order to understand Heaney's poem, the reader needs 'to know something not only about the Twin Tower attacks but also about Horace, Jupiter, the River Styx, and classical Fortune; you have to have some context for the poem's literariness and difficulty, its classical mythology, and elevated diction'. In other words, '[t]he poem acknowledges its deep embeddedness within literary tradition, instead of presenting itself as a history-free report of current reality.' This 'intensity' is achieved by 'deploying a variety of poetic resources' including syntactic complexity, apostrophe, enjambment, mixed registers, chiasmus, metaphor, simile, and alliteration. 'As memorable speech that remembers prior memorable speech, and yet that also evokes contemporary reality, the poem freely translates Horace to point up references to 9/11, dropping Horace's first stanza and adding a new final stanza.'[21]

Ramazani's analysis is undoubtedly accurate, but Heaney's poem only 'evokes' the 9/11 attacks or contemporary reality more generally insofar as it is read by readers who, having experienced those globally broadcast images and knowing the context of the poem's production, project that information onto the text. In the same way that the Latin poem does not necessarily evoke

20 Jahan Ramazani, *Poetry and its Others: News, Prayer, Song, and the Dialogue of Genres* (Chicago: University of Chicago Press, 2014), pp. 68–69.

21 Ibid., pp. 70–71.

Epicureanism nor even the Roman Empire, if the reader does not know anything about the poet Horace. Therefore, what is needed for the reader's response may not be, in the first place, 'some context for the poem's literariness and difficulty' nor the poem's 'deep embeddedness within literary tradition', but rather the recognition of a certain use of language which does exactly the opposite, that is, it subtracts the utterance from contextual referentiality. Horace's 'nunc' can be doubled in Heaney's 'just now' because there is nothing within the text that fulfils that act of temporal deixis, just as there is no individuated subject to whom the 'I' in Horace and the 'you' in Heaney refer. Before any production of meaning and any supplement of contextual information, the 'transhistorical durability and transnational adaptability' of Horace's lyric poem, as much as Heaney's, is based on its open referentiality. The words of Horace's ode are applicable to a different external context because the text does not provide any context for the utterance within itself. The news, on the contrary, seems to rely heavily on that immediate external referentiality whose transience makes it short-lived.

A lyric poem does not take the reader to an alternative space nor, as Jonathan Culler maintains following Käte Hamburger, does it project a fictional world;[22] it rather needs a larger world in which to happen as a performance, a world which it can *point to*.[23] The gesture underlying the text is not embedded in a world that the text itself brings forth as usually happens in narratives. If it had its own

22 Jonathan Culler, *Theory of the Lyric* (Cambridge, MA: Harvard University Press, 2015), pp. 106–08.

23 On lyric indexicality see Daniel Tiffany, 'Lyric Poetry and Poetics', in *Oxford Research Encyclopedia of Literature*, 30 April 2020, Oxford University Press <https://doi.org/10.1093/acrefore/9780190201098.013.1111>.

fictional world, the gesture could have been a fully accomplished action and it could be more easily transmitted in association with the meaning it would have acquired in that world. In contrast, this peculiar situation allows for a quite radical re-semantization of the gesture underlying the text in each of its contexts of reading and re-writing. Finally, the gesture readers recognize while reading a poem is likely to carry with it previous or subsequent instantiations of that gesture and this coalescence or accretion plays a crucial role in the *act-event* of reading and in the process of recognition.

GESTURAL COMMUNITIES

In 'What is Epic Theater?' (1939), Walter Benjamin famously describes Bertolt Brecht's epic theatre on the basis of a notion of gesture defined in opposition to the unity of action that Aristotle requires for tragedy in his *Poetics*. For Benjamin, gesture *interrupts* action and plot. As Samuel Weber explains, gesture 'involves not the fulfilment or realization of an intention or of an expectation but rather its disruption and suspension.'[24] Gesture also needs to be *quotable* and, as Benjamin affirms, '[q]uoting a text entails interrupting its context.'[25] According to Weber, gesture gives form because, while interrupting an 'ongoing sequence', it 'fixes it by enclosing it in a relatively determined space, one with a discernible "beginning" and "end." But at the same time, the closure brought about by gesture remains caught up in that from which it has partially extric-

24 Samuel Weber, *Benjamin's -abilities* (Cambridge, MA: Harvard University Press, 2008), p. 98.

25 Walter Benjamin, 'What is Epic Theatre? (II)', trans. by Harry Zohn, in his *Selected Writings*, 4 vols (Cambridge, MA: Harvard University Press, 1996–2003), IV: *1938–1940*, ed. by Howard Eiland and Michael W. Jennings (2003), pp. 302–09 (p. 305).

ated itself: in the "living flux" of a certain temporality'.[26] Benjamin ascribes a dialectical dimension to the tension embodied in gesture, and Weber comments,

> 'gesture' does not merely interrupt something external to it: the expressive intentionality of an action, the teleology of a narrative, or the causal necessity or probability of a sequence of events. It does all of this, but it also does something more: insofar as it is citable, it interrupts itself, and indeed, only 'is' in its possibility of becoming other, of being transported elsewhere.[27]

The theatrical space, from which discourse is directed at others and even at the future, is a virtual medium that 'causes the borders of all interiority — and be they those of the interval itself — to tremble'. This 'trembling' exposes both spectators and actors 'to the afterthought that, *after all*, they share the *same* trembling space of singularity. It is a space not of *Einfühlung* but of *Exponierung*, of exposure to the possibility of separation and detachment.'[28]

Benjamin's reflections bear a resemblance to Rainer Maria Rilke's lyric meditation on the 'ununterbrochene Nachricht' (uninterrupted message; l. 60) that calls upon the 'now' from the past and his exhortation to a trembling endurance in the first of the *Duineser Elegien*, written in 1912 (ll. 49–53):

> Sollen nicht endlich uns diese ältesten Schmerzen
> fruchtbarer werden? Ist es nicht Zeit, daß wir liebend
> uns vom Geliebten befrein und es bebend bestehn:
> wie der Pfeil die Sehne besteht, um gesammelt im Absprung
> mehr zu sein als er selbst. Denn Bleiben ist nirgends.[29]

---

26 Weber, *Benjamin's -abilities*, p. 100.

27 Ibid., p. 103.

28 Ibid., p. 108.

29 Rainer Maria Rilke, *Werke*, ed. by Manfred Engel, Ulrich Fülleborn, Horst Nalewski, and August Stahl, 4 vols (Frankfurt a.M.: Insel, 1996),

What Rilke seems to be proposing here, by way of exhortation, is the formation of a 'we' (wir) based on the repetition of the gesture of praising the beloved, which involves a suspension of knowledge ('Beginn | immer von neuem die nie zu erreichende Preisung'; Begin, always anew, the unattainable praise; ll. 39–40). This repeatability interrupts the particular individuality of each lover and of each beloved to inscribe each of them into a transtemporal citable gesture. At the same time, however, that potential gesture is 'fruitful' inasmuch as it enables the praising of each individual. In Rilke's elegy, the 'I' and the 'you' are brought together in a collective 'we' by this shareable gesture. Different individuals can enact it and in this way participate in a form of transtemporal choral community. Therefore, what can be shared — both synchronically and diachronically — is neither a particular object of love nor a specific text, but rather the gesture of praising and thus a certain modality of loving.[30]

Yet, following Brecht, Benjamin is well aware that gestures cannot be re-enacted a-historically.[31] Their viability depends on the social, cultural, and political conditions of the poets and their epoch, and different gestures contribute to the formation of different communities. In his 'Commentary on Poems by Brecht', written between the

---

II: *Gedichte 1910 bis 1926*, ed. by Manfred Engel and Ulrich Fülleborn, pp. 201–04. 'Shall not these oldest pains finally become | more fruitful for us? Is it not time that, loving, we | free ourselves from the beloved and endure, trembling, | as the arrow endures the bow, tightened in the leap, | to be more than itself? For staying is nowhere'; my translation.

30 See Francesco Giusti, 'Reversion: Lyric Time(s) II', in *Re-: An Errant Glossary*, ed. by Christoph F. E. Holzhey and Arnd Wedemeyer (Berlin: ICI Berlin, 2019), pp. 151–61 <https://doi.org/10.25620/ci-15_19>.

31 See Walter Benjamin, 'Notes from Svendborg, Summer 1934', trans. by Rodney Livingstone, in his *Selected Writings*, II.2: *1931–1934*, ed. by Michael W. Jennings, Howard Eiland, and Gary Smith (1999), pp. 783–91 (pp. 783–84).

fall of 1938 and March 1939 and partially published in the *Schweizer Zeitung am Sonntag* (April 1939), Benjamin engages with a sonnet by Brecht, 'Über die Gedichte des Dante auf die Beatrice' (On Dante's Poems to Beatrice):

> Noch immer über der verstaubten Gruft
> In der sie liegt, die er nicht vögeln durfte
> So oft er auch um ihre Wege schlurfte
> Erschüttert doch ihr Name uns die Luft.
>
> Denn er befahl uns, ihrer zu gedenken
> Indem er auf sie solche Verse schrieb
> Daß uns fürwahr nichts anderes übrig blieb
> Als seinem schönen Lob Gehör zu schenken.
>
> Ach, welche Unsitt bracht er da in Schwang!
> Als er mit so gewaltigem Lobe lobte
> Was er nur angesehen, nicht erprobte!
>
> Seit dieser schon beim bloßen Anblick sang
> Gilt, was hübsch aussieht und die Straße quert
> Und was nie naß wird, als begehrenswert.[32]

This sonnet problematizes exactly the traditional lyric gesture of praise that Rilke had retrieved from the past as a possibility for poets and for the formation of a choral 'we'. Past gestures need to be recognized and evaluated in the light of the conditions of the present in order to assess

32 'Even today, above the dusty crypt | In which she lies—the woman he could never screw | No matter how often he trailed after her— | For us, her name still makes the air tremble. || For he commanded us to remember her | By writing such poems about her | That we in truth had no choice | But to lend an ear to his beautiful praise. || Alas, what a bad habit he brought into vogue! | By praising with such mighty praise | What he had merely seen and had not tried! || Since he sang after just a glimpse | Whatever looks pretty and crosses the street | Without getting wet, passes for something to be coveted', in Walter Benjamin, 'Commentary on Poems by Brecht', trans. by Edmund Jephcott, in his *Selected Writings*, IV, pp. 215–50 (pp. 237–38). Yet, one could suppose that the present does not need to be considered as a unitary context and that different situations in the present could allow for the viability of different gestures.

their viability, but as Benjamin observes, those gestures are tested in a form transmitted from the past. The form of the sonnet helps to 'prove' the extent to which gestures and the values with which they have traditionally been associated are, or are no longer, viable in the present.

Relevant in this context is Daniel Tiffany's distinction between the generality of form, which cannot be forged, and the indexicality of diction, which points to social identities: 'One could no more fake the form of a sonnet than produce a forgery of the number 2. Only the style and diction of a particular sonnet — which possesses specific personal and social characteristics — can be faked'.[33] Thinking of Giacomo's 'Madonna, dir vo voglio' and Heaney's 'Anything Can Happen', one could wonder if the iterable gestures re-enacted in those poems could function as a medium between the 'potency as an index of social identities and desires'[34] that pertains to diction — pointing both to contemporary reality and back to the past — and the abstract generality of form, this way allowing for the transcontextual repeatability of those poems. Brecht retrieves the form of the sonnet, but breaks the traditional, now stereotypical diction with a popular, even vulgar, style, to mockingly contest the gesture of praise for a distant beloved authoritatively transmitted by Dante's poetry. Yet, there is still something captivating about this gesture, which implies a specific kind of desire.

Giorgio Agamben detects two different ontologies in the Western tradition: the ontology of the indicative or apophantic assertion and the ontology of the imperative or non-apophantic speech. According to the Aristotelian distinction in the *De interpretatione* (17a 1–7) to which

33 Tiffany, 'Lyric Poetry and Poetics'.

34 Ibid.

Agamben attends, non-apophantic is that speech which cannot be said to be true or false, because it does not manifest the being or not being of something in this world.[35] Command, prayer, exhortation, and possibly praise, so widespread in lyric poetry, belong to this type of speech. Indeed, as Ramazani remarks,

> As speech acts directed to an other, yet an other more veiled than a human interlocutor, poetry and prayer function simultaneously as acts of address, albeit partly suspended (hence address modulating into apostrophe), and as forms of meta-address, or images of voicing, because of the decontextualization of address from normal lines of human communication.[36]

Agamben identifies the command with the performative in J. L. Austin's sense of the word.[37] But at this point, it is helpful to introduce a distinction advanced by Culler between *performativity* in Austin's sense and *performance* as an enunciation that exposes only itself and that, in the lyric, finds a central rhetorical device in apostrophe.[38] Prayer, exhortation, and praise belong to this category of performance, which does not actualize something external to its enunciation, but exposes only itself and remains waiting in

---

35 Giorgio Agamben, 'Che cos'è un comando?', in his *Creazione e anarchia. L'opera nell'età della religione capitalista* (Vicenza: Neri Pozza, 2017), pp. 91–112.

36 Ramazani, *Poetry and its Others*, pp. 128–29.

37 J. L. Austin, *How to Do Things with Words* (Cambridge, MA: Harvard University Press, 1975).

38 Culler, *Theory of the Lyric*, pp. 125–31 and, on apostrophe, pp. 211–43. See also Jonathan Culler, 'Apostrophe', in *The Pursuit of Signs: Semiotics, Literature, Deconstruction*, 2nd edn (London: Routledge, 2001), pp. 149–71; Paul de Man, 'Lyrical Voice in Contemporary Theory', in *Lyric Poetry: Beyond New Criticism*, ed. by Chaviva Hošek and Patricia Parker (Ithaca, NY: Cornell University Press, 1985), pp. 55–72; William Waters, *Poetry's Touch: On Lyric Address* (Ithaca, NY: Cornell University Press, 2003).

its openness. Never reaching the ultimate limit of its actualization in an accomplished act, as in the performative, nor the limit of truth or falsity with respect to the state of things in the world, as in apophantic speech, prayer, exhortation, and celebration offer themselves to re-enactment as language that finds its realization only in its re-enunciation. In this sense, Culler is right in affirming that the lyric functions as a memorable language available for repetition in different contexts and as a potential vehicle for a variety of meanings.[39] Perhaps not only memorable verbal formulations but also certain selected gestures — such as the gesture of praise which Rilke re-proposes and Brecht condemns (but probably its historical dubiousness was already implicit in Rilke's exhortation) — can reach the status of lyric 'cliché', and maybe even of 'poetic kitsch' as described by Tiffany.[40]

The lyric, therefore, would be an enunciation that does not actualize anything but itself. From its utterance, one cannot know if the prayer, exhortation, or command will be heard, obeyed, and executed. It can only solicit a response from the external world; it establishes a relation between language and world that is held in suspension in

39 Culler, *Theory of the Lyric*, pp. 336–48.

40 Baudelaire's ambition to create a cliché is discussed in Daniel Tiffany, *My Silver Planet: A Secret History of Poetry and Kitsch* (Baltimore, MD: Johns Hopkins University Press, 2014), pp. 23–24. Culler, too, refers to Baudelaire's contention arguing that the highest success for the memorability of lyric language is to become a cliché, Culler, *Theory of the Lyric*, p. 131. In *My Silver Planet*, Tiffany explores the functions and potentialities of 'poetic kitsch' in connection with diction for the formation of a common language and collective experience. With respect to the link between 'poetic kitsch' and 'minor literature', it is interesting that, in his elegy, Rilke mentions the Italian Petrarchist poet Gaspara Stampa as a precursor, instead of Petrarch or Dante's 'style of praise', although he had been considering translating Dante's *Vita nova* and eventually renounced doing so just before starting writing the first elegy, see Giusti, 'Reversion'.

its potentiality.[41] This suspended relationship, which underlies lyric speech, calls for an external world in which to take place and the repetition of its performance in the attempt to bring it forth. In such language re-enacted in its pure mediality, an idea of *gestural communities* can be envisioned: communities based on the shareability of gestures, not on reciprocal identification among individuated subjects nor on communal knowledge nor on identical responses to literary works. This process of community formation based on the transferability (or *quotability* to use Benjamin's term) of certain gestures may allow us to think of the transcontextual dimension of literary texts differently.[42] This kind of gesture, in fact, comes before the production of any contextual meaning and before the fulfilment of the utterance's referentiality; its transference, therefore, does not necessarily require the translatability of meaning.

In the encounter of a reader (and potential future writer) with a lyric poem, what Attridge aptly dubs an *act-event*, the process of individuation is counteracted by a process of dis-individuation. While reading, 'I' come to inhabit the open position of the poem's speaker making the utterance my own, but at the same time, 'I' inscribe myself into a recurrent gesture, into a transindividual medium. I have been suggesting that the most basic lyric gesture is *deixis*, an open deixis that never fills the gap it points to with a fixed 'now', 'this', or 'that'. One could advance the hypothesis that it bears similarities with Agamben's no-

41 Francesco Giusti, 'Temporalità liriche. Ripetizione e incompiutezza tra Dante e Caproni, Montale e Sanguineti', *California Italian Studies* 8.1 (2018) <https://escholarship.org/uc/item/87x199p7> [accessed 23 May 2020].

42 Perhaps also of the transtemporal co-agency of texts as explored in Rita Felski, *The Limits of Critique* (Chicago: University of Chicago Press, 2015), pp. 151–85.

tion of gesture, a type of action in which 'nothing is being produced or acted, but rather something is being endured and supported'.[43] This gesture is neither a means to an end nor an end in itself. As dance would be gesture 'because it is nothing more than the endurance and the exhibition of the media character of corporal movements',[44] the lyric might be gesture because it might be nothing more than the endurance and the exhibition of the media character of linguistic movements.

When one looks at the lyric transhistorically and subtracts contextual functions and meanings from poems, what is left to be handed over to readers and future writers is the pure mediality of certain gestures that the lyric use of language exposes primarily through its open referentiality. Such language with no ends nor functions, which calls for a world without creating it but rather holding ontology in suspension, provides a sort of shareable linguistic present for readers across different epochs and places. Readers can inscribe themselves into this present by re-enacting the poem. Two different poems as cultural artefacts or two events of the same poem as acts of reading can be connected based on the 'disappropriated', and for this reason common, presence of the medium itself. What the lyric has to offer, when readers voice its words or poets rewrite previous poems, is a shareable position with no fixed individual identities.

If Rilke exhorts 'us' to welcome and re-perform the gesture of praise, Brecht subjects it to ironic criticism, but he too must acknowledge its endurance. In fact, as Brecht

---

43 Giorgio Agamben, 'Notes on Gesture', in his *Means without End: Notes on Politics*, trans. by Vincenzo Binetti and Cesare Casarino (Minneapolis: University of Minnesota Press, 2000), pp. 49–61 (p. 56).

44 Ibid., p. 57.

makes clear with respect to Dante's poetry, 'uns fürwahr nichts anderes übrig blieb | Als seinem schönen Lob Gehör zu schenken' (we in truth had no choice | But to lend an ear to his beautiful praise; ll. 7–8). Readers can decide how to respond — whether to make those words their own or refuse to do so — only insofar as they are called upon to respond. When readers inhabit that space by uttering the poem in their own present, they find themselves participating in a gestural community — a rather demanding position. Something similar could be said about the transnational character of poetic 'mourning' explored by Ramazani, which can be and has often been exploited for nationalist purposes.[45] Our decision on the level of meaning — about the meaning of the poem but also of the community in which we find ourselves — is predicated upon the sharing of that transcontextual gesture that first constitutes us as a 'we' and puts us in common.[46]

Investigations in world literature often have to take the transcultural applicability of the notion of 'literature' for granted. This procedure may be understandable when engaging with contemporary literary production in a globalizing world, but proves problematic when deployed in or across different epochs. Therefore, it may be helpful to observe how recurrent gestures are presented by texts, before they acquire context-based values and functions that

45 Ramazani, *A Transnational Poetics*, pp. 71–93.

46 Interesting here is Eric Hayot's use of the term 'gestural' to describe the process of 'worlding': 'Worlding is gestural; it is an attitude, by which one adjusts oneself, symmetrically, to one's inclusion in a whole that does not belong to one. Worlding creates worlds because it bespeaks the part's relation to the whole, but also because in that speaking it imagines (or recreates) the whole that opens to the part. The whole neither precedes the part, nor succeeds it'. See Eric Hayot, 'World Literature and Globalization', in *The Routledge Companion to World Literature*, ed. by Theo D'haen, David Damrosch, and Djelal Kadir (London: Routledge, 2012), pp. 223–31 (p. 228).

can pertain to a significant variety of symbolic realms, from religious rituals to aesthetic objects, passing through social performance, commercial entertainment, and political protest. These realms can intersect, overlap, or mingle in a certain text, but also remain separate. Apter seems to hint at a possible solution when she explores the untranslatability of *fado* and *saudade*.[47] Despite their different historical meanings, behind the web of interrelated words that Apter brings together, such as *saudade, acedia, Sehnsucht, spleen, melancholia,* there might be a transcultural gesture of lament for a painful separation from an unrelinquishable object of desire. These gestures are not primarily offered as meaningful actions directed to a specific goal; they come before any acquisition of contextual meaning and socio-historical purpose, and thus they are made culturally available for re-enactment in different times and places.

47 Apter, *Against World Literature*, pp. 137–55.

The World after Fiction

J. M. Coetzee's *The Childhood of Jesus*

BENJAMIN LEWIS ROBINSON

> Fiction, being a serious affair, cannot accept prerequisites like (1) a desire to write, (2) something to write about, (3) something to say. There must be a place for a fiction of apathy toward the task of writing, toward the subject, toward the means.[1]

Coetzee's note dates from October 1973 and is the first of a collection of notes and drafts towards what would have been his second novel entitled *Burning the Books* — the novel was unrealized. This concern — call it a concern about *indifference to fiction* — remains, I would argue, a persistent preoccupation of Coetzee's literary production. His

* My thanks to J. M. Coetzee and the Harry Ransom Center, the University of Texas at Austin, for permission to cite from the J. M. Coetzee Papers.

1 J. M. Coetzee, Draft of *Burning the Books* (unrealized), 19 October 1973, Manuscript Collection MS-0842, Container 33.1, Handwritten notes, and unfinished draft, 19 October 1973–4 July 1974, J. M. Coetzee Papers, Harry Ransom Center, The University of Texas at Austin.

fiction is profoundly informed by a sense that fiction, and the institution of literature more broadly, cannot assume significance in contexts, specifically colonial/postcolonial contexts, in which the European or Eurocentric character of the literary tradition may with good reason be considered questionable, or even suspect. Speaking in 1987 upon receiving the Jerusalem Prize, Coetzee contrasted the South African situation with that of Cervantes, who in the figure of Don Quixote and at the beginning of the tradition of modern fiction 'leaves behind hot, dusty, tedious La Mancha and enters the realm of faery by what amounts to a willed act of the imagination'.[2] In South Africa such a Quixotic undertaking was not only impossible, but also unjustifiable: 'In South Africa there is now too much truth for art to hold, truth by the bucketful, truth that overwhelms and swamps every act of the imagination.'[3] His Australian writings, in contrast, are more directly, which is to say often metafictionally, concerned with figures and scenarios that would prefer not to have anything to do with fiction, least of all the fictions of which they find themselves a part. These fictions stage in different ways iterations of the indifference to fiction, which paradoxically turns out to present a profound provocation of fiction. It is as if Australia were the new La Mancha — and it is no coincidence that *Don Quixote* in one form or another is increasingly present in the Australian writings. *The Childhood of Jesus* is, among other things, an interpretive translation into a new time and a new place — into a new world, I am inclined to say — of *Don Quixote*. I'll return to this at the end of the essay.

---

2 J. M. Coetzee, 'Jerusalem Prize Acceptance Speech', in his *Doubling the Point: Essays and Interviews*, ed. by David Attwell (Cambridge, MA: Harvard University Press, 1992), pp. 96–100 (p. 98).

3 Coetzee, 'Jerusalem Prize', p. 99.

In the sketches for *Burning the Books,* Coetzee imagined a censor in some future time of political oppression and civil unrest. Working in a glass tower, he reads and promptly incinerates the canon of Western literature, unmoved by the texts except to wonder why such things never happen to him. His work destroying works of literature and thought was to be interspersed with scenes of 'real life' in the city below that he observes through his binoculars. The conceit was, to quote from Coetzee's notes:

> A consciousness inhabiting a tower of glass in a burning city, reading the mind of the West and amusing itself by turning a pair of binoculars of magically high power on scenes of the street (violence) and bedroom (sex) about it — [4]

In Coetzee's 2013 book, *The Childhood of Jesus,* a very different, but not altogether unrelated, scenario is played out: The figures in this book are transported on a boat and arrive in a new life 'washed clean', without histories, memories, or identities. They are washed clean, I would suggest, of the Western 'tradition' or rather, referring to the title of the book, of the Christian tradition insofar as this continues to inform modern Western culture.[5] Indeed, there is indication that the 'old life' the migrants are fleeing from is nothing other than the history of the West. There is a kind of inversion of contemporary geopolitics. If the migrants are not European (it is not clear where exactly they come from and they can't remember), they are refugees from the idea of Europe, from a world defined by Europe.

One compelling consequence of this new beginning in a new life is an utter indifference to the institution

---

4 Coetzee, Draft of *Burning the Books,* p. 3.

5 J. M. Coetzee, *The Childhood of Jesus* (London: Vintage, 2014), p. 24. Subsequent citations in-text.

of literature and specifically to fiction. *The Childhood of Jesus* presents a world without fiction, with no need for fiction, without the least interest in fiction. If in 1973, Coetzee considered presenting the destruction of the Western tradition, but perhaps also its culmination, in scenes of political suppression, graphic violence, and censorship, in the 2013 book, the challenge to fiction is more thoroughgoing because less explicit. And this perhaps speaks to a change in fundamental mood in the forty years between 1973 and 2013 (and not just in Coetzee's writings). In the latest novel, there is no censorship, no political violence, no suppression, no discrimination, no injustice — just indifference.

And it is not a cold, calculating indifference. On the contrary: the new polity, Novilla, in which the novel is set, is characterized by a *benevolent* indifference. What is strangest about this strange land to which we are transported in Coetzee's fiction is that everyone is 'so decent, so kindly, so well-intentioned' (p. 36). One can speculate that the indifference exhibited by the inhabitants of Novilla, and perhaps also their benevolence, is the first outcome of the forgetting of the European tradition that is not mourned but simply missing in Coetzee's novel — if a novel about a world without literature, which has no interest in the sort of things that happen in literature and that get literature going, can remain itself recognizable as a work of literature at all.

The plot is quickly told: a man and a boy, strangers to each other, arrive in a strange land, where they have to learn a foreign language (Spanish) and begin their new lives with new birthdates and new names — the man, Simón, the boy, David. David has (supposedly) lost a note he was carrying from or to his parents during the passage and

Simón, at least as he remembers it, has committed himself to take care of the boy and to find his mother. Although the boy has no memory of her, Simón is convinced he will recognize David's mother. Early in the novel he does so in the figure of Inès (the chaste, the virgin), to whom he offers the child and who then assumes the role of or, alternatively, if we are to credit Simón's intuition, *becomes what she is,* David's doting and indulgent mother.

The boy and the man are bound by the lost message that fell, by accident, into the sea — 'The fishes ate it' (p. 34), says the boy. It was, so to speak, lost in translation between the old life and the new. Nonetheless, it is the memory of this lost communication across the seas that distinguishes the two new arrivals from the other migrants who populate Novilla, who 'have washed themselves clean of old ties' (p. 24). 'Why are we *here*?' asks David shortly after their arrival:

> His gesture takes in the room, the Centre, the city of Novilla, everything.
>
> 'You are here to find your mother. I am here to help you.'
>
> 'But after we find her, what are we here for?'
>
> 'I don't know what to say. We are here for the same reason everyone else is. We have been given a chance to live and we have accepted that chance. It is a great thing, to live. It is the greatest thing of all.'
>
> 'But do we have to live here?'
>
> 'Here as opposed to where? There is nowhere else to be but here.' (p. 21)

Both Simón and David have questions of a 'metaphysical' sort that don't seem to trouble others in Novilla. But I want to suggest that their respective concerns are in fact of altogether different orders. Simón retains a relation to the 'old life'; he has what he calls 'shadows of memories'

(p. 77) that he cannot or will not let go. David, the child protagonist of *The Childhood of Jesus*, seems in contrast to be altogether new. He comes to present a perplexity to all those around him — and certainly to the reader of the book. If he is, as even the most pedantic of the adults he encounters are prepared to admit, an 'exceptional child' (p. 253), is he a true exception transcending the order of things in Novilla or is he just a child with a 'lively imagination' (p. 265) who is rather over-indulged?

Simón, for his part, feels that there is something missing in the new life. What is missing is a sense of yearning, desire, longing; he finds life in Novilla too anodyne (p. 76). Novilla is a state of benevolence. Everyone, he observes, is so decent, kindly, and well-intentioned, but as a result social relations seem to him strangely 'bloodless' (p. 36) and lacking in 'passion' (p. 75). Life in Novilla, he complains, 'lacks the substantiality of animal flesh, with all the gravity of bloodletting and sacrifice behind it. Our very words lack weight, these Spanish words that do not come from our heart' (p. 77). Everyone else, however, appears quite content in the new life. For them nothing is invisible, nothing missing, and not even irony, the minimal sense that things may be other than they seem, can be made out in the Spanish in which the inhabitants of Novilla communicate. As Simón remarks of two of his closest acquaintances:

> Álvaro does not trade in irony. Nor does Elena. Elena is an intelligent woman but she does not see any doubleness in the world, any difference between the way things seem and the way things are. An intelligent woman and an admirable woman too, who out of the most exiguous of materials — seamstressing, music lessons, household chores — has put together a new life, a life from which she claims — with justice? — that nothing is missing. It is the same with Álvaro

> and the stevedores: they have no secret yearnings he can detect, no hankerings after another kind of life. (pp. 76–77)

Only Simón is 'the exception, the dissatisfied one, the misfit' (p. 77). Because he finds this life to be lacking, Simón represents the 'old life' — as if this 'lack' is precisely what he dimly remembers of the old life.

So Simón presents the alienated figure of the 'old life' insofar as the essence of the old life consisted in the hankering for another kind of life. Whereas what is new about the new life is that there is no *other* life that has been lost or is longed for or is even possible. The new polity of Novilla is a community of migrants that operates on the basis of universal hospitality. But what is strange about this place is not that all strangers are welcome but that no one is interested in strangeness. Strangeness has no pull, no secret, no element of mystery; it generates no angst. Simón observes: 'His fellow stevedores are friendly enough but strangely incurious. No one asks where they come from and where they are staying' (p. 26). Strangers are welcomed because they are not treated as strange — they are simply expected to adapt to the language, the diet, and everyday regime of the new dispensation. There is no expectation of, no longing for, no hostility towards, and ultimately not even a sense of otherness in Novilla. Here: *every other is like the other*.

One consequence of this indifference to strangeness is that Novilla presents a world without literature, or more precisely a world without the 'work of literature'.[6] It is not simply that 'Spanish literature' is not listed among the course offerings at the Institute and is not to be found

6 See Derek Attridge, *The Work of Literature* (Oxford: Oxford University Press, 2015).

among the books — *Teach Yourself Carpentry, The Art of Crocheting, One Hundred and One Summer Recipes* — at the local library (p. 179), but the minimal and most innocuous, because fictional, 'otherness' of literary invention does not appear to pique the interest of the inhabitants of Novilla. I will not say they are *deprived* of the work of literature because for the most part, for most of its inhabitants, this lack is not experienced as a lack; they do not seem to register a cultural or spiritual impoverishment but live lives of collegiality and contentment. Nothing is missing — not another life, not the promise of another life, not even the fiction of other lives. The 'work of literature', insofar as it facilitates a pleasurable singular encounter with otherness, belongs to the 'old life'. The implication is that literary fiction is more implicated in the metaphysics of the old world than readers and literary critics such as ourselves would like to acknowledge.

To reiterate: What is strange — perhaps uncanny — about Coetzee's fictional presentation of Novilla is that nothing is experienced as strange. It is no coincidence that this fictional world resonates with a number of anxieties expressed by those who have reservations about the progress, if not the imperial procession, of World Literature as a catch-all and all-consuming discipline in literary studies. Already in his canonical 1952 essay, translated by Maire and Edward Said as 'Philology and *Weltliteratur*' in 1969, Erich Auerbach had speculated that world literature was threatened by the global standardization of language, culture, and forms of life with which, he writes, 'the notion of *Weltliteratur* would be at once realized and destroyed.'[7] In writings following her *Death of a Discipline* (2003) Gayatri

7 Erich Auerbach, 'Philology and *Weltliteratur*', trans. by Maire and Edward Said, *The Centennial Review*, 13.1 (1969), pp. 1–17 (p. 3).

Spivak speaks in positively apocalyptic tones of the loss, perhaps we could say, the forgetting of the 'ethics of alterity' for which the take–over of Comparative Literature by World Literature is symptomatic.[8] Emily Apter echoes such concerns in *Against World Literature* (2013), speaking of the 'oneworldness' attendant on the principle of universal translatability.[9] Such a project of translation is realized after a fashion in Coetzee's novel, which furthermore presents an ironic fulfilment of Aamir Mufti's claim in *Forget English!* (2016) that World Literature belongs to a broad and systematic effacement of the hegemony of English.[10] The novel, written in English by the South African now Australian Nobel Laureate, presents a world in which English has literally been forgotten but in which a single, universal language is nevertheless exclusively operative. In Novilla, 'Spanish' is the new English. Meanwhile, in *What Is a World?* (2016), Pheng Cheah worries that the *world-making* capacity of literature will be occluded by the attention to the *inner-worldly* production and circulation of what is called 'world literature'. If, as Cheah argues, the world as a standardized space defining all that is given risks superseding the 'other possible worlds' to which literature attests and in a certain sense brings forth,[11] then Coetzee has written a novel about a possible world (is it this one?)

---

8 Gayatri Chakravorty Spivak, *Death of a Discipline* (New York: Columbia University Press, 2003).

9 Emily Apter, *Against World Literature: On the Politics of Untranslatability* (London: Verso, 2013).

10 Aamir R. Mufti, *Forget English! Orientalisms and World Literatures* (Cambridge, MA: Harvard University Press, 2016). In a more affirmative sense, Rebecca L. Walkowitz treats Coetzee's novel as exemplary of a novel 'born translated' in an 'age of world literature', see the Introduction to Walkowitz, *Born Translated: The Contemporary Novel in an Age of World Literature* (New York: Columbia University Press, 2015).

11 Pheng Cheah, *What Is a World? On Postcolonial Literature as World Literature* (Durham, NC: Duke University Press, 2016), p. 129.

in which the world exists oblivious to literature, that is to say, without the possible worlds or modes of worlding afforded by fiction.

For many literary critics, the advent of World Literature seems quite literally to be the end of the world! At the end of *Against World Literature*, Apter diagnoses a 'psychopolitics of planetary dysphoria' in our time, defined by what she calls the 'depression of the globe or the thymotic frustration of the world'.[12] This fundamental mood, characterized by a 'total evacuation of euphoria', is legible in a series of works of contemporary philosophy and criticism but epitomized in Lars von Tier's 2011 film *Melancholia*, in which the end of the world is the end of the film.[13] Insofar as it presents a world — perhaps the world after the end of the world and certainly the end of World Literature — emptied of *eros* and *thymos*, of passion and spiritedness, *The Childhood of Jesus* can be seen as contributing to, or reflecting on, this atmosphere of 'planetary dysphoria'. In this context, what is unsettling about Coetzee's novel is that Novilla is not so very far away. Novilla is the world that the depressed opponents of World Literature fear the world is becoming or has already become.

There is, I want to say, an 'old world' reading of *The Childhood of Jesus* — a reading that, like Simón, finds Novilla, if not the book about Novilla, to be somehow lacking. Exemplary in this regard would be Robert Pippin's reading of the text. For Pippin, an unabashed proponent of the Western canon, the dysphoria of the novel presents the contours of longing, of properly human longing 'for more than bodily satisfactions, for the beautiful, for philosophy, for self-knowledge' that is exhibited precisely in its

12 Apter, *Against World Literature*, p. 8.

13 Ibid., p. 338.

absence: 'We can see such yearning and what it entails better, by virtue of its absence'.[14] Such a reading, however, fails to acknowledge that the serious and thoughtful inhabitants of the city show no symptoms of depression — quite the contrary. In any case, as we all know and as Simón keeps being told, there is much to be said for leaving the old life and its longings behind. As Elena remarks at one point: 'You may want more than goodwill; but is what you want better than goodwill?' (p. 67). The question thus arises: Is there a 'new world' reading of the novel? Is there a space in the 'new life' for something like a literature that does not correspond to the questionable longings of the old? This would be the question of a new world literature, absolved, if this were possible, from the tradition that it cites.

I have yet to explicitly approach the significance of the title — *The Childhood of Jesus*. The old life as a longing for another life is a caricature of Christianity and recites a certain critique of Christianity — the account, for example, of how the 'true world became a fable'.[15] In contrast to his sensible and secular counterparts in Novilla, Simón turns out to be, on account of his longings, an unreconstructed 'Christian'. This presents one line of approach to the curious title of Coetzee's book. I have suggested that Coetzee's book presents an attempt to write a fiction of a world beyond or before and in any case freed from complicities with 'Christianity', where Christianity is understood to extend

14 Robert Pippin, 'What does J. M. Coetzee's Novel *The Childhood of Jesus* Have to Do with the Childhood of Jesus?', in *J. M. Coetzee's* The Childhood of Jesus*: The Ethics of Ideas and Things*, ed. by Anthony Uhlmann and Jennifer Rutherford (London: Bloomsbury, 2017), pp. 9–32 (p. 26).

15 Friedrich Nietzsche, *The Twilight of the Idols, or How to Philosophize with a Hammer* (1888), in his *The Anti-Christ, Ecce Homo, Twilight of the Idols, and Other Writings*, ed. by Aaron Ridly and Judith Norman (Cambridge: Cambridge University Press, 2005), p. 171.

to and encompass the theological residues that continue to inform ostensibly post-Christian secular Western culture, not least literature. And perhaps it goes still further back. That literature is prefigured in scripture, that it inherits a theological tradition which it also disavows, that it exhibits despite itself a 'religious remainder', is at the centre of Derrida's various reflections on Kierkegaard's 'Christianized' reading of the episode of Abraham responding to the command to sacrifice Isaac in *Fear and Trembling*:

> be it understood that literature surely inherits from a holy history within which the Abrahamic moment remains the essential secret (and who would deny that literature remains a religious remainder, a link to and relay for what is sacrosanct in a society without God?), while at the same time denying that history, appurtenance, and heritage. It denies that filiation. It betrays it in the double sense of the word: it is unfaithful to it, breaking with it at the very moment when it reveals its 'truth' and uncovers its secret.[16]

Kierkegaard's reading is too 'Christian' because he takes the absolute other to be the voice of a transcendent God, whereas as Derrida insists: '*tout autre est tout autre*' — *every* other is *altogether* other.[17] Every encounter with *an* other has therefore the form of a struggle, in Kierkegaard's terms, between the universal laws of the 'ethical' and the unspeakable singularity of the 'religious'. The secret kept and revealed in Abraham's silence, the silence that expresses the singular injunction of the altogether other, is structurally shared by literature, which unapologetically exhibits the

16 Jacques Derrida, 'Literature in Secret', in his *The Gift of Death* (Second Edition) *& Literature in Secret*, trans. by David Wills (Chicago: University of Chicago Press, 2008), p. 157.

17 Derrida, *The Gift of Death*, p. 77–78.

secret as the very logic of its ironic operation. Literature is forever, rather frivolously, asking forgiveness for the secret significance it seems to promise, but withholds. To cite Derrida again, literature is always saying: 'Sorry for not meaning to say...' (Pardon de ne pas vouloir dire...) — or simply, with Bartleby, whose secretive formula Derrida takes to exhibit the paradigm of literature: 'I would prefer not to.'[18]

Coetzee's experiment, very much in the tradition of betrayal Derrida describes, involves producing a fiction that brackets the 'holy history', the very tradition upon which literature is supposed to rely for its efficacy. In Novilla, where the food is so bland and bloodless, there is no 'taste for a secret' — and also, significantly, no interest in sacrifice. A general law or norm (as it does not appear to be violently enforced) governed by the principle of good-will seems to be the order of the day. In a benevolent world ruled by the universal imperatives of 'the ethical', how might the other, the absolutely other, appear? Would such a singularity be recognizable at all, and if so in what terms, by what means of expression? Or in words that would be altogether foreign to the inhabitants of Novilla: Were the messiah, were Jesus Christ himself to arrive, how would he be recognized? These are the sorts of questions prompted by the open secret betrayed in the title: *The Childhood of Jesus.*

How in this world does 'the other' appear in their singularity? One answer, and it is doubtless as slippery as Derrida's 'Sorry for not meaning to say...' or Bartleby's 'I would prefer not to', is: *like a fish*. At one point, Simón finds himself looking into David's eyes:

---

18 Derrida, 'Literature in Secret', p. 119; also *Gift of Death* 77–78; and Jacques Derrida and Maurizio Ferraris, *A Taste for the Secret*, trans. by Giacomo Donis (Malden: Polity, 2001), pp. 26–27.

> For the briefest of moments he sees something there. He has no name for it. *It is like* — that is what occurs to him in the moment. Like a fish that wriggles loose as you try to grasp it. But not like a fish — no, like *like a fish*. Or like *like like a fish*. On and on. Then the moment is over, and he is simply standing in silence, staring.
>
> 'Did you see?' says the boy.
>
> 'I don't know. Stop for a minute, I am feeling dizzy.' (p. 222)

When something is like, like, like…and one cannot grasp what it is that it is like, one might say: it is like a fish. To do so, however, is to revert to a metonymy that relates to the *experience* (of failing to grasp) rather than standing for an intentional object. But what then does it mean to say it is like *like like a fish* — on and on? Is there a difference between *like a fish* and *like like like a fish*? Is the second formulation more 'fishy' than the first or is it rather the experience of *likeness* that is intensified? David would appear as absolute *likeness*.

Certainly, something of the vertigo of Simón's experience is expressed in his grasping for words. Something is missing — he lacks the name, indeed, lacks so much as a metaphor for what he sees in David's eyes. There is, however, a distinction between what he feels habitually to be *lacking* (the occasion of his 'old world' longing) and what he here experiences as *like*. If David presents someone *other*, who cannot be accounted for and ultimately accommodated in Novilla, he does not stand as an instance of transcendence (for another life, something other than this life), instead he is *like*, as if excavating an alterity *inside* of this life as it is given. Not coincidentally Señor León, David's teacher, observes, 'In all that time I have not had a like case' (p. 271).

The *altogether other* (*tout autre*) is in fact not altogether *other*, as in the tradition of religion and of literature Derrida refers to, but absolutely *like*. Coetzee's experiment in presenting a fiction about a world indifferent to fiction — indifferent to fiction of the sort that belongs to the tradition that relates life to another life that is felt to be lost or longed for — exposes, in the figure of David, another principle by which otherness expresses itself in the world, which is also to say, another principle of fiction: *like-ness*. Ironically, in a novel that supposedly presents a 'new life', such fiction recovers or saves the strangeness of this life without reference to, in the suspension of, the longing for a new one. Alternatively, to distinguish these two types of fiction, 'old world' fiction from 'new world' fiction, one can say: there is no *secret* in *The Childhood of Jesus,* the form of the secret does not structure the reading experience, there is just an unfolding of an ungraspable *like-ness*. *The Childhood of Jesus* is *like* nothing I have ever seen before.

Like Simón, the boy too claims to remember, but his memory is of a different order altogether. For David remembers *every single thing*. This is in any case how it sometimes seems to the reader. He sees singularity. Ironically, the one thing he does not see, on account of this otherwise exceptional faculty, is *like*. For David, it would seem, because of the precision of his memory and perception, there is no basis for resemblance. And this is at the root of the cosmological and mathematical misunderstandings between him and Simón.

There is a lot of philosophical, perhaps even Platonic, dialogue in Coetzee's novel. Much of it, however, is, to quote a figure in the book, 'schoolboy philosophizing' (p. 296). And this is part of the challenge, also the irritation, of the book: are we to take the exchanges between Simón and David as addressing, or at least indicating, serious philosophical questions, or are these simply discussions between a strong-willed infant with a 'lively imagination' and a well-meaning adult attempting, by the limited means available to him, to show the child how to make his way in the world? And this ambiguity of course has larger ramifications for the reading or readability of the novel. In short: is Simón responding to the needs and demands of a child or to the even more obscure communications of a god? Is David just a child, or is he also something else altogether? *Or* is perhaps *every* child a Jesus-child until — for better or worse? — the normalizing processes of education and upbringing set in?

In contrast to Simón, for whom 'something is missing', David, exceptional although everyone agrees he is, is usually described as lacking in some way. Señor León suggests he has a deficit, 'a specific deficit linked to symbolic activities' (p. 243). The expert called in by the school to assess his case relates this deficit to environmental factors, referring principally to the boy's uncertain parentage: 'The real, I want to suggest, is what David misses in his life' (p. 246). As a result, she proceeds, he feels special, even abnormal; this contributes to his insubordination, and she recommends that the boy be removed from the school, as well as from Simón and Inès, and taken into the care of a Special Learning Centre.

David himself does not seem to feel anything missing in his life. He is instead preoccupied with the gaps or cracks that seem to traverse his world or seem to prevent it from cohering into a stable world of norms and conventions. When Simón impatiently tells the boy to keep his 'game' avoiding the cracks on the pavement for another day, the boy responds that he doesn't want to 'fall into a crack' —

not a visible crack but 'another crack', one that 'nobody knows' (p. 43). If one only sees singularity, there are no connections, or only contingent ones, between everything that is the case. David's world, one can speculate, is a collection of discrete instances and events which are not bound by similarity or contiguity habitually constituted by the 'normal' forms of experience; instead phenomena are separated by yawning gaps.

When they return to this anxiety some time later, Simón attempts to draw a distinction between gaps, which are part of the 'order of nature' — and are therefore nothing to worry about — and cracks which break with it: 'It [a crack] is like cutting yourself with a knife, or tearing a page in two. You keep saying we must watch out for cracks, but where are these cracks? Where do you see a crack between you and me? Show me' (p. 209). The occasion of this second discussion is the constellation of stars known as the 'twins' — the space between them is a gap rather than a crack. In this regard, Simón ventures, they are *like* numbers. But David knows no 'like': '"Are all the stars numbers?" he asks brushing off Simón's attempts to correct him. Far from introducing the idea of lawfulness and continuity into David's world by means of the comparison, the boy sees the stars just like he sees numbers — as absolutely discrete. For the boy claims to 'know' the numbers although he cannot count: '"I know all the numbers. Do you want to hear them? I know 134 and I know 7 and I know" — he draws a deep breath — "4623551 and I know 888 and I know 92 and I know —"' (p. 177). Does he just know the *names* for random numbers, or does he actually *see* the numbers he names? Later, asked by Señor León to do some basic arithmetic (adding fish as it happens), he will say, 'I can't see them' before with much effort, or show of effort, coming up with the right answer: 'This time...this time...it is...eight' (p. 266). In any case, the exchange regarding gaps and cracks ends with Simón stating: 'There is never any crack between the numbers. No number is ever missing', and the boy responding: 'There is! You don't understand! You don't remember anything!' (p. 211).

It is not only numbers that the child has trouble with — David also exhibits a peculiar relation to language. The day that Simón sees the 'like-ness' in his eyes, David had asked: 'Why do I have to speak Spanish all the time?' (p. 221). David's dissatisfaction with speaking Spanish is not the same as Simón's. Simón feels constrained by a foreign language in which he cannot authentically express himself and by a use of language that does not, even in the minimal form of irony, acknowledge that things may be other than they seem. David on the other hand, struggles in the Spanish language to express *the way he sees things*; he struggles, namely, to convey singularity in the generality of everyday language. He takes to expressing himself in a private language, speaking 'gibberish', while Simón patiently tries to explain the necessity of communication if he is not to be ostracized in the community (pp. 221–22). It is with his first encounter with reading, specifically reading fiction, that David begins to find ways to use the Spanish language in a new way. It is not the either/or of irony that he discovers — that what is meant can be other than what is said — but rather the errant adventure of signification — that what is expressed always means more than what is meant. In his reading, without fear of contradiction or incoherence, he perversely affirms the least likely interpretation.

In the local library, in which otherwise no literature is to be found, Simón uncovers *An Illustrated Children's Don Quixote* (p. 179) with which he proposes to begin to teach the child to read. '*Don Quixote* is an unusual book', Simón explains to David after reading the first chapter to him:

> 'It presents the world to us through two pairs of eyes, Don Quixote's eyes and Sancho's eyes. To Don Quixote, it is a giant he is fighting. To Sancho, it is a windmill. Most of us — not you, perhaps, but most of us nevertheless — will agree with Sancho that it is a windmill.' (p. 182)

David, however, insists on reading the book through the eyes of Don Quixote: 'He's not a windmill, he's a giant! He's only a windmill in the picture' (p. 182). After all, he points out, 'It's not the adventures of Don Quixote and Sancho. It's the adventures of Don Quixote' (p. 183). What does it mean to read *Don Quixote,* not just in a manner sympathetic to what he stands for, for example the struggle between the bounty of the imagination and the barrenness of reality, but to read *Don Quixote* like Don Quixote?

When David claims later that he can read, Simón berates him:

> 'No, you can't. You can look at the page and move your lips and make up stories in your head, but that is not reading. For real reading you have to submit to what is written on the page. You have to give up your own fantasies. You have to stop being silly. You have to stop being a baby.' (p. 196)

The boy does not practice the discipline of reading fiction, but does that mean he cannot read? What does it mean after all to do justice to a book like *Don Quixote*? If the point of the novel, as many readers would agree, is precisely the opposite of the one stated by the narrator of the novel, namely, to show the dangers of reading fiction, if it presents rather an extended plea for the powerlessness of fiction against the domination of reality, then what could be more appropriate than a fictional reading of fiction? David is to be sent to a Special Learning Centre because he would rather persist with the fiction, than submit to the discipline of reading, to reading as a discipline. When Simón takes him to see Señor León in a last-ditch attempt to save him from the special school, the teacher interviews him on the meaning of the story of *Don Quixote*. The parallels between Don Quixote's fate at the hands of his benevolent companions and David's at those of the well-meaning authorities of Novilla could not be more explicit:

> [David] 'They lock him up in a cage and he makes poo in his pants.'
>
> 'And why do they do that—lock him up?'
>
> 'Because they won't believe he is Don Quixote.'
>
> 'No. They do it because there is no such person as Don Quixote. Because Don Quixote is a made-up name. They want to take him home so that he can recover his senses.' (p. 265)

Later the boy expresses perplexity at Señor León's reaction, after all Don Quixote exists. To which Simón replies: 'True, there is a man in the book who calls himself Don Quixote and saves people. But some of the people he saves don't really want to be saved. They are happy just as they are' (p. 268). For someone like Señor León, Don Quixote upsets the social order, 'He likes order in the world. There is nothing wrong with that' (p. 268).

In Coetzee's text, *Don Quixote* stands for two possible comportments to fiction: there is a disenchanted reading of fiction that brings one back to one's senses, back home to reality, restoring one's sense of order in the world; and there is an enchanted reading of fiction that sends one on a laughable quest to save oneself from reality (from what is called 'reality'), a necessarily futile quest insofar as it inevitably runs up against the compulsions of said reality. One could also say, there is a reading of fiction that understands the *institution* of literature, that it consists in a certain suspension of reality; and there is a reading of fiction, which is actually not a reading of *fiction* at all, for the fiction is taken to be more real than reality. There is a world-preserving reading of fiction and a world-upsetting one, a universal and a singular, or, with Kierkegaard, an ethical and a religious, or finally a sensible and a mad reading. While, to be sure, a world consisting only of the second kind of readers would descend into sheer chaos; would a world without some of the madness of reading *really* be a world? Is that ultimately the difference (the source of the strange like-ness) between the fictional Novilla and the world we still inhabit? We may be no better prepared to entertain the arrival of the messiah than the inhabitants of Novilla, but it is still possible to be entertained by *The Childhood of Jesus*.

When David shows Simón that he can read and write, he transcribes the following line from Don Quixote: '*Deos* [sic] *sabe si hay Dulcinea o no en el mundo*' — 'God knows whether there is a Dulcinea in this world or not' (p. 259). Is Don Quixote here betraying a first trace of doubt regarding his entire fictional enterprise? Or is his undertaking in fact sustained by such ambivalence? Reality or fiction? — that is a matter not for a mere man, or knight errant, but for a god. Or alternatively, reading the 'god knows' in the more colloquial sense: Reality or fiction, no one knows. It would not, in other words, be the absolute conviction in the reality of his enchantments that makes Don Quixote Don Quixote, but a readiness to concede the fictionality of all reality. In Coetzee's novel, the line takes on a further ambiguity: not even a god could save us from such confusion. For if David is indeed divine, then what he knows, is precisely not communicable, at least not in a sensible way, in the life and times of Novilla. He appears like an 'exceptional' child with a 'lively imagination', like a child with special needs, like an infantile Don Quixote, like like like a fish. Señor León tells him to write on the board: '*Conviene que yo diga la verdad,* I must tell the truth.' David writes: '*Yo soy la verdad,* I am the truth' (p. 266). Is he telling the truth or is he just being silly? *Deos sabe.*

Extracting Indigeneity

Revaluing the Work of World Literature in These Times

RASHMI VARMA

Extractivism has emerged as a new form of ecological imperialism truly graspable only on a world scale. Some go further to argue that it is 'a constitutive feature of the current operations of capital'.[1] In its delimited sense it involves the extraction of 'huge volumes of natural resources, which are not at all or only very partially processed and are mainly for export according to the demand of central countries'.[2]

* I would like to thank Francesco Giusti and Benjamin Lewis Robinson for inviting me to Berlin for their symposium on the Work of World Literature in June 2019, for their thoughtful comments on my paper and for all the practical help I have needed in getting this ready for publication.

1 Verónica Gago and Sandro Mezzadra, 'A Critique of the Extractive Operations of Capital: Toward an Expanded Concept of Extractivism', *Rethinking Marxism*, 29.4 (2017), pp. 574–59 (p. 579).

2 Alberto Acosta, 'Después del saqueo: Caminos hacia el posextractivismo', *Perspectivas, Análisis y Comentarios Políticos América Latina*, 1 (2015), pp. 12–15 (p. 12), cited in Gago and Mezzadra, 'A Critique of the Extractive Operations of Capital', p. 576.

This definition points to the ways in which extractivism feeds on and extends pre-existing centre-periphery relations in the contemporary world order. For although colonial regimes relied heavily on extracting raw materials from the colonies, extractivism now forms a crucial element of many postcolonial economies, and is often carried out in the name of development. As Verónica Gago and Sandro Mezzadra argue about the Latin American case, 'the intensification of extractive activities primarily linked to non-renewable resources [...] have returned Latin American economies to their classical role as the providers of raw materials, except that now raw materials are mainly directed to China.'[3] Equally, it is important to point out that the contemporary phase of capitalist accumulation consists of not only the increasing power of extractivism as an 'economic model' that fuels development in neo-liberal conditions but also that it coincides with, or even that it is currently being produced by, a global turn to authoritarian populism, from Latin America to India. This of course has far-reaching implications for the depletion of democracy as such and for the instrumentalization of democratic processes to smooth the flows of extraction.

My essay draws on extractivism as a political and economic project to argue that it is always already also a cultural project. Extractivism as a project that has its own specific process focalizes critical questions of cultural value, for what is being extracted on a global scale is not just the bauxite from the Niyamgiri mountains of Odisha or coal from the fields of Jharkhand in India, copper from Zambia, or gold and silver from Patagonia, but also memory, history, art, as well as 'cultural values that are tied to entire

3 Gago and Mezzadra, 'A Critique of the Extractive Operations of Capital', p. 576.

ecosystems of survival and existence'.[4] Heterodox economists such as Joan Martinez-Alier have contributed their scholarship towards developing theories of the domain of 'non-economic epistemes' that produce values that are incommensurable with those of the utilitarian economic realm.[5] In a different vein I argue that extractivism draws in the conflicts and collisions between different kinds of value in ways that may help us work out the tenuousness of those divisions, beyond the classic base-superstructure framework that plots the relations between culture and economy.

The concept of incommensurability presupposes a problematic exteriority of culture, especially primitive or indigenous culture, to the operations of global capitalism. But Marxist theorists like Rosa Luxemburg, David Harvey, and others have pointed out that capitalism requires and depends on a non-capitalist outside to serve as resource to be extracted for its development.[6] From this perspective, the outside (or the commons, as in the history of primitive accumulation), far from constituting some kind of natural external domain, is produced by capital itself.

In the context of such a conceptualization of extractivism as pertaining to both economic and non-economic

---

4 Ibid., p. 580.

5 See, for instance, Joan Martinez-Alier, *The Environmentalism of the Poor: A Study of Ecological Conflicts and Valuation* (Cheltenham: Edward Elgar, 2003). See also Martin P. A. Craig, Hayley Stevenson, and James Meadowcroft, 'Debating Nature's Value: Epistemic Strategy and Struggle in the Story of "Ecosystem Services"', *Journal of Environmental Policy & Planning*, 21.6 (2019), pp. 811–25.

6 Rosa Luxemburg, *The Accumulation of Capital* (1913), trans. by Agnes Schwarzschild (London: Routledge and Kegan Paul, 1951); David Harvey, 'The New Imperialism: Accumulation as Dispossession', *The Socialist Register*, 40 (2009), pp. 63–87. See also Rashmi Varma, 'Primitive Accumulation: The Political Economy of Indigenous Art in Postcolonial India', *Third Text*, 27.6 (2013), pp. 748–61.

realms and constituting the intertwining of the two within the always emergent logic of capital, literary theory must then also attend to the problem of representation that attaches to the projects and processes of extraction. Within dominant postcolonial theory, one way of approaching this issue of representation has been via a theorization of an unassimilable subaltern otherness that is relentlessly exploited but cannot ever be adequately represented within elite frames of representation such as literature. This has in fact led to a wholesale scepticism towards, if not outright rejection of, representation itself in some quarters.[7] This is in sharp distinction to the materialist modes of conceptualizing the constitutive outside as also the materially submerged or the ideologically invisibilized within canonical literary frames. After all, the coal underneath our fields or the bauxite in the belly of our mountains offer not only material value that is subjected to relentless extraction within the neoliberal world order, but also signify the domain of cultural difference in a world that thirsts for the invisible and the other to be corralled for extracting value. Macarena Gómez-Barris in her work on extractivism has called out the 'Eurocentric, high modernist, and totalizing visions of differentiated planetary life that rendered natives invisible and illegible'.[8] Literature that is written either as a registration of the depleting life-worlds of the extractive zones or as resistance to the ongoing onslaught mounted

7 See Neil Lazarus, *The Postcolonial Unconscious* (Cambridge: Cambridge University Press, 2011), especially pp. 114–60. See also Rashmi Varma, 'Beyond the Politics of Representation', in *New Subaltern Politics: Reconceptualising Hegemony and Resistance in Contemporary India*, ed. by Srila Roy and Alf Nilsen (Delhi: Oxford University Press, 2015) for a more detailed explication of the point that I am making here.

8 Macarena Gómez-Barris, *The Extractive Zone: Social Ecologies and Decolonial Perspectives* (Durham, NC: Duke University Press, 2017), p. 16.

on the poor and the indigenous communities can be read then as mediating global regimes of extraction that rely on conditions of invisibility. In this same vein, Achille Mbembe has pointed to extractivism as a historically racialized mode of accumulation. He writes:

> Extraction was first and foremost the tearing or separation of human beings from their origins and birthplaces. The next step involved removal or extirpation, the condition that makes possible the act of pressing and without which extraction remains incomplete. Human beings became objects as slaves passed through the mill and were squeezed to extract maximum profit. Extraction not only branded them with an indelible stamp but also produced the Black Man, or [...] the subject of race, the very figure of what could be held at a certain distance from oneself, of a *thing* that could be discarded once it was no longer useful.[9]

What anti-extractivist literary theory asks us to do is to go beyond the call for the search for a radical otherness that resides outside the bounds of capitalism. It calls instead for the embrace of what Gómez-Barris calls a 'cognitive and embodied mode of seeing' that can help us apprehend 'submerged modes' of existence in the lifeworlds of the peripheries.[10] Like the lining of coal dust on the lungs of miners.

In the following sections I analyse two short stories of Indian indigeneity where extractivism provides 'the formal literary condition' of indigenous writings. Through these readings I hope to illustrate the ways in which the liter-

9 Achille Mbembe, *Critique of Black Reason*, trans. by Laurent Dubois (Durham, NC: Duke University Press, 2017), p. 40

10 Gómez-Barris, *The Extractive Zone*, pp. xiii and xvi.

ary work of resisting extractivism can find formal shape.[11] Extractivism in the South Asian region has been central both to the unfolding of the European colonial project and to the subsequent postcolonial state formation. As Sharae Deckard puts it: 'The subcontinent has functioned as a testing-ground for large-scale environmental engineering, from the tea plantations, cash crop monocultures, and mass hydraulic schemes and river diversions of the colonial period, to the modernization schemes and Green Revolution in the twentieth-century, to transnational extractivism and bio-piracy in the neoliberal era'.[12] For India, in particular, extractive industries have been viewed as providing 'shortcuts to progress', with masses of people rendered landless and pushed into precarious labour in cities. Deckard rightly points out that this has continued well into the twenty-first century, triggering 'a wide spectrum of resource conflicts over pasture, fish, forest, the siting of hydro-electric mega-dams, and open-cast mining'.[13] As the project of extractivism reshapes and ravages the countryside's material and social composition, the indigenous community is subjected to both spectacular moments of displacement (as when dams are constructed and millions are rendered homeless) as also to what Rob Nixon has termed 'slow violence'.[14] This involves disrupting what

---

11 Christine Okoth, 'Extraction and Race, Then and Now: Ecology and the Literary Form of the Contemporary Black Atlantic', forthcoming in special issue of *Textual Practice*.

12 Sharae Deckard, 'Land, Water, Waste: Environment and Ecology in South Asian Fiction', in *The Oxford History of the Novel in English*, 11 vols (Oxford: Oxford University Press, 2010–19), x: *The Novel in South and South East Asia since 1945*, ed. by Alex Tickell (2019), pp. 172–86 (p. 172).

13 Ibid., 176.

14 Rob Nixon, *Slow Violence and the Environmentalism of the Poor* (Cambridge, MA: Harvard University Press, 2013).

Sudhir Puttnaik has called the 'ecological collectives'[15] of indigenous communities. Virginius Xaxa has pointed out that the common predicament of these communities is 'characterised by steady erosion of their control and access to land, forest and other resources'.[16]

Two short stories from the collection titled *The Adivasi Will Not Dance* by Hansda Sowvendra Shekhar provide illustrative sites where the full force of extractivism is registered and worked through the frame of the literary.[17] Shekhar, who is a medical officer in the small town of Pakur in Jharkhand in eastern India, has been hailed as a pioneering adivasi (from the Santhal tribe) writer writing in English, even as that nomination does grave injustice to his stature as an emergent writer of considerable heft writing in English.[18] Given the troubled history of how adivasis have been represented in mainstream literary and cultural narratives, one would think that he would be carrying a heavy burden of this representational history. After all, he is writing not only against the dominant representational frameworks of the colonial archive but also against postcolonial perspectives in which adivasis are seen as savage, backward, primitive, dangerous, and criminal. Or, inno-

15 Sudhir Puttnaik, 'Tribal Rights and Big Capital', in *Adivasi Rights and Exclusion in India*, ed. by V. Srinivasa Rao (Delhi: Routledge India, 2019), pp. 142–152 (p. 148).

16 Virginius Xaxa, 'Isolation, Inclusion and Exclusion: The Case of Adivasis in India', *Adivasi Rights and Exclusion in India*, ed. by V. Srinivasa Rao (Delhi: Routledge India, 2019), pp. 27–40 (p. 29).

17 Hansda Sowvendra Shekhar, *The Adivasi Will Not Dance* (New Delhi: Speaking Tiger, 2015). Subsequent citations in-text.

18 Santhals are the largest group of adivasis in Jharkhand. Adivasi is the Hindi word referring to India's indigenous people (about 8 percent of the population, and among the most marginalized and exploited). In neoliberal India, their lands are under constant threat by capitalists, both national and global, as the forests and mountains where many adivasis still live are sources of rich raw materials.

cent, naïve, simple, pristine, liberated. In either case, they are the quintessential Other of modern India.

But Shekhar bears this burden critically and unsentimentally, and with a sharp eye on possibilities of imagining it otherwise, as freedom, in fiction. In his writing, adivasiness is re-signified from its essential outsider status as an undefinable difference, as an object that is barely glimpsed in the rear-view mirror of the vehicle of development. Rather, it is patiently registered through words, names, turns of phrase, and cultural allusions that are woven into the narratives whose unevenness registers the stark disparities and concurrent inequalities within the time-space of being adivasi. In these stories, humour, parody, and satire carry as much weight as gritty realism committed to representing the lives of India's most marginalized citizens. In other words, these stories are not 'about adivasis' as much as they are stories in which adivasis are the protagonists and the story-tellers.

Shekhar narrates the everyday lives of adivasis who work as bank clerks, performance artists, migrant workers, sex workers, and landless peasants. The stories narrate the loves, fears, desires, intimacy, aspirations, as well as greed and prejudices of these ordinary adivasis. They are marked by a profound unsentimentality that in itself constitutes the political stakes of fictionalizing adivasi lives today. These are tales of dispossession in the context of the collapse of adivasi agrarian society and adivasi culture. Adivasis have been turned into unskilled labourers, seeking migratory jobs, eking out a precarious existence or have been forced to perform their adivasi-ness for mainstream society whether as dancers or craftspersons. In so many ways, they are the quintessential victims of the development logic that renders modernity as trauma. They endure multiple forms of violence on land ('they turn our land upside down, inside out, with their heavy machines […]. They sell the stones from our earth in faraway places', p. 172), culture ('we are becoming people from nowhere', p. 173), body ('we cough blood and remain forever bare bones', p. 172), environment. But what characterizes Shekhar's fiction that seems to take in the totality of adivasi life through the fragment of the short story is a dialectical method in which a worldly narratorial consciousness becomes critically aware of the depleted material but culturally rich worlds of adivasi lives.

Although many of the stories are set in rural India's tribal heartland of Jharkhand, the 'mineral-rich core of the Indian subcontinent' (p. 114), Shekhar's characters live in spaces that span from remote villages to urbanized mining towns and large, populous cities. What unites their disparate locations and situations is the fact that their experiences are enmeshed in a complex web of structural and everyday oppression that operates at several scales all at once, from the local networks of societal taboos and prohibitions to the depredations of national and multinational capital that have been given a free hand to extract raw materials in places where adivasis reside, regions rich in mineral wealth and forest cover. As Xaxa points out, tribal communities in India have been subjected to 'twin colonialism'. Having suffered at the hands of British attempts to control them, they are now subjected to the newly imposed atrocities of the postcolonial neoliberal order.[19] As Hari Charan Behera states: 'The tribal territories were annexed, their resources were exploited, and the people were forcefully evicted from their territory in the name of development since colonial administration'. But now the 'LA (Land Ac-

19 Xaxa, 'Isolation, Inclusion and Exclusion', p. 29.

quisition) Act has been introduced for acquisition of land', in the name of a 'so-called public purpose'.[20]

The appropriation of resources by corporations and the postcolonial state certainly recalls colonial relations in Shekhar's stories, particularly in the title story 'The Adivasi Will Not Dance' where the protagonist laments: 'They turn our land upside down, inside out, with their heavy machines [...]. They sell the stones from our earth in faraway places' (p. 172). The gap between the (post)colonial capitalist world and tribal India shapes the sense of 'they' — the agents and beneficiaries of global capital — wreaking havoc on 'our' — Santhal — lands. The writing is imbued with an enduring sense of alienation from the 'faraway places' and shadowy figures who profit and who are estranged from the lives of the characters in the stories.

'The Adivasi Will Not Dance' is narrated as a monologue by the 60-year old Mangal Murmu who speaks as 'a foolish Santhal'. That of course is just a ruse, as the story reveals a highly politicized consciousness of the different geo-political scales — the region, the nation (Dilli) as well as the world — and the layered historical memories of revolutions past impinging on the lives of the adivasis. Set in Matiajore, near the mining towns of Pakur, Sahebganj, Godda, Ranchi, and Dumka, Mangal and his community of share-croppers have been displaced by mining. As he says poetically, 'we are becoming people from nowhere' (p. 173) — losing our roots, faith and identities.

The story uses a first person voice that lends a diegetic mode to the narration which is nevertheless constantly broken up by the intrusive worldly consciousness that

20 Hari Charan Behera, 'Land, Property Rights and Management Issues in Tribal Areas of Jharkhand: An Overview', in *Shifting Perspectives in Tribal Studies*, ed. by Maguni Charan Behera (Singapore: Springer, 2019), pp. 251–71 (pp. 254–55).

bears on the story and exceeds what the displaced farmer actually 'knows' and can comprehend within the limits of his experience. The story of Mangal Murmu is closely interwoven with that of the materials of extraction.[21] The narrative is infused by an anti-extractivist aesthetic at the level of both form and content, as characterized by the dry dust of coal that envelops the entire world and forms a film through which the narrative eye perceives it. The coal's blackness 'is deep, indelible' (p. 174) and seeps into both material space and consciousness:

> The trees and shrubs in our village bear black leaves. Our ochre earth has become black. The stones, the rocks, the sand, all black. The tiles on the roofs of our huts have lost their fire-burnt red. The vines and flowers and peacocks we Santhals draw on the outer walls of our houses are black. Our children — dark-skinned as they are — are forever covered with fine black dust [...]. (pp. 174–75).

The black coal dust that envelops everything, from the earth to the trees and stones to art and the body is draining out the blood (embodied in the ochre earth, the red tiles, and flowers) from adivasi life. But extractivism does not operate on an economy of exchange. Accumulation and dispossession are its currency. As Mangal Murmu asks rhetorically, for there is no one responsible for responding: 'What do we Santhals get in return? Tatters to wear. Barely

21 Citing Upamanyu Pablo Mukherjee, Sharae Deckard writes: 'Environment, as a web of relations between both human and non-human agents, is not only a prominent thematic presence in the content of South Asian fiction, but "a formal and stylistic presence" mediating uneven development, ecological imperialism, and environmental degradation', Deckard, 'Land, Water, Waste: Environment and Extractivism in South Asian Fiction', p. 172.

enough food. Such diseases that we can't breathe properly, we cough blood and forever remain bare bones' (p. 172).

However, these same adivasis whose very blood is blackened by the dust of extraction are recruited to showcase the nation's diversity through cultural performance — dance, music, craft. Mangal asks poignantly: 'What has our art given us? Displacement, tuberculosis' (p. 178). The purportedly sacred and ritualistic nature of adivasi art is opportunistically commodified, as adivasis are made to dance on land from which they have been evicted for a thermal plant whose benefits are most likely to be siphoned off elsewhere.

In the end, Mangal Murmu's impassioned monologue and his courageous refusal to perform his indigeneity, collapses in defeat as the government's henchmen descend on him for his impertinence in speaking to the President of India. The spectacle of a landless adivasi addressing the highest office holder in the nation is one that can only be conjured through and in fiction. It also doubles up on the meaning of representation that Gayatri Chakravorty Spivak had written about in her famous essay 'Can the Subaltern Speak?'.[22] In staging a powerful confrontation between the adivasi and the state, the narrative suggests that power also lies in refusal. The eloquent address of the protagonist simultaneously expresses the anguish of the dehumanized, proletarianized, and commoditized people, while giving literal voice to the communities that are submerged beneath the radar of global social justice movements.

---

22 Gayatri Chakravorty Spivak, 'Can the Subaltern Speak?', in *Can the Subaltern Speak? Reflections on the History of an Idea*, ed. by Rosalind C. Morris (New York: Columbia University Press, 2010), pp. 21–78.

The story 'Baso-jhi' operates on a different register and narrates the story of a character who is the classic figure of a scapegoat for the traumas of modernity that her community undergoes. It is told almost entirely from the perspective of a narrator who has the worldly knowledge of the long history of adivasi exploitation. In Baso-jhi's story the private, communal, and public worlds of exploitation collide in such a way that the story is best read and understood as an allegory. It is the allegorical form that reveals the gaps that are left unrevealed in the narration of the private trauma of an adivasi woman.

The story is set in the village of Sarjomdih in Jharkhand, on the large forested plateau known as Chhotanagpur. It is the quintessentially in-between kind of place, the kind of borderland that extractivism produces and thrives on. A predominantly Santhal village that worships Sarna, deity of the 'aboriginal faith' of the area, it has grown into a semi-urban conurbation with the establishment of a mine and a copper factory on its southern outskirts. This 'Copper Town', which was forever 'illuminated and throbbing with life', was 'now gradually threatening to swallow all of Sarjomdih' (pp. 114–15). As it turns out, it becomes the epicentre for a chain of events that are to destroy the community in the village. Since its establishment 'few people farmed in Sarjomdih anymore' (p. 115). Having been forced to give up their 'fecund land' for the building of roads and factories, the villagers had turned into 'coolie' and 'reja', wage labourers in the factory and mines. Those who succeeded in garnering some measure of upward mobility gratefully accepted low level jobs in banks, the army, and government offices, exercising power in a community now riddled with class hierarchies.The narrative's unevenness is brought to the fore when in parts it reads like a litany of opposition to development as an elite ideology, in part as sociological discourse: the village, we are told, is 'standing testimony to the collapse of an agrarian Adivasi society and the dilution of Adivasi culture, the twin gifts of industrialisation and progress' (p. 115). For 'Sarjomdih, which bore the repercussions of development' had now acquired 'all the signs of urbanity' — concrete houses, cable tv, two-wheelers, hand pump, a primary school, and a narrow winding tarmac road called the 'main road' (p. 115). In spite of these ragged signs and 'gifts' of an unevenly distributed modernity, the narrator concedes: 'Still, this was progress, considering how the Adivasis had lived so far' (p. 115).

But as much as the outer frame of the story is narrated by an urbane adivasi who is critical of the depredations of development, the story belongs to its eponymous protagonist. It privileges her consciousness, her feelings, the ways in which she perceives things and the social relationships that she forges and that are in the process of tumultuous change. It is in the gap between the two frames that we can read how this story operates as an allegory of extractivism itself, narrating the multiple levels at which extractivism functions to create alienation both of adivasi society from the dominant, mainstream society and within adivasi society itself whose ravaged condition is held in place by the production of internal boundaries between inside and outside, with catastrophic consequences for both the individual and her community.

The story paints an idyllic scene at the outset at the centre of which is the figure of Basanti, or Baso-jhi. Dressed in a white cotton saree, she cuts an impressive figure as the narrative eye zooms in on her tall, strong, dusky figure standing among a group of women who seem to have some sort of social bond. The description of her physical features is accompanied by the declaration that she had become 'an integral part of the day to day life of the village' (p. 114). She seems to possess a reservoir of stories of Bidu, the Santhal hero who slayed demons 'a long, long time ago', that she narrates to the children around her (p. 113). But it is precisely in the way in which the narrative draws attention to the process of becoming 'integral' that we first note the presence of an outsiderliness that haunts the ideal of community in this village.

As the narrative sweeps away from Baso-jhi to take in the broader rural topography, it brings into view all the contradictions of industrialization and progress as they strike roots in a place like Sarjomdih. The very basic infrastructure of water delivered through hand pumps, a main road built to connect the village to Copper Town and a primary school combines unevenly with the Cartoon Network playing on cable television and the increasing availability of chowmein as a desired culinary option, producing a deeply uneven experience of modernity in the village.[23]

But what is obviously simmering just below the surface of these tantalizing slivers of progress are the ravages of dispossession through mining that are evident not only at the level of the political and economic dispossession of adivasi land and rights, but in the sphere of social reproduction. For it is through a process grounded in the labour of unremunerated care work that Baso-jhi had become 'an integral part' of life in the village. And it is through a tearing of that fabric of care and community that she becomes

23 See Warwick Research Collective (WReC), *Combined and Uneven Development: Towards a New Theory of World-Literature* (Liverpool: Liverpool University Press, 2015) for a proper explication of this point.

doubly dispossessed. As the narrative backtracks to fill us in on her life story we learn that Baso-jhi had been brought into the household by Soren-babu, a bank clerk who lives in the village with his wife and children on a salary that does not afford him paid household help. He had found her destitute at a railway station, and his memory of having met her at a family wedding years prior ignited his sympathy for her. So it is that through a process grounded in the work of social reproduction that Baso-jhi becomes 'an integral part' of life in both the household and in the village. She sets about making herself useful — cleaning, washing, looking after the children: 'In Baso-jhi, Pushpa [Soren-babu's wife] found a baby-sitter, a house-keeper, a laundrywoman, a vegetable-chopper, a masala-grinder, a fish-scaler, a back-scrubber, a scalp-masseuse, a confidante and a companion' (p. 117). The complex work of social care allows for the creation of a different kind of family that traditionally made space for 'surplus women' like Baso-jhi who takes care of the household in return for shelter and participation in family life, albeit from its margins.

This precariously carved out social world is shaken to the core when Baso-jhi is accused of possessing witch-like powers that are causing deaths in the village. It is then that we get the first glimpse of her inner consciousness: 'When Basanti had first heard of the accusation, she had been shocked. A long-buried, agonizing recollection had assaulted her, like a thin rubber band which snaps as one is tying a chignon, and stings the fingers' (p. 119). The narrative voice claims access to Baso-jhi's inner consciousness and her 'agonizing recollection'. It now shifts gears and moves alongside her memories that connect this moment of expulsion from the social network of Sarjomdih to what had occurred just before she had arrived. Back then she had been blamed for her grandson's death that was followed by a brutal eviction by her sons that left her a destitute widow. These two linked catastrophic events open up space in the narrative for the reader to glimpse her back story through memories mediated by the narrative voice. Married off at age 14 to a farmer twice her age from the village of Chapri in Bengal, Baso-jhi had stepped out for the first time into the world. Boarding the train that is a foreign object to her, she is transported to Salbani, his village. There she gives birth to two sons and leads what we understand to be a happy life, visiting the weekly market to buy things for herself and her family and enjoying consuming the small luxuries of life. When she tragically loses her husband and becomes a young widow, she is cheated of her farmland. Left with a small but fertile piece of land on which she grows vegetables to sell at the market, she finds work in construction sites and rice-mills, and gathers maha and tendu leaves to supplement her income. She becomes the quintessential 'gritty Santhal widow'. Alas her sons' greed and selfish disregard for her 'lifetime of struggle' (p. 126) renders it without value. When her grandson dies due to diarrhoea, Baso-jhi is held responsible. She is seen to be sacrificing children for evil gods and is brutally evicted from the family home. It is then that she arrives at the Copper Town railway station, spending nights on the platform until she catches Soren-babu's eye. What is evidenced in both moments of eviction is the pressure placed on the formation of the nuclear adivasi family that is coming into being. The non-productive widow who is now an economic and social burden becomes the scapegoat in the face of death, illnesses, and conditions of precarity shaping adivasi lives caught in the maelstrom of desiring a modernity that is held up by a still backward infrastructure of health and education.

When her friend Maino's grandson dies in Sarjomdih, it is the third death in the village in the two years since Baso-jhi's arrival (the other two were old men). The child had been to Copper Town in the days before to celebrate a festival. With his death, the narrator points to an unexpected rupture in the fabric of village life: 'All of a sudden, Basanti's presence began to matter' (p. 121). Chorus-like voices of villagers now proclaim: 'She was a dahni — a witch. She'd killed her own grandson and, for that, her sons had disowned her. How could she expect strangers to accept her? She truly was a witch' (p. 122). This time she leaves Soren-babu's home before she is asked to vacate the small room she occupies outside the main homestead.

The narrative registers a simmering sense of unease as Baso-jhi's plight comes to represent the wider situation of women — widowed as well as educated young women — who are decried as sorceresses and witches. They are the scapegoats for an emergent modernization of adivasi life under extractive capitalism. The dominant modes of capitalist exploitation extract every last grain of value from reproduction, making outcast all those who threaten the structures of the emergent nuclear family and normative heterosexuality that harbours Brahmanical notions of female beauty (light complexion) and female subservience. These go against long-standing adivasi traditions where women historically held freedoms unimaginable in mainstream Hindu society. Thus Baso-jhi feels empathy for Bijoya, a young woman in the village who is a graduate in history and aspires to be a teacher. But she has 'the wrong sort of complexion', in addition to being burdened with a degree such that 'she didn't have too many chances' in finding a suitor. Although Bijoya could cook, clean, sew, take care of the elderly, 'even clean cowsheds and split firewood when required' (p. 119), her economic value is purportedly overshadowed by her social burden in a society that hopes to mimic dominant social formations such as the nuclear Hindu family. In reality, however, she is needed to perform unremunerated care. For although rumours of her power of sorcery persist, smeared with accusations of how she had contributed to 'her mother's death, her brother's disability, her father's failed paddy crop' (p. 119), her marriage would leave the men in her family without her double labour of economic and social care.

Shekhar's stories attest to the ways in which modernity ushers in new social relations and economic arrangements that emerge alongside pre-existing modes of domination. A depleted adivasi society is the object of both economic and cultural extractivism, and older forms of community and resistance are eroded in the process. Baso-jhi as the village witch and Mangal Murmu, the mad, hysterical Santhal who refuses to dance are symptoms of a deeply traumatized society as a whole. In his 1986 essay on third-world literature as national allegory, Fredric Jameson had written of the combined and uneven spatio-temporal conjunctures of third-world literature in which 'archaic customs' are 'radically transformed and denatured by the superposition of capitalist relations', contributing to significant generic discontinuities that are the hallmark of such literature.[24] When Jameson writes that 'the primordial crime of capitalism is exposed: not so much wage labour as such, or the ravages of the money form, of the remorseless and

24 Fredric Jameson, 'Third-World Literature in the Era of Multinational Capitalism', *Social Text*, 15 (Autumn, 1986), pp. 65–88; reprinted in *Allegory and Ideology* (London: Verso, 2019), pp. 159–86 (p. 182).

impersonal rhythms of the market but rather this primal displacement of the older forms of collective life from a land now seized and privatized', the power of his theorization is borne out in Shekhar's fiction.[25]

To recall Jameson's famous essay on third-world literature as national allegory in the era of world literature is also to recall Jameson's pronouncement that 'the allegorical spirit is profoundly discontinuous, a matter of breaks and heterogeneities, of the multiple polysemia of the dream rather than the homogeneous representation of the symbol'.[26] This then points to the necessity of a more materialist conceptualization of the crisis of representation that my essay alluded to before. But what does a crisis of representation mean in an era in which world literature has come to stand in for the world-system as a whole? This is where the *work* of world literature comes into play, especially when the task is to represent extractivism as the ongoing colonial dimension of our times.

Jameson himself recalls the fury that his earlier essay had generated even among Marxists who saw him moving away from the classical Marxist position in his pointing out 'that the international class situation of the period could be mapped as an insurrection of the international peasantry of Third World countries surrounding the international city bourgeoisie of the rich countries'.[27] Always preoccupied with the project of cognitive mapping in times of late capitalism, he goes on to point out that class struggles within nation-states are now displaced on to a global scale, creating a new 'representational dilemma'.[28] He writes: 'Its two

25 Ibid.

26 Ibid., p. 184.

27 Fredric Jameson, 'Political: National Allegory B. Commentary', in *Allegory and Ideology*, pp. 187–216 (p. 188).

28 Ibid., p. 189.

dimensions — class struggle with a given national situation and the globalized forces at work outside it on a world scale — are at least for the moment incommensurable: which is to say that it is their very disparity and the difficulty of finding mediations between them that is the fundamental political problem for the Left today'.[29] Allegory in this situation can serve as 'a diagnostic instrument to reveal this disjunction'.[30] That precisely is the work of world literature in our times when extractivism provides the dominant framework for accessing the world's resources that are material and cultural at the same time.

29 Ibid., p. 190.

30 Ibid.

Being Taught Something World-Sized

'The Detainee's Tale as told to Ali Smith' and the Work of World Literature

DIRK WIEMANN

In 'The Detainee's Tale as told to Ali Smith' (2016), the narrator (whom we are encouraged to identify with the author herself) recollects her encounters with a Ghanaian *sans papiers* asylum seeker in Britain, and later on the same day with a young Vietnamese who is held in indefinite detention in a removal centre.[1] These are not chance meetings but organized interviews prearranged by a refugee relief group. A person named Anna, who is a member of that relief organization, accompanies the narrator through the maze-like corridors of the university, where the first interview takes place, and later through the numerous security checks at the detention centre. Anna is also present

1 Ali Smith, 'The Detainee's Tale as told to Ali Smith', in *Refugee Tales*, ed. by David Herd and Anna Pincus (London: Comma Press, 2016), pp. 49–62. Subsequent citations given in-text.

during the interviews. The text that ensues is a meticulous account of these two encounters. The speaker/author constantly addresses the man from Ghana as 'you', so that the report as a whole reads like a letter to that person — a 'letter' written with the hope that the addressee will approve of it as a token of the writer's faithful documentation of all that has been said, but also as testimony to the writer's responsible reading of the detainee's tale.

'The Detainee's Tale as told to Ali Smith' is part of a slim volume titled *Refugee Tales,* edited by David Herd and Anna Pincus in 2016. While Ali Smith, especially since the 'four seasons' quartet on Brexit Britain comprising the novels *Autumn, Winter, Spring,* and *Summer,* requires no introduction, David Herd and Anna Pincus are not likely to be household names. Herd is a professor of Modern Literature at the University of Kent, Pincus is a civil rights activist working with the Gatwick Detainees Welfare Group. She may well be the 'Anna' character in Smith's report. Their project, *Refugee Tales,* offers an occasion to engage with both the vexed issue of world literature and, more specifically, with the ethico-political implications of the notion of the literary work as event.

WORKING WORLD LITERATURE

Smith's text lends itself easily (perhaps deceptively so) to multiple readings as world literature according to the different criteria elaborated and proposed by influential actors in the arena of current world literature studies. If, as David Damrosch suggests, world literature is primarily defined by its capacity to open 'multiple windows on the world',[2] then Ali Smith's exposure of/to the excruciating

2 David Damrosch, *What Is World Literature?* (Princeton, NJ: Princeton University Press, 2003), p. 15.

plight of the asylum seeker can obviously be read as an ideal example of such an opening that allows us 'a form of detached engagement with worlds beyond our own'.[3] In this respect it cannot be denied that the specifically powerful appeal of 'The Detainee's Tale' may to some extent derive from its subject matter: after all, the predicament of *sans papiers* refugees is clearly an urgent 'world theme'[4] that puts the literary text under the ethical pressure 'to find an adequate representation'.[5] Nor is this obligation a matter of the world-literary text alone but just as much an effect on the reader; indeed, one could argue that the dialogic structure of Smith's text, and the very sincere urge of the white privileged narrator to 'reach out' to the illegalized asylum seeker, is designed as a staging of Gayatri Spivak's agenda to conceive of world literature as an exercise in 'suspending oneself into the text of the other', 'striving for a response from the distant other, without guarantees'.[6] If thus no 'guarantee' ensures that a responsive encounter of reader and text will occur, the possibility of failure looms large here marking the putative point at which the irreducible alterity of the other appears to put a limit on all translational expectations, which all the same remain the driving impulse of any world-literary preoccupation. Reading, therefore, has to proceed from what Emily Apter has called 'a dispossessive ethics'[7] that not only eschews the appropriative and accumulative stance of the collector of worlds but

3 Ibid., p. 281.

4 Mads Rosendahl Thomsen, *Mapping World Literature: International Canonization and Transnational Literatures* (London: Continuum, 2008), p. 138.

5 Ibid., p. 114.

6 Gayatri Chakravorty Spivak, *Other Asias* (Oxford: Blackwell, 2008), p. 23.

7 Emily Apter, *Against World Literature: On the Politics of Untranslatability* (London: Verso, 2013), p. 329.

actually engenders processes of actively unlearning proprietorial logics. Perhaps this imperative resonates with the idea put forth by Stephen Heath who suggests that world literature be conceived of as the effect of a particular kind of reading that unmoors and unsettles the reader, enabling her to read 'migrationally and impurely': 'to read with [...] a migrant's-eye perspective, which is another definition of "world literature"'.[8] No doubt, Smith's narrator undergoes such a process of 'dispossession' (Apter) or 'unmooring' (Heath) in the course of her exposure to the detainees' tales, effectively disidentifying her with the status of citizen/subject that the text of the other has so forcefully revealed as exclusive privilege rather than universal right. World literature in this sense works as 'an ethical project because, like the larger project of cosmopolitanism to which it belongs, it asks us to imagine or act out an ethical relation to the world as a whole'.[9] Pheng Cheah, in a similar vein, suggests that 'world literature must work toward receiving a world or letting it come':[10] a process that Smith's text, again, virtually stages by tracing the narrator's insight into how, in the course of her exposure to the refugees' accounts, she is 'being taught something world-sized', without any self-congratulatory claim that she has adequately 'learned' this lesson, or ever will.

I am aware that my configuration of 'The Detainee's Tale' with a range of snippets from contemporary propositions on world literature is criminally loose and has done

8 Stephen Heath, 'The Politics of Genre', in *Debating World Literature*, ed. by Christopher Prendergast (London: Verso, 2004), pp. 163–74 (p. 174).

9 Bruce Robbins, 'Uses of World Literature', in *The Routledge Companion to World Literature*, ed. by Theo D'haen, David Damrosch, and Djelal Kadir (London: Routledge, 2012), pp. 383–92 (p. 391).

10 Pheng Cheah, *What Is a World? On Postcolonial Literature as World Literature* (Durham, NC: Duke University Press, 2016), pp. 211–12.

justice neither to literature nor to theory, neither to Ali Smith's text nor to the critical models that I have merely referenced here but hardly unpacked. All the same this is not meant to be a wilful assemblage but a pointer toward one of the dominant problems of current engagements with the work of world literature. For what hopefully emerges from the above configuration is how all these discrepant voices have one crucial concern in common, namely, their preoccupation with the *ethical* dimension of world literature, if not of the literary as such. In this sense they can be read as indicative of how intensely the practice (both literary and critical) of world literature is involved in what Michael Eskin has dubbed the 'turn to ethics' in literary studies in general.[11] Among the major protagonists of this 'turn', Eskin identifies Derek Attridge, who indeed has, for the past two or three decades, influentially and consistently argued for a very specific ethics of reading. Sketching the basic outlines of his theory may help to clarify the potential and potential limitations of the 'ethical turn' in (world) literature studies.

Attridge highlights the singularity, alterity and inventiveness of the literary text, which he posits not as a fixed object but emphatically as an event. He is concerned with the radical newness of 'something extra' that the literary text qua singular event imports into the routine procedures of the everyday. As in Alain Badiou's delineation of the irruptive 'truth-event', this event cannot be deliberately forced but is 'something that happens without warning to a passive, though alert, consciousness'.[12] More specifically,

---

11 Michael Eskin, 'The Double "Turn" to Ethics and Literature?', *Poetics Today*, 25.4 (2005), pp. 557–72 (p. 557).

12 Derek Attridge, *The Singularity of Literature* (London: Routledge, 2004), p. 26.

the text-as-event '*happens to the reader*' as an event '*for the reader*'[13] in their strictly individual historicity for which Attridge coins the term 'idioculture':

> The term 'idioculture' refers to the embodiment in a single individual of widespread cultural norms and modes of behaviour. [...] Idioculture is the name for the totality of the cultural codes constituting a subject, at a given time, as an overdetermined, self-contradictory system that manifests itself materially in a host of ways.[14]

Idioculture thus comprises the specific and idiosyncratic appropriations and articulations of historically available cultural resources by/in the individual. It is into this idiocultural continuity that the text as event of reading irrupts, effecting an immanent break (to adopt a term from Badiou's theory of the event) inasmuch as the encounter with the other re-calibrates the reader's idioculture and thus 'remakes the actor'.[15] As a consequence, 'the norms of my idioculture' are by the literary event 'so freed up that the truly other finds a welcome'.[16] What is that 'other'? It is certainly not a property of the text as object nor some unconscious substratum already latent in the reading subject; it is instead the hitherto unheard-of, the theretofore '*unencounterable*',[17] which in the event of reading is allowed to emerge on the condition that the reader to some extent abandon their 'intellectual control': 'The coming into being of the wholly new requires some relinquishment of intellectual control, and "the other"

13 Ibid., p. 59; p. 45.

14 Ibid., p. 22.

15 Ibid., p. 126.

16 Ibid., p. 24.

17 Derek Attridge, *The Work of Literature* (Oxford: Oxford University Press, 2015), p. 55.

is one possible name for that to which it is ceded'.[18] As a result, something may emerge that — again translated into Badiou's terminology — had no significance in the dominant language of the given situation: 'The other, the unprecedented, hitherto unimaginable disposition of cultural materials comes into being in the event'[19] as a pure singularity — a singularity that, for all its intense inventiveness, emphatically concerns no one but the individual(ized) reader to whom it happens. In short, the event cannot be shared or communicated *as event*. It is first and foremost the encounter with the other as singularity, where 'singularities are sites of resistance to the universal'.[20]

It is precisely because of this emphatic uniqueness that the literary event attains a dissident character, on the condition however of its being categorically incommensurate and, indeed, ultimately irreconcilable with meaning as such. Attridge makes this clear when he contrasts 'literature' with 'allegory': while the latter 'deals with the *already known*, [...] literature opens a space for the other. Allegory announces a moral code, literature invites an ethical response'[21] whose appropriate technique is 'literal reading', that is to say: 'a reading that defers the many interpretive moves that we are accustomed to making in our dealings with literature, whether historical, biographical, psychological, moral, or political'.[22] Literal, moral, allegoric: the very terms collated here make it well-nigh impossible *not* to associate Attridge's theory with the age-old tradition of

18 Attridge, *The Singularity of Literature*, p. 24.

19 Ibid., p. 63.

20 Attridge, *The Work of Literature*, p. 133.

21 Derek Attridge, *J. M. Coetzee and the Ethics of Reading: Literature in the Event* (Chicago: University of Chicago Press, 2004), p. 64.

22 Ibid., p. 60.

patristic hermeneutics, whose fourth level of interpretation, though, is conspicuous in its absence: the anagogic, which traditionally was the locus of the *sensus communis*. As I will try to argue later on, the recuperation of this dimension (whose omission is definitely not specific to Attridge!) might be a worthy project for an ethico-political practice of world literature. To be very clear, such recuperation can only come about as a substantial redefinition of the anagogic itself. To some extent, 'The Detainee's Tale', and the *Refugee Tales* project to which it is a contribution, may serve as a concrete example pointing in that direction.

REFUGEE TALES

Refugee Tales is the extension of an outreach event that has been organized by the Gatwick Detainees Welfare Group annually since 2012. The multiple-day group walk is intended to publicly express solidarity with migrants and refugees seeking asylum in the UK: those who either are involuntarily living a life on the run, or worse, are incarcerated in the limbo of indefinite detention. It is especially the latter issue which has sparked significant civil-society protest and campaigning all over the UK, including the *Refugee Tales* project, which has constituted itself primarily as an attempt to enact a counter-logic to the established procedures of indefinite detention. For in fact the UK is likely, at the time of writing, to leave the European Union as the only (ex-)member state that practices the indefinite detention of non-passport holders, i.e. 'illegal' immigrants. What is impossible even in Hungary or Slovakia is indeed daily routine in the land that boasts of having given the world *habeas corpus*: in Britain, and only in Britain, is it possible to lock away refugees, migrants, and asylum seekers without time limit, sometimes for periods of years, with no indication of whether and when they will be released or whether and when their case will be decided. It should be added that detention centres are profitably operated not by the state, but by multinational corporations, with little transparency or meaningful accountability. The Brook House 'immigration removal centre' at Gatwick Airport, for instance, is operated by the multinational G4S corporation on behalf of the Home Office, while Yarl's Wood, arguably the most notorious of Britain's ten detention centres, is run by the Serco Group, which has faced recurrent charges of sexual abuse, unlawful detention of minors and children, and numerous cases of suicide.

Herd and Pincus's *Refugee Tales* project is part of the sustained and substantial protest that has been raised against such practices in Britain. It is an activist intervention but its activism is first and foremost literary. While it unabashedly harnesses literature to a political cause, it simultaneously insists on its status *as literature,* and to being received as such. In close collaboration with the Gatwick Detainees Welfare Group and the Kent Refugee Help initiative, Herd and Pincus further developed the idea of the public solidarity walk by adding a literary dimension to the walking demonstration. Modelled on the mythical founding text of English Literature — Geoffrey Chaucer's *Canterbury Tales* — the event combines walking with storytelling and is meant thereby to re-enact and re-appropriate Chaucer's poem for the immediate present. Moreover, the multiple-day walking-and-storytelling tour through mythical 'Chaucer country' is intended to recode the landscape of southern England from a hostile environment into a space of welcome; but most fundamentally, to reclaim the work of literature as an act of sharing and conviviality. In the words of Ali Smith, patron of *Refugee Tales*:

> The telling of stories is an act of profound hospitality. It always has been; story is an ancient form of generosity, an ancient form that will tell us everything we need to know about the contemporary world. Story has always been a welcoming-in, is always one way or another a hospitable meeting of the needs of others, and a porous artform where sympathy and empathy are only the beginning of things. The individual selves we all are meet and transform in the telling into something open and communal.[23]

Setting out from Southwark in a series of walks to Canterbury, a group of participants including asylum seekers, pressure-group activists, writers and sympathizers from all walks of life rehearse the pilgrims' progress as told in Chaucer's poem. By the mere act of walking, they produce a public and political performance in its own right, 'crossing part of the country that is integral to a certain sense of English cultural identity, and that is also now the first sight of the UK for those who arrive via the road, rail and ferry routes between Calais and Dover'.[24] Clearly the idea is not just to raise awareness about the outrage of indefinite detention but symbolically and performatively to instantiate a solidary and hospitable Britain 'to come' as an alternative to the then Prime Minister Theresa May's vision of a 'hostile environment'. 'As the project walked', recalls David

---

23 Ali Smith, 'Welcome from Ali Smith' <https://www.refugeetales.org/about> [accessed 22 September 2019].

24 Tom White, 'Lives Suspended: An Essay on "Refugee Tales" and "Refugee Tales II", edited by David Herd and Anna Pincus', *Glasgow Review of Books* (21 September 2017) <https://glasgowreviewofbooks.com/2017/09/21/lives-suspended-an-essay-on-refugee-tales-and-refugee-tales-ii-edited-by-david-herd-and-anna-pincus/> [accessed 22 September 2019].

Herd, 'it reclaimed the landscape of South England for the language of welcome and everywhere it stopped it was greeted with hospitality and enthusiasm.'[25]

The general principle of the project consists of a tandem structure in which the 'walk in solidarity' is two things at once: first, a publicly visible manifestation of a community underway not just towards Canterbury but towards a more welcoming Britain, 'walking towards the better imagined'[26] as the slogan of the project has it; and second the occasion to tell and listen to tales en route. It thus is both 'real' and 'symbolic':

> Real as the walk is, and acutely real as are the experiences presented in the tales, there is a significant sense in which Refugee Tales is also symbolic. What it aims to do, as it crosses the landscape, is to open up a space: a space in which the stories of people who have been detained can be told and heard in a respectful manner. It is out of such a space, as the project imagines, that new forms of language and solidarity can emerge.[27]

It is important to point out that these 'stories of people who have been detained' are presented not by those experts-by-experience themselves but by established writers, many of them leading figures on Britain's literary scene — from Jackie Kay to Marina Warner, Iain Sinclair to Evaristo, Ben Okri to Kamila Shamsie. It would, at one level, be misleading to call any of these literary celebrities the *authors* of these stories, since these are obviously stories

25 David Herd, 'About Refugee Tales' <http://refugeetales.org/about-refugee-tales/> [accessed 22 September 2019].

26 Refugee Tales <http://refugeetales.org> [accessed 22 September 2019].

27 David Herd, 'Afterword: Calling for an End to Indefinite Detention', in *Refugee Tales II*, ed. by David Herd and Anna Pincus (London: Comma Press, 2017), pp. 113–25 (p. 115).

that 'belong' to somebody else. The Chaucerian titles indicate this by way of grammar: 'The Arriver's Tale' — 'as told to Abdulrazak Gurnah'; 'The Dependant's Tale' — 'as told to Marina Lewycka'; 'The Lorry Driver's Tale' — 'as told to Chris Cleave' etc. The involved writers have been told 'a tale' beforehand, in extensive dialogue with a person immediately affected by or involved in the issue of refuge and detention in Britain: (former) detainees as in Ali Smith's case, asylum seekers, immigrants, lawyers, clergymen, support workers. The tales are in that sense the outcome of a close collaboration between the person whose story it is, and the writer they are working with and who gives that story a specific shape. In the best of cases, the writer succeeds in translating the 'tale' into literature in the emphatic sense insisted on by Derek Attridge, but the ensuing event is meant to exceed the strictly circumscribed horizon of idioculture.

'The Detainee's Tale as told to Ali Smith' from the first volume of *Refugee Tales* opens *in medias res*: 'The first thing that happens, you tell me, is that school stops' (p. 49). The opening sentence not only marks the beginning of the 'tale' — the 'first thing that happens'; it also establishes a text-as-dialogue structure that allows the narrator to recurrently address her interlocutor directly, even if in retrospect, as 'you' — namely the detainee whose tale she is processing, reflexively, cautiously, but not preciously. Moreover, the abruptness of the two alliterative monosyllabic words — 'school stops' — that terminate this first sentence conveys the non-negotiable finality of the occurrence they denote. This finality of something having been terminated has its effect on the subsequent paragraphs of the text: the detainee's tale is blocked for the time being and what immediately follows instead is a detailed establishment of the setting within which the prearranged meeting of the two dialogue partners takes place — 'in a room in a London university so that you can tell me, in anodyne safe surrounding, a bit of your life so far' (p. 49). It is only one and a half pages further down that the narrator interrupts herself: 'Here's what you tell me. It's all in the present tense, I realise afterwards, because it's all still happening' (p. 50).

This, then, is neither a report (even though we were led to expect this) nor even a 'tale' (as the title of the text misleadingly announced); instead of the belatedness that both reports and stories as 'past-tense' forms have in common, the 'tale' comprises a number of narrative fragments that, even while *re*-collected, urgently point to the fact that they refer to something on-going, even if the informant himself has escaped some of these ordeals for the time being. But inasmuch as this story is not only an individual's story, all that is being related is 'still happening', as if eternal, and therefore incompatible with the preterit so typical of storytelling. Hence, nothing in the following account allows for the expectation of that putatively consoling resolution that narrative closure appears to guarantee according to narratologists like Peter Brooks, Frank Kermode, or Walter Benjamin. This withholding of narrative pastness is particularly disorienting since the text configures the static eternity of the 'all still happening' not only with the incompatible act of posterior recognition of this eternal present ('I realise afterwards') but, more strikingly, with the attempt to reconstruct a chronology at least at the level of the individually biographic:

> You arrive at the farm when you're six and you run away when you're 21. That's not the first time you run away. The first time you're fifteen. Hunger. Beatings. Headaches. You have a headache, you have it quite often, and you have to have

> the right medicine or leaves for it or you hit the ground. (p. 51)

After his escape from the farm, the informant gets trafficked to Britain where he is kept imprisoned in 'a shut room. The shut room is all mattresses on the floor and there are six others and you in the room' (p. 53). From the room the illegals are transported every morning at four a.m. in a van to work in a warehouse:

> Room, van, warehouse. Warehouse, van, room. Four in the morning. Nine at night. Packing shoes. Ladies bags. Sorting dresses. Cleaning microwaves. [...] Room, van, warehouse. Warehouse, van, room. Five years. Most weeks all week, 18 hours a day. You sit in silence now, with me. (p. 53)

The absence of verbs intensifies the sense of stasis, the scrambling of time that continues since, as we have been told at the outset, nothing of this is over — 'it's all still going on' — even while being rehearsed 'now' in an interview in a room in some London university *and* read by me in a text that I have happened upon by coincidence at some indeterminate point in time. Whatever is being conveyed here thus attains a permanence that is as indefinite as detention itself. Later in the account, the informant finds some assistance and is encouraged to inform the Home Office about his situation as a victim of human trafficking and present-day enslavement. As a consequence, he is first arrested and imprisoned for six months as an illegal immigrant and then detained for two years, then released but re-detained after six months, then released again. But 'any moment now they can arrest you again' (p. 54). Detention, whether actually inflicted or 'only' a threatening potentiality, becomes eternal: 'It's all like still being in detention. Detention is never not there' (p. 55).

READING NOT ALONE

Regardless of its passionate involvement and topical immediacy, 'The Detainee's Tale' is not in the first instance mere testimony or documentation, let alone a political call to action, even though it is all that too. Its primary affordance is to enable the very *event* that it painstakingly stages: the encounter with singularity, alterity, and newness. For this encounter is both the theme of the narrative and the effect of the text on the reader. The narrator/scribe is here pretty obviously functioning as a surrogate reader trying to decode and reconcile with her idioculture what her interviewee relates. This input, however, exerts an extraordinarily immense pressure on the recipient to 'do justice to', to responsibly receive, such a narrative. It is something that effects or requires an abandonment to the 'eye-opening novelty'[28] of what is being told, and it is this abandonment that Ali Smith's narrator testifies to when she acknowledges: 'A mere hour or two with you in a university room and I'm about to find out that what I've been being taught is something world-sized' (p. 55). If temporality is again out of joint here, it is now not the infernal eternity of recurrent or potentially recurrent iterations of the always-same (whether as excruciating work routine, as dehumanizing detention, or as the general plight of refugees) but instead, the expectation or anticipation — 'I'm *about to* find out' — of something extraordinary irrupting. It might be misleading, though, to speak of an irruption here: the expected insight to come will not be epiphanic but laborious, not instantaneous and yet compressed into a conspicuously incongruous timespan. It does not come as a flash but a lesson, again in scrambled time: 'what I've been being taught'.

28 Attridge, *The Work of Literature*, p. 196.

This 'what' remains a *je ne sais quoi*, an *Unverfügbarkeit*, an irreducible singularity; it 'includes the provocation of what cannot be fully understood by being situated back into its historical context'.[29] But at the same time, this world-sized 'what' spells out an imperative to be translated into something that would have consequences beyond its mere acknowledgment as singularity and alterity: while the text aspires to a responsible reading — to be received as hospitably as the narrator receives the account of her interviewee — it ultimately hopes to transcend the horizon of the idiocultural.

This thrust manifests itself in two (para)textual moves. First, the detainee does not allow the interviewer to get away with her responsible reception. Indeed, the text works towards an understanding of hospitality that goes beyond the mere acknowledgment of the other's singularity. *As literature* it demands more than being responsibly 'received' as a literary work. It takes the risk, in other words, of dispelling at the very end the appeal to an ethics of reading by an appeal to a politics of social transformation without fearing to lose an iota of its literariness. The scrambling of time and tenses goes on (even as the narrative resorts to the past tense now) but more importantly a shift in appeal occurs:

> On the train home, and all these weeks and months later, I'll still be thinking of the only flash of anger in the whole of your telling me a little of what's happened to you in this life so far. It was a moment of anger only. It surfaced and disappeared in less than a breath. Except for this one moment you're calm, accepting, even forgiving — but for these six syllables, six words that carry the weight of a planet [...]

29 Ibid., p. 141.

> But when I came to this place, when I came
> to your country, you say.
> I sit forward. I'm listening.
> You shake your head.
> I thought you would help me, you say.
> (pp. 61–62)

With this ending, 'The Detainee's Tale' poignantly stages how all attentive openness to the singularity of the other ('I sit forward. I'm listening'), all intention, all responsible attempts to be a good reader can only ever be 'the beginning of things', and how from that beginning the actual work of conviviality has to proceed. Perhaps this work is no longer the work of literature in the strict sense but rather the transfer of the ethics of reading to an ethics of the interpersonal, if not the social. This would roughly correspond to Gayatri Spivak's notion of the 'teleopoietic', where the lesson of responsible reading is ultimately meant to prepare for responsible action in the world; or, in other words, where reading figures as 'an imaginative exercise in experiencing the impossible — stepping into the space of the other — without which political solutions come drearily undone into the continuation of violence'.[30] In this understanding, the work of literature would consist in making it, if not impossible, then at least harder, for readers to feel comfortable with being *only* good readers. Herewith the event of literature need not primarily be grasped as an intervention into the idioculture (Attridge) of an individualized reader who precedes the event and gets recalibrated by it. Rather it would provoke what Spivak refers to as an '*uncoercive* rearrangement of desires'[31] in the course of an encounter that, as Sara Ahmed puts it, does 'not presuppose a meeting

30 Gayatri Chakravorty Spivak, 'Terror: A Speech After 9-11', *boundary2*, 31.2 (2004), pp. 82–111 (p. 94).

31 Spivak, *Other Asias*, p. 17.

between two already constituted beings' and can better be thought of 'as collective in its very singularity'.[32]

This, it seems, is the horizon that Ali Smith opens up in her second move, which is a strictly paratextual one. For importantly, in her mission statement on the *Refugee Tales* homepage, Smith frames the notion of hospitality in a way that lodges it not (only) with the reader but, prior to reception itself, with the story and its teller: before the *reading* it is the *telling/writing* of stories that is an act of 'profound hospitality and generosity', a welcoming-in, a hospitable meeting of the needs of others. In this light it is first of all the detainee whose generosity constitutively enables a reception that, it is true, is then no less generous. But the latter could not have happened without the former, without, that is, the story-teller's prior act of 'welcoming-in'. Before the work comes as an arrivant, therefore, it has already taken the recipient in, unconditionally, that is, with no guarantee that that reader will behave responsibly. Moreover for Smith, the telling of stories re-instantiates a text-event that is not an encounter between a work and an individual reader; instead the work here becomes a contact zone in which the boundedness of the individual reader is overcome: 'The individual selves we all are meet and transform in the telling into something open and communal.'[33]

Thus, while Attridge rests his ethics of reading on the literal (as distinct from the moral and the allegorical), Smith takes recourse to the communal, thereby reintroducing the level of textual engagement that, for traditional hermeneutics, used to demarcate the ultimate horizon of interpretation. Even though Smith does not mention

---

32 Sara Ahmed, *Strange Encounters: Embodied Others in Postcoloniality* (London: Routledge, 2000), p. 143; p. 179.

33 Smith, 'Welcome from Ali Smith'.

'meaning' here; and even though the 'open and communal' status of literature does not appear to reside in anything that has to do with shared meanings at all, I find it nonetheless useful to link Smith's assertion with the time-worn hermeneutic tradition of the *sensus communis,* that emerges in the anagogic phase of exegesis.

Medieval Christian and Judaic systems of interpretation converge, as it were, on the idea that the (sacred) text opens itself in four distinct tiers of significance. These four levels are not to be confused with distinct textual properties: Scripture was believed to hold a unified total meaning which, however, disclosed itself only in distinct 'steps' due to the limitation of human understanding. Patristic hermeneutics does not assume four distinct 'meanings of the text but modes of "understanding" and "interpreting"; its concern is, in short, the four-fold exegesis of the text according to the historical, the allegorical (in the narrower sense), the moral, and the anagogical approach'.[34] While the *sensus literalis et historicus* pertained to the *res gestae* that the text literalizes, the second (allegorical or typological) level of understanding was supposed to name the 'meaning' of that historical narrative, often by way of typological cross-references to other biblical or Talmudic passages. The third level of interpretation, the *sensus moralis,* concerns the individual soul and its edification, while the ultimate step of interpretation, anagogy, refers to the eschatological dimension of the text's significance for the whole world. It is not particularly forced to translate the first three levels of this medieval edifice into interpretative paradigms that would be easily acceptable in various

34 Marius Reiser, *Bibelkritik und Auslegung der Heiligen Schrift: Beiträge zur Geschichte der biblischen Exegese und Hermeneutik* (Tübingen: Mohr Siebeck, 2007), p. 114; my translation.

nooks and crannies of secular criticism today. In such a transfer, the literal level would become plain referential analysis including, for example, the narratological dissection of story and plot elements etc., while the allegorical level would cover all kinds of procedures that colloquially go by the name of 'interpretation' proper. The *sensus moralis* could be secularized into the manifold psychological modes of inquiry that focus on the effect of the text on the reader, whether empirical or not. What is more difficult, obviously, is to envisage an equivalent of the anagogic in modern conceptions of exegesis: partly because anagogy requires that the textual event be placed within the context of a 'total' world, and partly because anagogy's *sensus communis* emerges not at the site of the individual reader that is so central to Western notions of literature but instead as a communal event. Of course, the notion of a 'total' world must appear simply incompatible with a prevalent doxa that 'rejects any idea of pretraced destiny, whatever name is given to it — divine, anagogic, historical, economic, structural, hereditary, or syntagmatic'.[35]

All the same, secular critics like Fredric Jameson or Edward Said, among others, have repeatedly brought up propositions as to how to recuperate some kind of anagogic dimension of literature. Jameson translates the transcendental figure of a divinely ordained universal order into an unabashedly universalist Marxist metahistory — no doubt a strong claim to some 'pretraced destiny' — according to which 'the human adventure is one' so that the task of interpretation consists in the rewriting of individual textual events as so many 'vital episodes in a single vast unfinished

35 Gilles Deleuze and Félix Guattari, *A Thousand Plateaus: Capitalism and Schizophrenia*, trans. by Brian Massumi (London: Continuum, 2002), p. 14.

plot'.[36] 'Unfinished' but somehow unified, history is thus a series of events that, for all practical purposes, can only be approached by way of prior textualization; it is therefore accessible only as a 'continuous sign-chain'[37] made up of event-fragments that anagogical readings will articulate as elements of a coherent 'plot'. In this perspective, then, individual texts are tributaries to an encompassing social text to which they contribute 'vital episodes'. Similarly, Edward Said suggests 'that texts are worldly, to some extent they are events'.[38] As such they should be grasped, according to Said, as 'significant forms, in which worldliness, circumstantiality, the text's status as an event having sensuous particularity as well as historical contingency, are incorporated into the text, an infrangible part of its capacity for conveying and producing meaning'.[39]

The event here figures clearly as an antidote to the reifying tendency of conceiving of texts as fixed structures that can be retrospectively extricated from the historical dynamics that inform not only their production or creation, but also each individual moment of reading. Texts are events inasmuch as they are part of a world that consists of nothing but events; while in turn, that world is itself linguistically constituted as a 'huge whispering gallery' (pace *Middlemarch*) resulting in a 'worldly textuality'[40] as the necessary mirror image of that 'textual worldliness' in whose name Said had embarked on his theoretical ruminations at

---

36 Fredric Jameson, *The Political Unconscious: Narrative as a Socially Symbolic Act* (London: Methuen, 1982), p. 19.

37 Fredric Jameson, *The Cultural Turn: Selected Writings on the Postmodern, 1983–1998* (London: Verso, 1998), p. 40.

38 Edward Said, *The World, the Text, and the Critic* (Cambridge, MA: Harvard University Press, 1983), p. 4.

39 Ibid., p. 39.

40 Ibid., p. 41.

the outset. This, then, engenders a virtually holistic worldview in which a continuous 'chain of humanity' is enacted and maintained through the iterated 'transmission of actual speech'.[41] Jameson and Said thus attempt to recover the anagogical by way of envisaging a social world whose continuity is that of an undelimited, open-ended, dynamically unfolding, and internally conflicted text, in which no symphonic cooperation but polemical dissonance prevails such that a 'polemical common world' emerges.[42]

Such attempts at re-appropriating the *sensus communis* for and in a horizon of 'worldly' criticism resonate strongly with Ali Smith's evocation of narrative as an essentially communal event in which the individual reader who is so central to Western notions of literature — the 'individual selves we all are'— may transform into 'something open and communal'. What is at stake here is a rethinking not only of 'the subject' but also of literature as such. This rethinking could arguably be the prerogative of world-literature studies, as soon as one assigns to that 'discipline' the capacity (and the task) to pluralize the possible/permissible ways of conceiving of literature both as an institution and a 'species-wide faculty'.[43] Such a project would probably proceed from Aamir Mufti's observation that the term '*literature*' may 'now provide the dominant, universalizing, *but by no means absolute* vocabulary for the comprehension of verbal-textual expression worldwide'.[44] From there it could begin to take into account

41 Ibid., p. 44.

42 Jacques Rancière, *Dissensus: On Politics and Aesthetics*, trans. by Steven Corcoran (London: Continuum, 2010), p. 151.

43 Wai Chee Dimock, *Through Other Continents: American Literature Across Deep Time* (Princeton, NJ: Princeton University Press, 2006), p. 78.

44 Aamir R. Mufti, 'Orientalism and the Institution of World Literature', *Critical Inquiry*, 36 (2010), pp. 458–98 (p. 488).

that in fact manifold alternative concepts and practices of multiple forms of 'verbal-textual expression' have existed in history and continue to coexist with 'literature' even today. This holds true for traditional non-European terms like the Chinese *wen* or the ancient Egyptian *medet nefret* that are routinely translated as 'literature' even though they do not really coincide with the term at all.[45] With respect to the Sanskrit-derived lexicon of modern Hindi and adjacent North Indian languages, Anand observes that the word *sahitya*, which has been widely accepted as the equivalent of 'literature', in fact resonates with entirely different connotations and associations that converge with Ali Smith's emphasis on the collective dimensions of storytelling rather than the strictly individualistic exclusivism of mainstream understandings of literature:

> While 'literature' of English deals with letters, language, compositions expressed through writing etc., 'sahitya' of Sanskrit denotes a social activity. The Sanskrit dictionary gives approximately the following meanings to sahitya: To be together; joining together various dharmas in one deed; participation of a large number of people on equal basis in one act; a kind of kavya. We see that the first set of meanings talk about a collective activity involving different kinds of people with different roles and attributes.[46]

Obviously, whether to speak of 'literature' or of 'sahitya' is not merely a question of nomenclature but of an entire worldview. The becoming-dominant of 'literature' worldwide is therefore one of many instances of the expansive

45 See David Damrosch, *How to Read World Literature* (Chichester: Wiley-Blackwell, 2009), p. 7.

46 Anand [P. Sachidanandan], 'What is sahit in sahitya?', *Indian Folklife*, 1.3 (2000), pp. 12–14 (p. 12).

globalization of modern Western paradigms at the expense of all other epistemologies, increasingly occluding the 'diverse ways of being human' that actually coexist and persist on the planet.[47] Responsible, ethical reading that is attentive to the singularity of literature is a first and indispensable step in such a project. This is precisely the step that Ali Smith's narrator takes, suspending herself in the text of the other without guarantees: a demanding and risky venture for sure and yet only a first step. For the detainees' tales demand from their listener not only the virtual self-effacement of attentive ethical reading but also the cultivation of an ethics of commitment — an 'infinitely demanding ethics' that, as Simon Critchley puts it, 'moves the subject to action'.[48] Ali Smith's rendition of the detainees' tales and of her narrator's/her own struggle with the infinite demands that these tales exert may be a particularly promising starting point for such an endeavour.

47 Dipesh Chakrabarty, *Provincializing Europe: Postcolonial Thought and Historical Difference* (Delhi: Oxford University Press, 2000), p. 254.

48 Simon Critchley, *Infinitely Demanding: Ethics of Commitment, Politics of Resistance* (London: Verso, 2007), p. 130.

Working Conditions

World Literary Criticism and the Material of Arvind Krishna Mehrotra

JARAD ZIMBLER

What are the conditions of contemporary literary experience? What are its limits? In posing these questions, I have in mind the account that Derek Attridge gives of readings in which texts become works.[1] I have in mind also the particular challenges posed by an expanded literary totality which is roughly equivalent with 'world literature' as the term is used today. It is the task of this essay to explore these questions by tracking my own responses to the writings of a single author, Arvind Krishna Mehrotra; and of

* Work on this essay was supported by the European Union's Horizon 2020 research and innovation programme under Marie Skłodowska-Curie grant agreement No. 708030. I am grateful to several readers for their comments and recommendations, even when I have not been equal to them: Derek Attridge, Rachel Bower, Ben Etherington, Benjamin Robinson, Nicola Sayers, Vidyan Ravinthiran. I am grateful also to Arvind Krishna Mehrotra for permission to quote from his work.

1 This account is elaborated over several books, but I rely especially on Derek Attridge, *The Work of Literature* (Oxford: Oxford University Press, 2015).

its introductory section to expand on what I have in mind when asking them.[2]

I

In his account of literary experience, Attridge describes acts of reading which convert texts into works, or, rather, which make them work. Whether a text can be made to work depends on what is activated in reading, and specifically on the reader's encounter with otherness, which entails a modification of one 'idioculture' (a way of speaking and thinking) by another.[3] Which is not to say that all texts are amenable to such activation, or that any reading practice is capable of it. From the perspective of the reader, the text must be somehow distinctive, unknown. To use Attridge's terms, it must be creative and above all inventive. But difference is not enough — in the act of reading, a dialectic of proximity and distance unfolds. The text must first appear in a legible medium, language, script, form, and genre, even as it modifies some or all of these.

The bar to this kind of literary encounter is high but surmountable, and while they must be largely unpredictable, such experiences are by no means uncommon. Nor

---

2 In our Introduction to *The Cambridge Companion to World Literature* (Cambridge: Cambridge University Press, 2018), Ben Etherington and I explore 'world literature' as only one of many conceptions of literary totality, and pose questions about its value though a reading of Mehrotra's verse. The project of a world literary criticism is fundamentally indebted to this collaboration, and to its previous and subsequent articulations, especially in Ben Etherington and Jarad Zimbler, 'Field, Material, Technique: On Renewing Postcolonial Literary Criticism', *Journal of Commonwealth Literature*, 49.3 (2014), pp. 279–98, and Ben Etherington, 'World Literature as a Speculative Literary Totality: Veselovsky, Auerbach, Said, and the Critical Humanist Tradition', *Modern Language Quarterly*, 82.2 (2021).

3 Attridge, *The Work of Literature*, pp. 60–62.

are they the preserve of literary critics. For Attridge, they depend on the reader's 'willingness to be surprised' and her 'effort to clear the mind of preconceptions'.[4] Yet legibility — and especially the legibility of inventive texts — will depend also on a training, both informal and formal, that begins in early childhood, and endows readers with the requisite linguistic capabilities, as well as the appropriate disposition and practical knowledge, including knowledge of the conventions of specific media and forms.

As for the text's *workability*, this demands still more: familiarity with the histories of these conventions, and with what is practically possible; though quite how much familiarity is a matter of debate. According to Attridge, a responsible reading, which will do justice to the text's inventiveness, is one that 'brings to bear on the work all the relevant cultural resources available to the reader'.[5] But which resources will be relevant? Although concerned not with inventiveness but with truth-content, Theodor Adorno's position seems pertinent: a text's workability depends on its own, and by implication its readers', embeddedness in what he calls the material.[6] As Ben Etherington has explained, what Adorno means by the material is anything that the artist has to hand in making, which is not *anything at all*, but anything that can in fact be utilized for artistic expression.[7] Of necessity, this changes over time: a

4 Ibid., p. 190.

5 Ibid., p. 191.

6 Theodor Adorno, *Aesthetic Theory*, ed. by Gretel Adorno and Rolf Tiedermann, trans. by Robert Hullot-Kentor (London: Continuum, 2004), p. 194. For Attridge's reflection on the distinction between inventiveness and truth-content, see *The Work of Literature*, pp. 82–83.

7 Ben Etherington, 'What Is Materialism's Material? Thoughts toward (Actually against) a Materialism for "World Literature"', *Journal of Postcolonial Writing*, 48.5 (2012), pp. 539–51. At the minimum, 'artistic expression' entails labour undertaken in what Henry Staten describes

technique, genre, or medium can be worn out as much as a subject-matter, banalized by the passage of time, emptied of meaning, and even of the potential for meaning. What an artist has to hand in making, then, is not the sum total of all media, forms, genres, techniques, subject matters, but only those which remain, or which have become again, alive to the touch, instinct with the spirit.

In Adorno's sense, then, the material may be conceived as the horizon of possibilities and expectations that, in each moment, determines aesthetic judgement, decision-making, and experience, as well as the capacity of literary works to convey their truths. Attridge's account is by no means aligned with Adorno's, but there are certainly moments of congruence. In describing the artist's idioculture, Attridge says it will incorporate 'the appropriate techne governing, and providing resources for, the art form in question', which, 'in conjunction with the physical matter specific to the particular art form, constitutes the material out of which the artist creates the work'. This congruence persists even in Attridge's important qualification: 'in all the arts, the material possibilities and limitations are significant only to the extent that the artist understands — or, more often, perhaps, discovers in practice — what can be done with them', since, in Adorno's sense, the material is precisely that which is discovered in practice.[8]

Is the same true for the reader? Will the material possibilities and limitations conditioning a work be significant only insofar as they are understood? If so, the question of relevant cultural resources returns in a different form:

---

as 'the realm of the "well done"', and which is subject to the given art's 'techne limit', its canons of correctness. See Henry Staten, *Techne Theory: A New Language for Art* (London: Bloomsbury, 2019), pp. 17–22 and 36–43.

8 Attridge, *The Work of Literature*, pp. 183–84.

how much must we appreciate of these possibilities and limitations in order for a text to be workable? Must text and reader be mutually embedded in the material? If so, how do we account for literary experiences of texts that arrive from beyond those domains that we inhabit and in which we easily move about? The question seems not to arise for Adorno, but it certainly troubles Attridge, who helpfully distinguishes between historical and cultural distance.

With regard to historically distant texts, one answer may be that, since the material itself, as an agglomeration of decisive decisions, is historical through-and-through, and since literary education has for centuries entailed exposure to significant authorships and practices, a proportion will remain workable without any noticeable effort on the part of readers. There are, however, two qualifications: first, not all practices enter lastingly into the material; second, it may be possible to reanimate practices that have expired by reconstructing their horizons of expectation and possibility. Attridge is sceptical of 'archaeological' literary criticism, and especially of the notion that research might allow us to inhabit the perspectives of historically distant readers.[9] 'Reading a literary work with an openness to its singularity', he says, 'is not, clearly, an exercise in historical reconstruction'.[10] All the same, if one does happen to be a literary scholar, the nature of one's responsibility to a text surely changes, and while an experience of inventiveness may not always require the recovery of a text's originality, without such a recovery certain texts will remain wholly unworkable. Indeed, Attridge's own research into Elizabethan quantitative metres is a powerful example of how critics might provide the means for others to attune

9 Ibid., p. 17.

10 Ibid., p. 194.

themselves to a very different set of aesthetic conditions.[11] This does not mean they will encounter Edmund Spenser's quantitative verse in the manner of his original readers, but only that, through acts of scholarship, deadened texts may be reanimated.

What then does one do with texts that are *culturally* distant? Practically speaking, the fact of a text's legibility means that it has already been somewhat domesticated. If it originates in an alien linguistic environment, this domestication is achieved chiefly through translation, though there are also editorial and bibliographic processes that give the text a familiar appearance, making it look, feel and read as if it were like others published in our language and time.[12] But translation may be responsible for more than domestication: depending on the manner in which it responds to the target literary culture's codes and conventions, it may ensure that an otherwise unworkable text becomes available for literary experience.[13]When thinking about the problem of cultural distance, it is therefore

---

11 See Derek Attridge, *Well-Weighed Syllables: Elizabethan Verse in Classical Metres* (Cambridge: Cambridge University Press, 1974).

12 I use 'domestication' here to refer to processes by which an illegible object becomes a legible text, and is thereafter available for literary experience. The term is used in a narrower sense by Lawrence Venuti to describe a translation practice that aims at fluency and invisibility, and which he contrasts with a 'foreignizing practice' that registers 'the linguistic and cultural differences of the foreign text'. Although he favours the latter, Venuti acknowledges that, in order to carry the text across a threshold of legibility, all translation necessarily involves some degree of domestication. See Lawrence Venuti, *The Translator's Invisibility: A History of Translation* (London: Routledge, 2008), pp. 12–16.

13 This may be the case with Alaa al-Aswany's *The Yacoubian Building*, the text through which Attridge examines cultural distance in *The Work of Literature* (pp. 211–18). If the experiences of readers of the Arabic and of the English texts are so different, this is perhaps because the translation is somehow more responsive to the demands of inventiveness than the original.

worthwhile considering texts whose legibility does *not* depend on translation, because they originate in literary cultures which are distinct, but which make use of a language that is, in a general sense, our own (and which might therefore be described as 'homo-linguistic').[14] In being both familiar and strange, our own and yet other, such texts reveal more clearly the strains of reading across literary cultures. In so doing, they allow us to make explicit the kind of knowledge that conditions literary experience, and ask us to think carefully about our capacity for making texts work: about where this capacity comes from and how it can be developed; and about the resources that we activate in writing, and in reading, and in writing about reading. In short, such texts clarify what is at stake for any critical practice that aspires to be something like a world literary criticism.

It is here that I turn to Arvind Krishna Mehrotra, considering his own verse as well as his translations, and how, for non-Indian anglophone readers, a dialectic of proximity and distance unfolds across these texts.

II

Born in Lahore in 1947, Mehrotra has lived most his life in Allahabad. Abroad, he is best known for *Songs of Kabir*, a volume of translations published in 2011 in the New York Review of Books (NYRB) Classics series, the success of which has led to a selection of his poetry appearing in

14 As Attridge argues in this volume, the belief that a single language is shared by a great variety of speech communities relies on a widespread but inadequate notion of what a language is. In light of this inadequacy, we might understand 'homo-linguistic' literary cultures simply as those amongst which legibility does not depend on translation, so long as we also keep in mind that the threshold of legibility is by no means fixed.

the NYRB Poets series. Advertising the latter, the NYRB website states that 'until now his work has rarely been available in the United States and Britain', whilst assuring us that 'Mehrotra's poetry [...] reflects an intense and original engagement with American poetry, especially the work of William Carlos Williams and the Beats'.[15]

This characterization contributes to the kind of domestication that I describe in the previous section: it makes Mehrotra legible for British and American readers by relating him to recognizable metropolitan poets. But it is not without justification. Throughout his career, Mehrotra has seemed to enact with enthusiasm what we might describe as a cosmopolitan disposition. He reflects in a recent essay that he had, from the outset, taken his 'bearings from distant stars', and though he here specifies 'e. e. cummings and Kahlil Gibran',[16] he elsewhere notes the impact of first reading *Penguin Modern Poets 5*, which appeared in 1963 and included poems by Gregory Corso, Lawrence Ferlinghetti, and Allen Ginsberg.[17]

Songs of Kabir itself clearly signals Mehrotra's cosmopolitanism. For in translating 'the most outspoken' of the medieval Indian *bhakti* poets, whose performances mocked at pieties of caste, class, religion, and also language and script, Mehrotra follows a well-trodden

---

15 'Arvind Krishna Mehrotra, *Selected Poems and Translations*', *New York Review of Books* <https://www.nyrb.com/products/arvind-krishna-mehrotra> [accessed 8 November 2019].

16 Arvind Krishna Mehrotra, 'Introduction', *A History of Indian Literature in English*, ed. by Arvind Krishna Mehrotra (New York: Columbia University Press, 2003), p. 26.

17 Laetitia Zecchini, '"We Were Like Cartographers, Mapping the City": An Interview with Arvind Krishna Mehrotra', *Journal of Postcolonial Writing*, 52.1–2 (2017), pp. 190–206 (p. 191).

path.[18] Ezra Pound tried his hand at the beginning of the twentieth century, in a collaboration with Kali Mohan Ghose;[19] Rabindranath Tagore published his *One Hundred Poems of Kabir* in 1915, two years after his Nobel Prize in Literature;[20] and Robert Bly worked with Tagore's translations to produce his own versions in 1971.[21]

No less important, Mehrotra's translations seem to go out of their way to meet British and American readers on familiar linguistic and aesthetic territory. We can see this in his version of KG 179:[22]

> It take a man that have the blues so to sing the blues.
> — Leadbelly

> O pundit, your hairsplitting's
> So much bullshit. I'm surprised
> You still get away with it.
>
> If parroting the name
> Of Rama brought salvation,
> Then saying *sugarcane*
> Should sweeten the mouth,
> Saying *fire* burn the feet,
> Saying *water* slake thirst,
> And saying *food*
> Would be as good as a belch.

---

18 Arvind Krishna Mehrotra, *Songs of Kabir* (New York: New York Review of Books, 2011), p. xxiii.

19 Kali Mohan Ghose and Ezra Pound, 'Certain Poems of Kabir', *The Modern Review*, 13.6 (1913), pp. 611–13.

20 Rabindranath Tagore, *One Hundred Poems of Kabir* (London: Macmillan, 1915).

21 Robert Bly, *The Fish in the Sea is Not Thirsty: Kabir Versions* (Northwood Narrows, NH: Lillabulero Press, 1971). This was the first of several publications devoted to Bly's translations of Kabir.

22 Mehrotra, *Songs of Kabir*, p. 26. 'KG' here refers to Parasnath Tiwari's edited collection, *Kabir Granthavali* (Allahabad: Hindi Parisad, 1961), one of four source texts used by Mehrotra, though all but three of the *padas* he translates are from either this volume, or Mata Prasad Gupta's *Kabir Granthavali* (Allahabad: Lok Bharti Prakashan, 1969), identified by the acronym KGG.

> If saying *money* made everyone rich,
> There'd be no beggars in the streets.
>
> My back is turned on the world,
> You hear me singing of Rama and you smile.
> One day, Kabir says,
> All bundled up,
> You'll be delivered to Deathville.

In the volume's Preface, Wendy Doniger notes that 'Mehrotra tries to push the poems as far as he can towards Americanese, in the direction of the language that comes most naturally to him', using 'Slang, neologisms, and anachronisms', to produce some of the 'shock-effect that upside-down language would have had upon Kabir's fifteenth-century audiences', and to 'say what cannot otherwise be said about god and caste and Hindu-Muslim conflict'.[23]

As examples of what Doniger calls 'contemporary language' and 'colloquialism', she cites two words that appear in KG 179, *bullshit* and *Deathville,* to which we might add *getting away with it,* and *all bundled up,* as well as syntactic features, such as the contraction of *hairsplitting's, I'd, there'd,* and *you'll,* and the anachronistic Leadbelly epigraph. More than merely contemporary or colloquial, the language of the poem is tough, plain-speaking, and confrontational — effects achieved as much through lineation and prosody as through anaphora and rhyme. Breaks in the line mostly coincide with breaks in syntax, and where this is not the case enjambment is counteracted by some other feature. So, in the first verse paragraph, the cross-rhymes on *pundit, bullshit* and *with it* help to organize pauses consonant with the syntax. They also give the opening lines a punchiness felt on the lips and teeth.

---

23 Wendy Doniger, 'Preface' , in Mehrotra, *Songs of Kabir,* pp. vi-xviii (pp. xvii-xviii).

The energy of these lines is all directed against the *pundit,* a loan-word which contributes to the colloquial contemporaneity of the poem, whilst indexing the language of Kabir's original, so that its sights are set both on the Brahmin scholar of Hinduism's sacred texts as well as on the talking heads, public professors, and media experts of our own moment. The distinctions without differences, the speech without significance, the portentous prognostications, and rebarbative retrospectives: all are dismissed as empty verbiage in lines whose identical rhymes give them bite, whilst communicating a disregard for aural decorum.

It is therefore appropriate that instead of the opening's relatively complex structure, the two verse paragraphs that follow are made of quite simple conditional sentences, in which the repetition is chiefly grammatical and semantic. Which is not to say that there are no surprises, for the object of scorn is not simply a bankrupted scholasticism, but a broader error about the nature of language, made by the poets and critics of today as much as by the clerics of the past, who forget the limited power of words.

Yet if the poem seems headed towards a familiar complaint about needing to do rather than say, it swerves sharply at the end. First, because the Kabir persona turns away from the world, preferring song to action. Second, because the punchiness of the opening returns in the final two lines, which curse the self-satisfied expert with a fate somehow worse than mere death. Being 'all bundled up' and 'delivered' recalls a mob kidnapping, and 'Deathville', in figuring humanity's end as some kind of townlet or suburban neighbourhood, associates the experience of death with a semi-permanent lingering on the edges of life.

But the word that delivers the final blow also identifies Kabir's singing with a particular group of mid-twentieth-century American poets. For *Deathville* — which translates *jamapuri*, meaning, literally, the town or city of Yama, the god of death and the underworld — belongs more obviously to American English of this earlier moment than to American English of the new millennium. The *OED* informs us that '-ville' is chiefly associated with American colloquial speech, especially of the 1930s through to the 1960s, and the *Dictionary of American Slang* confirms that, from the mid-fifties to the mid-sixties, the suffix was 'in wide bop and cool use', often designating a place or a state as uninteresting, as in '*Dullsville*', '*Hicksville*', and '*squaresville*'.

Deathville, then, seems to cast Kabir as a latter-day Beat, identifying his song with an irreverent countercultural poetic idiom steeped in a mysticism of bodily ravishment and a language of the everyday, if not of the banal and bathetic, though it is by no means the only source of this identification. Other of the poem's colloquialisms, *bullshit* and *get away with it*, had likewise been in use since at least the 1930s, and this kind of mid-century American flavouring is found across the whole of *Songs of Kabir*: 'Brother', 'figure it out' (KG 116); 'bedroom eyes', 'all hell breaks loose', 'get the story' (KG 138); 'shortchanging' (KG 93); 'cleaned out by thieves', 'best part of town', 'won't be pretty', 'Fearlessburg' (KG 170); 'punditry', 'Keep cool', 'Wipe the bootlicker's smile / Off your face' (KG 77); 'check out the place' (KG 29); 'smart guys', 'the only / Dimwit in town' (KGG 1.146); 'Load of crap', 'Deathville' (KGG 3.53); 'get a big head', 'Be street-smart', 'screw up your life' (KG 73); 'you blew it', 'sticky spunk', 'Has you by the balls' (KG 60); 'Goners'

(KG 167); 'Ended up on the couch' (KG 2.23). Of course, few of these phrases are quite as precisely localized as 'Deathville', and Mehrotra's colloquialisms are anyway as much grammatical as lexical. However, taken together with certain attitudes and themes, they all contribute to the impression that, among the several Kabirs emerging from Mehrotra's volume, there is one who appears very much like a tough-talking, slang-relishing 'subterranean' American poet of the sixties, unafraid of the body's urges and its frailty, intimate with sexuality, insanity, and death.

III

Mehrotra's KG 179 seems to close the distances — cultural and historical — between talking heads and religious scholars, as well as between poet-mystics of medieval India and poet-mystics of mid-twentieth-century America. In this way, it domesticates Kabir for contemporary British and American readers, making his poetry newly workable,[24] and provides evidence of the kind of engagements that the NYRB website claims on Mehrotra's behalf. As an act of translation that facilitates the passage of a canonical authorship whilst identifying itself with cosmopolitanism, it also gives support to recent theories of world literature that emphasize circulation, whether of texts, forms or genres.

However, this reading of KG 179 is unsettled by the history of Mehrotra's interest in Kabir, which begins as early as 1967, but comes to fruition in 1970, when a selection of his translations appeared in *Vrishchik*, an Indian little magazine. Gathered under the heading 'Recastings

24 In contrast, reading them today, Tagore's translations strike me as distinctly unworkable.

from Kabir', they were accompanied by a note which confirms that, from the outset, Mehrotra intended his version of the *bhakti* poet to be confrontational and contemporary:

> I hope there's a scholar/reviewer who is already snooping around these recastings, smacking his lips, all set for the kill. I hope someone rushes excitedly to Kabir's oeuvre and comes back with the headline: THESE DAMN THINGS DON'T EXIST THERE. In all probability they don't. Yet. Between Kabir and me stand five centuries, and any number of vulgar translations of his poetry – mainly Tagore's and Bankey Behari's. All these and more had to be melted, purified, and cast again. So Kabir began living in the nineteen seventies, I in the fourteen hundreds.[25]

However, if the metallurgic metaphors explain Mehrotra's choice of heading, his insistence on Kabir's contemporaneity is somewhat belied by the poems themselves. Here is one, which, like KG 179, concerns itself with death's inevitability and lack of regard for rank and religiosity:

> you be pauper or prince
> or the mendicant-saint,
> once you have come
> you must then end
>
> riding his throne
> one reaches the grave,
> the other is in irons bound
> and limps towards it[26]

Moving decisively away from Tagore's odic lyricism, Mehrotra tends towards the epigrammatic. The verse is terse, an effect achieved by simplicity of diction and

25 Arvind Krishna Mehrotra, 'Recastings from Kabir', *Vrishchik*, 1.11–12 (1970), pp. 4–6 (p. 6).

26 Ibid.

abbreviated two-beat lines, with line-breaks replacing the formalized caesurae of the printed Hindi *pad*. And yet the poem's lexicon as well as its syntax create an impression that Kabir belongs very much to the past: *pauper* and *mendicant* are antiquating, as are the inversion of verb and prepositional phrase in the penultimate line, and the use of *you be* rather than *whether you are* in the first clause. The impression is reinforced semantically, in references to iron bonds, royal litters, and princes.

In short, this Kabir is quite different from the one we encounter in Mehrotra's later volume, the contrast nowhere clearer than in comparing 'in irons bound' with KG 179's 'all bundled up'.[27] And yet this 'recasting' was produced closer in time to the emergence of the Beats, and closer still to Mehrotra's discovery of them. If one of the achievements of *Songs of Kabir* really is to infuse the *bhakti* poet with the counter-cultural energy of Ginsberg and Corso, why does Mehrotra come so late to their idiom? Are we dealing here with the aesthetic time-lag attributed to the literary world's outlying provinces,[28] or with the asynchrony of the literary world-system?[29]

It is difficult to answer these questions without turning to Mehrotra's own verse, beginning with 'Bharatmata: A Prayer'. The first of his major mature poems, it was

27 In his comparison of two of Mehrotra's translations of KG 85, Peter McDonald likewise notes that the recent version creates 'a more supple idiomatic English', freed of 'the sonorous Yeatsian repetitions [...] and stilted syntactic inversions [...] of the first version', *Artefacts of Writing: Ideas of the State and Communities of Letters from Matthew Arnold to Xu Bing* (Oxford: Oxford University Press, 2017), p. 239.

28 Pascale Casanova, *The World Republic of Letters*, trans. by Malcolm B. DeBevoise (Cambridge, MA: Harvard University Press, 2004).

29 Warwick Research Collective (WReC), *Combined and Uneven Development: Towards a New Theory of World-Literature* (Liverpool: Liverpool University Press, 2015).

published in a 1966 pamphlet by the ezra-fakir press of Bombay, and then reprinted in a 1970 issue of *Mahfil*, an American journal devoted to South Asian writings. A reasonably long poem, 'Bharatmata' cannot be cited in full, but what follows is the first of its eight sections:

> O BHARATMATA
> O SOCIALIST MOTHER INDIA
> O BRIGHT STAR
> O LAND OF THE PEACOCK & THE LION
> LAND OF THE BRAHMAPUTRA & THE HIMALAYA
> OF THE BRAVE JAWAHAR
> OF THE MIGHTY GANDHI
> HOMAGE TO THEE
>
> india
> my beloved country, ah my motherland
> you are, in the world's slum
> the lavatory
>
> the septic tank where in paper gutters
> fall the
> marksrublesdollarspoundsyenslirasfrancs
> yet our stomachs remain sirens
> tooting pathetic messages
>
> i am so used to your cities with a
> chain reaction of suburbs
> where whole families live in bathrooms
> and generations are pushed out of skylights
> and the next one sticks out its head
> like a tapeworm through frozen shit.
> used to the village reduced to a bone
> and then swallowed.
> i am used to seeing pot-bellied children
> ride the dog with jockey's confidence.
> used to the old man pick his nose
> in prayerlike concentration.
> used to a hand
> rag like
> wiping the
> mouse like
> car

with a
leaf
outside
industry house[30]

As with the translations of Kabir, there is little in language or lineation to challenge a non-Indian anglophone reader, and certainly nothing to stifle the force of the invective, which rips away the mask of the opening incantations, reversing the poem's epideictical tenor from praise to blame. On the contrary, it seems that one of the poem's aims is to situate India in the world, subject to economic imperatives originating in the advanced economies. Thus the invocations of local power, whether in the domains of nature (Brahmaputra, Himalaya) or of politics (Jawahar [Nehru], Gandhi), are expelled as hot air, the 'pathetic messages' of empty stomachs.

And yet, even if the poem's progress deflates the localizing gestures of the opening paragraph, for any non-Indian reader the anaphoric stress on habituation — the four sentences in which 'used to' is the main verb — re-asserts a cultural distance, which grows towards the section's final lines, where the leaf is juxtaposed more jarringly with the productive technologies signalled by 'industry house' than with the mouse-like car. For what is only too familiar to the persona (and presumably to readers for whom such scenes are similarly commonplace) is likely to have struck the poem's non-Indian readers as very much unfamiliar; and though the shape of the verse imbues the final line with the qualities of the turn, it is difficult not to feel that something of the effect is lost if one does not know the precise location and significance of industry house.

30 Arvind Krishna Mehrotra, *Bharatmata: A Prayer* (Bombay: ezra-fakir press, 1966).

In truth, there is unease long before we reach this point, for though the rhetorical magic of the preliminary incantations may be dispelled, the very title of Mehrotra's poem invokes a liturgical tradition quite distinct from that of the siddur, psalter, and hymnal, and one embedded in religious beliefs and practices which will be present to a good number of American and British readers only as a sense of absence, a lack in knowledge and understanding. Likewise with the poem's opening dedications, to Indira Gandhi and Malay Roy Choudhury. The former had come to power as Prime Minister early in 1966, but if one initially suspects she is the object of praise — the SOCIALIST MOTHER INDIA — that interpretation is difficult to sustain as the poem unfolds, full of scorn for politicians. Full of scorn for poets too, so that, even if one knows that Choudhury had recently been imprisoned for the obscenity of his poem 'Stark Electric Jesus', the meaning of the dedication is opaque.

This sense of uncertainty continues throughout, for me, and perhaps for most readers who encountered 'Bharatmata' in the pages of *Mahfil*. This has to do with the manner in which the poem pulls one in — through the use of idiomatic and technical repertoires that are compelling but hardly uncomfortable — whilst periodically disturbing one's confidence, in ways small (the appearance of untranslated words, references to local places and practices), and large (the invocations, at the poem's beginning and its end, of a Hindu liturgical tradition). This effect is crystalized in the section which begins:

> ah
> walt whit
> wish you were around
> and tried to contain these multitudes

and tried being our Representative Man
your yankee tricks wont click with us[31]

The familiarity with which Mehrotra invokes Whitman (and thus, by implication the Ginsberg of 'A Supermarket in California') is countered by the gesture of refusal, most pointed in the possessive pronouns: 'our', with its added emphasis, followed by the 'your' qualifying Whitman's 'yankee tricks', leading back to 'us', in a line which displays a command of an American idiom — especially in the internally rhyming 'click' — whilst insisting on its unsuitability.

Of course, these moments of disorientation do not make the poem illegible. We easily skip over words and references we do not understand; we take for granted that we have only limited access to all the resources of a poem's idioculture. Nor does it make the poem unworkable. On the contrary, the play of proximity and distance may be central to its effects, and its strangeness may be the grounds of a properly literary experience, an encounter with otherness that leaves readers — that left this reader — captivated by its intensity, and particularly by its stark metaphors and blasphemously resonant incantations. Indeed, as Peter McDonald has remarked, a certain 'artful' obscurity is an 'essential element of Mehrotra's own foreignizing poetics', troubling even those readers endowed with a high degree of relevant '*cultural* competence'.[32]

And yet, there is a nagging sense that something important may be missing, exacerbated by the insistence that 'yankee tricks' cannot 'click' with Indian poets and subject matters. Is this a reflexive acknowledgement of the poem's deficiency? Or does it mean there may be something in-

31 Ibid.

32 McDonald, *Artefacts of Writing*, pp. 236–37.

herently faulty in a response to Mehrotra's verse that takes as its starting point his 'intense and original engagement with American poetry', using this as an alibi for overlooking the significance of cultural distance? Might we be guilty of misreading if we presume that the interplay of proximity and distance is central to the poem, when this interplay may be apparent especially (only?) for non-Indian readers of 'Bharatmata'?

IV

In *Well-Weighed Syllables*, Derek Attridge writes that, in order to understand the success of a poet like Richard Stanyhurst, as well as the interest of Spenser and Philip Sidney in classical quantitative metres, we need to know the poems and the 'discussion that surround them', and also 'just what an educated Elizabethan took to be the metre of a Latin poem', and 'how he pronounced the individual words, how he delivered the lines of verse, and how he had been taught Latin, and in particular Latin prosody, at school'.[33] More recently, and in a quite different vein, Timothy Brennan has lamented 'the misplaced sociological hermeneutic of world literature', and called 'for a different literary sociology that captures the affiliative networks of authors choosing, strategizing, carving out a space in a hostile commercial environment of circles, schools, and class fractions'.[34] However differently oriented, both Attridge and Brennan describe a project of research that is philological as much as historical or sociological, and

33 Attridge, *Well-Weighed Syllables*, p. 2.

34 Timothy Brennan, 'Cosmopolitanism and World Literature', in *The Cambridge Companion to World Literature*, eds. Ben Etherington and Jarad Zimbler (Cambridge: Cambridge University Press, 2018), pp. 23–36 (p. 34).

which entails a description of those horizons of expectation and possibility that condition any text's emergence into meaning. In very different ways, both also recall the work of Pierre Bourdieu, and his belief that literary texts are de-realized when abstracted from the literary fields from which they emerged, 'stripped of everything that attached them to the most concrete debates of their time', and thereby 'impoverished and transformed in the direction of intellectualism or an empty humanism'.[35]

Almost as a riposte to any kind of localizing criticism, Mehrotra has suggested that anglophone Indian 'writers have seldom acknowledged each other's presence', and that in 'Indian literature in English [...] there have been no schools, literary movements, or even regional groups [...]. Its history is scattered, discontinuous, and transnational. It is made up of individual writers who appear to be *sui generis*. They are explained neither by what went before them nor by what came after'.[36] This will be comforting to non-Indian readers, who may therefore be content with whatever knowledge they happen to possess of those metropolitan literary currents that washed over Mehrotra and his peers. However, almost in the same breath, Mehrotra has insisted — when speaking of 'the conditions that have recently made Indian writing something of a commodity' — that 'unlike Coca-Cola, a piece of writing is savoured best in the place where its secret recipe is from, and more often than not it is only really possible for it to be satisfyingly consumed in the same place too'.[37] If the suggestion here is that even transnationalism might be locally

35 Pierre Bourdieu, *The Field of Cultural Production: Essays on Art and Literature* (Cambridge: Polity Press, 1993), p. 32.

36 Mehrotra, 'Introduction', pp. 25–26.

37 Ibid., pp. 23–24.

inflected, it is borne out by an exploration of the print culture from which 'Bharatmata' and 'Recastings from Kabir' emerged; however, as we shall see, the same cannot be said of Mehrotra's claim that anglophone Indian literature has entirely lacked movements and groupings.

On its back-page, the 'Bharatmata' pamphlet describes the poem's provenance: 'passages from bharatmata have appeared in outcast. the whole poem will appear in klactoveedsedsteen (ed. carl weissner 1-3a muhltalstr, 69 heidelberg germany) in a special issoo which will feature the hungries and others of the indian avant'.[38] Here, Mehrotra takes pains to mark his metropolitan success but he also affiliates himself to a local avant-garde through its best-known exponents, the writers of the Hungry Generation. By then, the Hungryalists had achieved international as well as local notoriety, largely because of Malay Roy Choudhury's arrest in 1964. Criminal proceedings followed, generating coverage in the foreign press, precisely because Choudhury's cause was taken up by Allen Ginsberg and Howard McCord, who published an English self-translation of 'Stark Electric Jesus' towards the end of 1965, or the beginning of 1966, and then guest edited 'HUNGRY!', a special issue of *Salted Feathers*, featuring letters from Ginsberg and Gary Snyder.

If the 'Bharatmata' pamphlet declares Mehrotra's affiliations with both the Beats and a local avant-garde, it tells a similarly complex story about circulation. The back-page announces that the ezra-fakir press — Mehrotra himself in one of his several guises as publisher and editor — produced 'poetry mags poetry collections broadsides concrete poems and everything else which can be recreated on a stencil', and exchanged these with a striking

38 Mehrotra, *Bharatmata*, back-page.

number of overseas and especially American periodicals and presses: 'mother, rot, zebra books, manhattan rev, openings press, outcast, poetmeat, screeches pubs., poetry rev, klactoveedsedsteen, breakthru, avalanche, kritik, new measure, approches, poetry australia, weed, dust, keeper's voice, unilit, contra '66, origins/diversions, trace, dionysus, riverrun, wormwood review, hors commerce press, damn you'.[39] The list points out a network of exchange with nodes in cities across India (Bombay, Secunderabad, New Delhi, Allahabad) and around the USA, as well as in Paris, Heidelberg, and Sydney, and confirms that its currency was nothing other than the various little magazines and pamphlets themselves.

The ezra-fakir press might thus be understood as an instance of the mid-century mimeo revolution, during which poets became their own publishers and printers, using national postal services to market and disseminate their offerings. In these domains, Mehrotra demonstrated notable zeal: he was responsible not only for his press, but also, jointly or solely, for three little magazines, including *ezra* and *fakir*, as well as their predecessor, *damn you: a magazine of the arts*, which he had launched from Allahabad. Given the broad identification of the Beats with the mimeo revolution, all of these ventures attest to Mehrotra's engagement with American poetry, though *ezra* claims a particular intimacy with Pound, whilst *damn you* explicitly references *fuck you: a magazine of the arts*, put out by Ed Sanders in New York from 1962.

The nature of this engagement makes it impossible to sustain the view of Mehrotra's belatedness. Far from being a mere consumer or emulator, he was an active participant in a transnational field. His own magazines featured Amer-

39 Ibid.

ican, British, and Mexican poets, and he contributed to several of those overseas periodicals for which *damn you, ezra* and *fakir* were exchanged. And yet it is clear that all of Mehrotra's editorial efforts were engaged at the same time with a local poetry scene that was far less scattered and discontinuous than his own later remarks suggest. Without having to look far, we find evidence of position-takings which were, necessarily, relational, and which took for granted the existence of a national literary space, endowed with its own institutions, and dynamized by its own tensions (aesthetic, but also generational and regional).

The Hungryalists, for example, positioned themselves self-consciously against what had by then emerged as a literary establishment, whether identified with Purushottama Lal's Writers Workshop, set up in Calcutta in 1958, or the Bombay little magazines edited by Nissim Ezekiel, such as *Quest* and *Poetry India,* or the Bengali writers organized around the journal *Krittibas,* which had first appeared in 1953. The first issue of *Waste Paper: A Hungry Generation Newsletter* insists: 'No other group has any relation with the Hungry Generation because Hungry Generation is a Literary Movement. [...] Hungry Generation, from the beginning, is original and has no relation with any group or coterie'.[40]

In a similar vein, the inside-cover of *ezra* 3 quotes a review which declares: 'Anybody cheesed-off [with] the literary establishment in India will welcome these two magazines (damn you & ezra).. . ..... The Illustrated-Ezekiel-Lal axis if they are not already awake, ought to beware'.[41] Yet, if Mehrotra had at one point aligned himself

---

40 'Othe [sic] Groups', *Waste Paper: A Hungry Generation Newsletter*, 1 (1967), p. 5.

41 Arvind Krishna Mehrotra, ed., *ezra: a magazine of neo imagiste poetry*, 3 (1968), inside cover. The first term of this axis is a reference to

with the Hungryalists, the 'statement' included in *damn you* 6, positions the magazine's project not only against Lal and Ezekiel ('a bombay professor'), but also against this other faction of the Indian avant-garde:

> not the organ of a hungry generation, a clan of anti-poets, or a writer's workshop. not the public child of a bombay professor. we are illiterates. unaware of ists/isms. [...]
>
> a mag which gets out two issoos, survives the debacle, and goes on to a third fourth fifth can go on to a hundred. and now its time to solidify our position. dig in. make zigzag trenches. fire back. oil and set the mimeomachine like a machine-gun.[42]

The language of combat is striking, but also characteristic of the 'craft wars' that were being waged in other decolonizing poetry scenes at much the same time. Inevitably, these entailed confrontations with metropolitan poets as well as with local predecessors and peers. In *damn you* 6, Mehrotra drew lines of battle by describing the inability of British and American readers to think of the world of English poetry other than as one divided strictly between them: 'ken geering, ed. of breakthru, thinks we are yankee oriented, a yankee, eric oatman, who edits the manhattan review, writes "the name is too damn british". and so, we like to keep them guessing, and leave the capitals of the skyscraping earth to decide amongst themselves'.[43] Concurrently, the editorial statement of *ezra* 1 issued a more straightfor-

The Illustrated Weekly of India, which 'first started Indian poetry in English in the late 1940s'. Emma Bird, 'A Platform for Poetry: The PEN All-India Centre and a Bombay Poetry Scene', *Journal of Postcolonial Writing*, 53.1–2 (2017), pp. 207–20 (p. 210).

42 Arvind Krishna Mehrotra, 'statement', *damn you: a magazine of the arts*, 6 (1968), np.

43 Ibid.

ward refusal: 'the mag might smack of "beatness". you are wrong. it is gently avant garde.'[44]

Yet as much as the local poetry scene was structured by inter- and intragenerational tensions, and by claims to distinction, it was also a site of collaboration. Little magazines and presses could be vehicles for connection as much as contestation. Mehrotra had edited *damn you* together with Amit and Alok Rai; and, after moving to Bombay, began to interact with several poets there. The most important of these was Arun Kolatkar, who wrote in Marathi as well as English, but Mehrotra also developed relationships with Adil Jussawalla and Gieve Patel.

In the mid-1970s, Kolatkar, Mehrotra, Patel, and Jussawalla would create a publishing cooperative, Clearing House Press, to bring out their own important volumes of verse.[45] But something of their collective identity had already begun to emerge earlier in the decade. In a special issue of *Mahfil* published in 1972 and devoted entirely to Indian poetry in English, one of their contemporaries, Pritish Nandy, spoke dismissively of 'the arty-arty style of the ad-men poets', who belonged to 'esoteric coteries' associated with Nissim Ezekiel.[46] Nandy did not name any of these 'ad-men poets', but Kolatkar was then working in an advertising firm as an art director, and both he and Pa-

---

44 Arvind Krishna Mehrotra, Editorial Note, *ezra: an imagiste magazine*, 1 (1967), inside back page.

45 For an account of this venture, and important documents related to it, see Jerry Pinto, 'Key Document: Eight Books, Seven Poets, One Clearing House', *Journal of Postcolonial Writing*, 53.1–2 (2017), pp. 233–46.

46 Suresh Kohli and Pritish Nandy, 'Suresh Kohli Interviews Pritish Nandy: Tradition and the Individual Talent', *Mahfil*, 8.4 (1972), pp. 11–15 (p. 15). By way of contrast with Mehrotra, in the same interview, Nandy remarks: 'British poetry ceased with Auden and American poetry never started' (p. 13).

tel were practicing visual artists. Their involvements with Mehrotra and Jussawalla, as well as with Ezekiel, were also common knowledge. The elder poet had published all four in *Poetry India*, and, in the same issue of *Mahfil*, singled out Mehrotra, Patel, and Jussawalla for praise.[47]

Nandy's sense of their 'arty-arty' style perhaps also had something to do with their association with *Vrishchik*. Founded in 1969 and devoted to visual arts as well as poetry, the magazine 'brought poets, painters, translators, art critics onto a common platform'.[48] In fact, Kolatkar, Patel, and Mehrotra had appeared together in a special issue of September–October 1970. Ostensibly devoted to medieval verse, the actual focus was narrower, since it included translations only of *bhakti* poets: of Muktabai, Janabai, and Namdeo, by Kolatkar; of Vasto, by Patel; and of Kabir, by Mehrotra. Indeed, this was precisely the issue in which Mehrotra's 'Recastings' appeared.

By this point, all three poets had been working on the *bhaktas* for several years, though the *Vrishchik* special issue needs to be understood as the outcome of something more than happy coincidence or the meeting of minds. It needs to be understood, instead, as a significant collective position-taking in the anglophone Indian literary field, underwritten by shared principles and priorities. Laetitia Zecchini observes that 'in India, [...] most modern poets are translators'.[49] Certainly, they have a great deal to translate, including several millennia of Sanskrit texts; the Persian poetry of the Mughal court; long, deep, and durable traditions in multiple vernaculars, including Urdu/Hindi,

47 Suresh Kohli and Nissim Ezekiel, 'Suresh Kohli Interviews Nissim Ezekiel: A Search for Limits', *Mahfil*, 8.4 (1972), pp. 7–10.

48 Zecchini, 'An Interview with Arvind Krishna Mehrotra', p. 198.

49 Laetitia Zecchini, *Arun Kolatkar and Literary Modernism in India: Moving Lines* (London: Bloomsbury, 2014), p. 74.

Bengali, Kannada, Marathi, Tamil, and Telugu; and over a century of writings in English. However, this on its own does not explain the need for translation, which expressed itself most clearly in *Poetry India*, a journal devoted to English translations of texts in classical, medieval, and modern South Asian languages. Why were Indian poets so preoccupied with translating for one another from their own traditions?

A straightforward answer is that, since few Indian poets, if any, commanded more than two or three languages, translation became a means of sharing local traditions. But this makes translation a matter of mere circulation, when it is considerably more important, since even when texts and practices belonging to hetero-linguistic literary cultures are legible, for an entire community of readers as well as writers, they cannot be said to constitute the literary material — in Adorno's sense — until they are first translated. This is because each literary language, and each literary culture, is confronted and therefore structured by its own problematics and its own history, so that not only the solutions but also the challenges are particular to each.

Writing of the formation of vernacular literatures, Sanskritist Sheldon Pollock explains that their emergence always demands two processes: *literization*, by which a standardized written variety is abstracted from a dialect continuum; and *literarization*, by which a written language is made into a literary language. This second process tends, according to Pollock, to entail the emulation of works from the canon of the cosmopolitan literature against which the vernaculars define themselves.[50] What I am suggesting

50 Sheldon Pollock, *The Language of the Gods in the World of Men: Sanskrit, Culture, and Power in Premodern India* (Berkeley: University of California Press, 2009).

here is that the kinds of labour necessary for *literarization* are ongoing, because literary languages are always being remade; and are as much in evidence when materials (plural: meaning authorships, texts, genres, techniques, themes, etc.) are imported from one vernacular tradition into another — say, from the Marathi into the Gujarati tradition, or from the Hindi into the anglo-Indian tradition — and thus constituted as part of the latter's literary material (singular: as Adorno uses the term). It is, in other words, only by being converted into workable English poetry that non-anglophone Indian verse could begin to reshape the horizons of what could be made by anglophone Indian poets, contributing to what Mehrotra has recently described as a 'working, workable tradition'.[51]

The question facing such poets was therefore not *whether* to translate, but *what*, and the manner in which they answered said a great deal about their aesthetic priorities. In some cases, the source texts were contemporary, as with the Hungryalists' self-translations, and Nandy's work on his Bengali contemporaries Samar Sen and Subhash Mukhopadhyay. In other cases, they were historically distant but highly canonical, as in A. K. Ramanujan's translations of Classical Tamil verse, and Purushottama Lal's of Vedic Hymns. The choice to translate the *bhakti* poets was anything but neutral. On the contrary, it spoke of an investment in a practice characterized by spiritualism and personal devotion; the rejection of caste, class, and socio-religious authority; and a turn to orality. The *bhaktas*, as Pollock explains, belonged to a second and more radical

51 Arvind Krishna Mehrotra, 'Arvind Krishna Mehrotra on his translations of Kabir's Songs', online video recording of interview with Souradeep Roy of *Guftugu Journal*, YouTube, 13 September 2018 <https://www.youtube.com/watch?v=y2FdL4OSgnY> [accessed 19 June 2020].

wave of vernacularization, which rejected the cosmopolitan Sanskrit tradition, rather than seeking to emulate it. Using forms 'closely linked to folk song',[52] they 'rebelled against imposed brahmanical orthodoxy to reveal the inclusive, informal and experimental dimension of language and the sacred'.[53]

V

The previous section might be understood as an attempt to sketch some of the dimensions of the field from which Mehrotra emerged, and the constitution of the material to which he contributed. It may be understood, that is, to undertake the groundwork for a project of research that, in their different ways, both Brennan and Attridge describe, which attends not only to localized debates, but also to the institutions and networks of literary formation, publication, and circulation, and which thereby attempts to bridge cultural distance, not by striving towards the 'complete recovery of the original context', but by clarifying the distinctive stakes and problematics of a particular literary culture.[54] For this reason it begins with literary rather than with cultural, political, and social contexts.

Admittedly, the emphasis on print culture and position-takings begins to overshadow the verse, though even this relatively superficial account of Mehrotra's relations helps, I think, to reframe 'Bharatmata'. To begin with, it seems wrong to read the liturgical invocations

---

52 Charlotte Vaudeville, '*Sant Mat*: Santism as the Universal Path to Sanctity', in *The Sants: Studies in a Devotional Tradition*, ed. by Karine Schomer and W. H. McLeod (Delhi: Motilal Banarsidass, 1987), pp. 21–40 (p. 22).

53 Zecchini, *Arun Kolatkar and Literary Modernism*, pp. 78–79.

54 Attridge, *The Work of Literature*, p. 210.

as blasphemous, in the manner of Choudhury's 'Stark Electric Jesus', when they are properly iconoclastic, indicting as idolatrous the rhetoric that yokes nation-building to religious devotion. Indeed, a comparison with Choudhury's poem, and especially its own cloacal lexicon and metaphorics, brings into focus what we might describe as the 'worldliness' of 'Bharatmata', in Edward Said's sense of being 'situated in the world, and about the world', rather than in the more muted sense of being cosmopolitan.[55] For Mehrotra's poem is preoccupied with something other than the travails of the persona's body and mind.

In the case of KG 179, an account of the anglophone Indian literary field of the late 1960s and early 1970s demands an even greater interpretive adjustment, not least in the manner of treating Mehrotra as a standard-bearer of cosmopolitanism. This is because translation itself is recontextualized as a practice central to this field, but it is also because Mehrotra's occasional deployment of a Beat idiom in *Songs of Kabir* can no longer be taken as evidence of any straightforward kind of emulation, or of his belatedness. On the contrary, his own early verse reveals that the technical and linguistic achievements of the Beats, as well as the print technology and culture with which they were associated, had already been subsumed in the verse of anglophone Indian poets of the late 1960s. Mehrotra's use of this idiom must therefore be seen as a choice, one which has consequences for how we read KG 179. For, if it is not an effect of Mehrotra's 'generative situation', or of the peripheral status of the Indian literary field, then the belatedness of the idiom attaches not to Mehrotra, but

55 Edward Said, *Reflections on Exile, and Other Literary and Cultural Essays* (London: Granta, 2001), p. 375.

to the Beats and to Kabir. As such, making Kabir sound sometimes like one of the Beats becomes a means of identifying his iconoclasm with an American counter-cultural movement that now seems naïve as well as vital, genuinely disruptive but ultimately contained.

In this way, KG 179 becomes a poem about literature's materials, and also about its material, in Adorno's sense. It throws into relief certain of the sediments of anglophone Indian verse, by using the Beats to mark the moment in which both they and the *bhaktas* were absorbed, or re-absorbed. It throws into relief also certain of the sediments of anglophone American verse. For if we set aside the notion that Mehrotra is 'naturally' attracted to an undifferentiated 'Americanese', the poem's Leadbelly epigraph cannot be read simply as another shocking anachronism, or a consequence of Mehrotra's participation 'in the improvisational fluidity of Kabir'.[56] Instead, Leadbelly's own historicity comes into focus, and with it the significance of the blues as a vernacular tradition which was itself subjected to processes of literarization, first in the verse of the Harlem Renaissance, and then in the writings of the Beats, whose 'group vernacular', as Rosemarie Ostler explains, was 'largely a version of hipster slang spoken by African-American musicians and bebop fans in 1950s New York'.[57] Framing KG 179, Leadbelly's words thus establish analogies between Mehrotra and the Beats on the one hand, and the *bhaktas* and the blues on the other. These are mutually illuminating, reminding us in both cases of the manner in which vernaculars and folk arts are made into the materials

56 Susan Stanford Friedman, *Planetary Modernisms* (New York: Columbia University Press, 2015), p. 212.

57 Rosemarie Ostler, *Dewdroppers, Waldos, and Slackers: A Decade-by-Decade Guide to the Vanishing Vocabulary of the Twentieth Century* (Oxford: Oxford University Press, 2003), pp. 112–13.

of literature, but also, in the case of the *bhaktas*, of the fundamentally oral, musical, and communal dimensions of their compositions, and in the case of the blues, of the radicalism and even iconoclasm of the religious traditions from which it emerged.

KG 179's triangulation of the blues, Beats, and *bhaktas* also gives particular content to the epigraph's implicit distinction between those who merely *seem* to sing, and those who truly sing the blues; and to the principal condition for the latter, which is not any kind of technical mastery, but simply *having* the blues, which is to say having an acquaintance with suffering that is both spiritual and material, and that is inextricably linked with racial oppression and cultural marginalization. Thus weighted, the epigraph takes measure of the difference, otherwise unplumbed, between the pundit's 'parroting the name | Of Rama' and Kabir's 'singing of Rama': salvation requires not only words but song, and singing requires an intimacy with (though not necessarily an experience of) certain conditions of existence, including those material deprivations — of wealth, food, water, warmth, pleasure — which give urgency to apprehensions of spiritual destitution. Singing of Rama may be possible, in other words, only if one has confronted the inadequacy of speech in the face of 'beggars in the streets'.

If the Leadbelly epigraph is Mehrotra's way of signalling that the Kabir of KG 179 appears to parrot the Beats only if one ignores the origins of their idiom in vernacular song, then the final violence of the poem seems at least partly directed against those who traffic too blithely in the artefacts of cultures distant from their own: a warning about the Beats themselves, to be sure, but also to metropolitan readers. But the epigraph — which identifies Leadbelly with Mehrotra as well as with Kabir — is also a way of recalling the history of racial and class antagonisms, of imperial and colonial exploitations, that frequently underwrite the acquisition and appropriation of cultural materials, including languages, as well as the circulation of literary media, forms, and texts. Indeed, one way of reading the poem, and the volume more broadly, is as an effort to vernacularize English, to remind us that we ought not to take for granted the processes by which English becomes available across the globe as a material for literary making, inevitably by being re-made, or re-cast, though not without costs.

Which returns us to the question of the conditions of literary experience and the problem of cultural distance, the question, that is, of the workability of texts that originate in literary environments that are not those in which we, as readers, are embedded. It is a question I have tried to explore by considering two moments in the career of a single author, whose texts are clearly legible because he is a contemporary located in a homo-linguistic literary environment. This question can be formulated quite succinctly: can we experience texts as properly inventive without any familiarity with the worlds in which they originate? If I return to my initial reading, I think the answer must be affirmative. And yet, there is so much missing from this reading — so much of what the poem has to say about the world — that we must wonder whether it would not be worth distinguishing between different registers of literary experience, that is, between a reading that opens us to otherness, and a reading that, in opening us to otherness, also forces us to inhabit a truth of our world.

At the very least, we might ask again about the value of a criticism that I am tempted to describe as archaeological in spite of Attridge's reservations. For it begins by encountering an object that may well fascinate us, but which is given its full weight and meaning only when we dust away the layers in which it is embedded, revealing its relations with other perhaps less beautiful objects, as well as something of its purpose within the economy of the whole. However, since appeals to the social sciences are not only ubiquitous in theories of world literature, but also fraught with the perils of positivism, I would rather identify such a project — which I have only partially attempted here, and which entails the illumination of a distinct literary world giving its own perspective onto the world at large — as something like the work of world literature; or, rather, the work of world literary criticism.

Afterword

Towards a Theory of Reparative Translation

EMILY APTER

The 'work' of world literature, as this volume underscores in its title, and as Derek Attridge lays out in his case for translation as 'creative labour', points to theories of translational praxis that challenge the status of a nationally fortressed standard language. In my first foray into translation studies, *The Translation Zone: A New Comparative Literature* (2005), I was interested in non-standard tongues that lie in the hyphenated space of the inter-nation: dialect, creole, pidgin, patois, Rotten English, slanguage, argot, idiom. In their cuts across national borders, in their diasporic dissemination, these diglossia limned what Attridge (taking his cue from J. K. Chambers and Peter Trudgill's 'dialect continua') termed linguistic continua — porous language worlds marked by sites of mutual intelligibility (loan words, common grammar and syntax) as well as geolinguistic conflict zones where minoritarian languages struggle against majoritarian ones.[1] Such zones were occasions of a 'dialectics of dialect', an expression used by Giancarlo Tursi with reference to dialect translations (proliferating during the *Risorgimento*) of Dante's already dialectal vernacular in *The Divine Comedy*.[2] Antonio Gramsci's theory (in the last section of the *Prison Notebooks*) of 'vernacular materialism' — projecting a kind of South–South continuum in language politics — was equally dialectical, catalysed by the class struggle between the regional-popular ('imminent grammar') and the national-hegemonic ('normative grammar').[3] With this language dialectics come methodologies that pivot from genetic inheritance — language families and trees, rooted etymons, cognates, syntactic deep structure — to dynamical relation, with emphasis on how knowledge alphabets — vowel, letter, script, alphanumeric cipher, algorithm, bitmap, pixel, meme, RNA molecule, transliterative icon, acoustic value, meme, atomic predicates — are themselves epigenetically morphing.

***

Attridge's open society, out-in-the-wild vision of *linguisticity as such* fundamentally alters the view of translation relied on by institutions of international

---

1 J. K. Chambers and Peter Trudgill, *Dialectology*, 2nd edn (Cambridge: Cambridge University Press, 1998), p. 4. As cited by Attridge in this volume, p. 30.

2 Giancarlo Tursi, a Ph.D. student in the Department of Comparative Literature at New York University, develops the notion of 'dialectal dialectics' in his dissertation (in progress), provisionally titled *Dialectal Translations of Dante in the Risorgimento.*

3 'Vernacular materialism' is a term coined by Peter Ives to describe Gramsci's approach, in *Gramsci's Politics of Language: Engaging the Bakhtin Circle and the Frankfurt School* (Toronto: University of Toronto Press, 2004), p. 4.

diplomacy, academic language and literature departments, or the publishing industry (with its infrastructures of global marketing, distribution, and niche audience-targeting). This is because translation, in its conventional ascription, recurs to distinctions between *a* language of the original or 'source', (a kind of geo-Imaginary of the *Ursprung*), and *a* language of the target (a discretely sited 'elsewhere' or bounded linguistic territory). Attridge and I are on the same page in resisting the view that a nucleated language can be said to exist or assigned a distinct ontology. We are interested in language as a *political construction*, a nationalist contrivance, whose modern development through the lexical instruments of dictionaries and homogenizing grammars is profoundly imbricated in the history of western imperialism. The push to evict and exterminate indigenous tongues through forced linguistic assimilation to 'the one', (the conqueror's sovereign coin of speech), was integral to the eugenicist underbelly of historical philology; with its grammar roots soldered to myths of *ethnos*; to the regionalist, blood-and-soil identitarianism of distinct peoples and races. What we come to realize is the extent to which 'World Literature' and 'World Language' are reciprocally constitutive. As Pascale Casanova indicates in *La Langue mondiale: Traduction et domination* (2015), literature confers prestige-value on select languages (and not just the other way round), elevating them to world-historical significance. [4] In becoming-World Language, a language is further monolingualized.

***

4 Pascale Casanova, *La Langue mondiale. Traduction et domination* (Paris: Seuil, 2015).

In *Against World Literature: On the Politics of Untranslatability* (2013), my polemical sequel to *The Translation* Zone, I neglected to take full measure of how notions of vernacular materialism, language continua, and linguistic *mondialisation*, conceived as dialectical and dynamical processes, can be used to critique institutions of World Literature. I focused instead on 'World Lit' as an approach that promoted large-scale ventures in literary studies that had become (much like globally sited art biennials) 'too big to really succeed'.[5] For a number of critics who revived World Literature (among them David Damrosch, Franco Moretti, Djelal Kadir, Mads Rosenthal, Theo D'haen, Susan Friedman, Karen Thornberg, Alexander Beecroft), there was an underlying presumption that 'more is better': more languages, more literatures, more genres, more translations. Inclusion, pluralism, and infinite comparison, taken as given values, were married to world systems sorted by language type, and lent coherence by means of literary genealogy, literary ecology, and translingual analyses of pre- and post- modernities. While this ambition often produced compelling axes of comparatism, the scope of research, enhanced by new technological capabilities in the digital humanities, fostered, I argued, a kind of managerial approach to literary studies that reconfigured[6] Eurocentric dominance in the choice of style, period, and

---

5 Andrew Stefan Weiner, 'The Art of the Possible: With and Against *documenta 14*', pre-circulated review essay.

6 Pheng Cheah adds ballast to this thesis by stressing (in relation to Heidegger's notion of world), that the 'proliferation of interpretations' brought about by enhanced circulation together with the lack of a 'normative horizon' 'quantitative increase in the meaning of mobile literary works' leaves unexplained 'how a world brings into relation and how the world's meaningful unity comes about'. See his *What Is a World? On Postcolonial Literature as World Literature* (Durham, NC: Duke University Press, 2016), p. 103.

genre categories or in the geopolitics of reading, literacy, and comparative epistemology.

David Damrosch, one of the strongest advocates for a revived World Lit paradigm, was susceptible to falling into this flattened groove. In *What Is World Literature*? he had maintained that a work's translation into other languages was a gauge of its global traction. Texts with a high quotient of translation became worthy of comparison according to criteria of likeness: 'rich nodes of overlap', 'family resemblances', and 'emergent patterns'. The effect of this approach was to turn unruly groupings of texts into manageable, relatable entities.[7] Damrosch's expository smoothness, pleasurable to read, tended to foreclose the possibility of discordant textual encounters. Gone was the unsettling 'suspensive' effect in the experience of reading evoked by Derrida in an interview with Attridge in 1989 titled '"This Strange Institution Called Literature"'. Derrida insisted that 'poetry and literature have as a common feature that they suspend the "thetic" naivety of the transcendent reading'.[8] In Damrosch's *What Is World Literature?* it is hard to imagine how the estranging action of literarity could disrupt transcendent reading or resist the effects of 'irreducible intentionality', 'thetic and naïve belief in meaning or referent', as described by Derrida. In 'the play of foldings that is inscribed in the difference between literatures, between the different textual types or moments in non-literary texts', in the 'noematic' (ontologically inflected) structure of a text, Derrida gave us a version of literature — a Derridean world literature (without capit-

7 David Damrosch, *What Is World Literature*? (Princeton, NJ: Princeton University Press, 2003), p. 281.

8 Jacques Derrida, 'This Strange Institution Called Literature', in his *Acts of Literature*, ed. by Derek Attridge (New York: Routledge, 1992), pp. 33–75 (p. 45).

alization to demarcate it from the institutional form) — that resisted readability and propaedeutic story-telling.[9] When he confided to Attridge: 'I like a certain practice of fiction, the intrusion of an effective simulacrum or of disorder into philosophical writing, for example... [but] telling or inventing stories is something that deep down (or rather on the surface!) does not interest me particularly', he demarcated a space for a literary difference disruptive to philosophy, that World Literature, at least as it is promulgated by many of its adherents, would tend to ignore or to neutralize.[10]

The attention accorded by Derrida to literature's 'suspensive function', has, on the face of it, little to do with the World Literature debates in their contemporary guises, but it helped provide the terms for a theory of untranslatability that arises in the breach of literature's effect on philosophy. Literature, or at least a certain poetic function within some literary forms, deconstructs the transcendent, philosophical concept and points the way to 'philosophizing in languages'.[11] This last expression was coined by Barbara Cassin to define a particular way of doing philosophy that emphasized retranslation, non-translation, and mistranslation.[12] An example of this kind of work is found

9 Ibid., p. 45.

10 Ibid., pp. 39–40.

11 Barbara Cassin, 'Philosophising in Languages', *Nottingham French Studies*, 49.2 (2012), pp. 17–28.

12 In the context of her collaborative project titled the *Vocabulaire européen des philosophies: dictionnaire des intraduisibles* (2004), Barbara Cassin developed a nuanced account of the Untranslatable as a deterritorialized, site-sensitive, dynamically infused *term* (over and against the static *concept*). Cassin identified Untranslatables according to their nontranslation (a carry-over to other languages, as in the case of Heidegger's term *Dasein*), their mistranslation, and their perpetual retranslation. It is worth noting that Lawrence Venuti consistently misconstrues Cassin's notion of the Untranslatable in typecasting it

in François Jullien's *Entrer dans une pensée ou Des possibles de l'esprit* (2012) (translated as *The Book of Beginnings*), which draws out the meanings of the Mandarin word for the concept of the cosmos (yúzhòu) by focusing on perceptual coordinates of orientation and directionality: propinquity, propensity, declension, inclination, intending in imagined space or community.[13] In my own work, this kind of philosophizing in languages led to a renewed politics of translation in which 'political' is taken as a way of retrieving nonpolitical vocabulary that may be newly marked with political function, or as a way of judicially hearing language, such that one picks up its exclusionary and policing structures in border controls and shibboleth-testing.

World Literature as it has become institutionally embedded and vocationally vested, struck me as apolitical or political in problematic ways. In returning to a Goethean humanist project, it restituted the model of the translator as cultural universalizer, evangelizer of transcultural understanding. Though I was well aware that many partisans of World Lit endorsed it for sound political reasons — as a way of militating against the latest harmful forms of exclusionary cultural nationalism resurgent in the wake of mass migrations, heightened fears of economic destabilization, and the mainstreaming of racism by Trumpism and its ilk — they remained vulnerable to the charge of complacency toward market-driven models of literary culture

---

as 'invariant' and part of an 'instrumental' (as opposed to a 'hermeneutic') apparatus of translation praxis. See Lawrence Venuti, *Theses on Translation: An Organon for the Current Moment*, FlugSchriften, 5 (Pittsburgh, PA: Flugschriften, 2019), p. 9 <https://flugschriften.com/2019/09/15/thesis-on-translation/> [accessed 10 September 2020].

13 François Jullien, *Entrer dans une pensée ou Des possibles de l'esprit* (Paris: Gallimard, 2012), p. 31.

and education. They risked falling prey to a globalism that favours research protocols that zoom out (master of the universe-style): the manipulation of large data sets, statistical modelling and measuring, distant reading, algorithmic translations that benefit corporate monolingualism (a by-product of what Alexander Galloway calls 'digital chauvinism', a gendered privileging of algebraic mathematization over geometric, non-Euclidean intuition).

For Pheng Cheah, World Literature is salvageable as a *Weltliteratur* that renews the Kantian political program of perpetual peace (construable today as planetary justice). It redounds to Marx's conceptualization of praxis, or world-making, cast as a 'movement stirring in the current world and its actuality (*Wirklichkeit*)', that directly hails 'from the proletariat's effectivity as a material agent'.[14] Pressing further, I would replace the whole rubric of World Literature with a problem-based approach to 'literatures of the world' that takes up the issue of 'to relate to' within community. The emphasis is on the making and unmaking of affinate grammar: on undoing myths of *genos* and *Geschlecht*, that stipulate belonging to a species, kind, *anthropos*, people, race, nation, or *nomos* within a given language.

***

Robert Young has analysed how complicated it is to belong in language or to move between languages because, as the Soviet linguist Nikolai Trubetzkoy intimated, affining in language — what he called *Sprachbund*, 'linguistic alliance' or 'language union' — is a fluid process. Trubetzkoy posed *Sprachbund* against the biologically grounded concept of a

14 Pheng Cheah, 'What Is a World? On World Literature as World-Making Activity', *Dædalus*, 137.3 (Summer 2008), pp. 26–38 (p. 34).

Sprachfamilie, 'language family', that helped equip national languages with the kinds of gates and patrols that keep monolingualism intact. *Sprachfamilien* inscribe a raced genealogy of tongues that harks back to the ancient Greek consignment of 'barbarian' languages to the outback of the unintelligible. As Young reads him Trubetzkoy offers a countermodel of affinate affordances:

> a nonnational, nonracial union that operates across language borders [...] continually reacting and interacting, colliding and combining with other systems in its zone, compounding 'the processes of divergence (the breakdown of a language into dialects) and convergence (the rapprochement of languages in contact)' in a dialectical movement of centripetal and centrifugal forces.[15]

Following the work of Nicolay Smirnoff a rather more complicated political agenda emerges from Trubetzkoy's version of the language continua model. His promulgation of Eurasianism — a middle-continental (Russia-Eurasia) *geosophy* (positioned against Europe's imposition of 'Romano-German culture as universal, which it did through chauvinism and cosmopolitanism)' — turns out to be hardly exempt from regional chauvinism. Arguably, it merely substituted a supranational or extrastate version of language boosterism for the older nationalist one.[16] But let's for the sake of argument allow Young's tendential reading of Trubetzkoy as a voice for dialectal dialectics; for a language theory of mobile

15 Robert J. C. Young, 'That Which Is Casually Called a Language', *PMLA*, 131.5 (2016), pp. 1207–21 (p. 1215).

16 Nicolay Smirnoff, 'Left-Wing Eurasianism and Postcolonial Theory', *e-flux journal*, 97 (2019) <https://www.e-flux.com/journal/97/252238/left-wing-eurasianism-and-postcolonial-theory/> [accessed 10 September 2020].

decipherment across plurilingual entities similar in some respects to what Yuri M. Lotman ecumenically dubbed the 'semiosphere' and 'world semiosis'.[17] Young places renewed political emphasis on the possibilities offered by the philological continuum, no longer sectorized by ontological nationalism or oblivious to the political histories of, as he puts it, 'minoritized groups who choose to work with standard languages by breaking them.'[18] Young's projection of the continuum contains the kind of emancipatory thrust registered by the testimony of a speaker of Yenish, a dialect found in the Swiss and French Alps comparable to Yiddish or Romani insofar as its predominant speakers are travellers. Interviewed by Martin Puchner, the Yenish Chief denounces the desire on the part of normative grammarians 'to make distinctions within Yenish; to cut something into different parts'. He calls out such efforts as 'the vice of the city', conjuring a carceral, stiflingly domesticated architecture of standard language as roofed-over, blocked by the ceiling from the open sky and landscape vistas illuminated by the moon.[19]

As a dialect of the open road Yenish is posed as a continuum, a pick-up language of places names, country accents, outlier inflections harvested from other mar-

---

17 See Ilya Kliger's discussion of Lotman's 1984 essay 'On the Semiosphere' (or world semiosis) in 'World Literature Beyond Hegemony in Yuri M. Lotman's Cultural Semiotics', *Comparative Critical Studies,* 7.2–3 (2010), pp. 257–74. Kliger underscores Lotman's understanding of linguistic relatedness '"along the spectrum which runs from complete mutual translatability to just as complete mutual untranslatability"'. Yuri M. Lotman, *Universe of the Mind: A Semiotic Theory of Culture,* trans. by Ann Shukman (Bloomington: Indiana University Press, 2000), p. 125. As cited by Kliger, p. 264.

18 Young, 'That Which Is Casually Called a Language', p. 1219.

19 Quoted by Martin Puchner in his *The Language of Thieves: My Family's Obsession with a Secret Code the Nazis Tried to Eliminate* (New York: Norton, 2020).

ginalized bohemian communities. If we extrapolate here from language to literature, we discover a model that S. Shankar calls 'literatures of the world' that foregoes 'canons and lists' and emphasizes 'mystery' over 'mastery', or, as Michael Allan advocates, that levels the playing field between national traditions, genres, and scripts.[20] In place of triage efforts as typically found in World Lit anthologies — classifications of literary forms by national geographies, traditions, and styles, literary histories based on formal typologies hooked on to western classics — there would be attempts to read literatures through the lens of what impedes translation through incommensurability, nonequivalence, the history of violent erasure, carried-over silences, and nonwords, or the effects of non-translation. Rebecca Walkowitz gets it right when, in her book *Born Translated,* she hails the emergent field of 'non-translation studies', a term coined by Brian Lennon to highlight what Lennon calls 'a renewed emphasis on idiolectic incommensurability'. Walkowitz explains that Lennon 'values books that refuse to participate in standards of linguistic, typographical or semiotic accessibility'. 'The most original books,' according to Lennon, 'will be barely publishable. [...] [N]on-translation scholarship would eschew its own monolingualism by producing "plurilingual" works.'[21] Lennon and Walkowitz gesture toward a utopian horizon of *translation continua* that register the happening

20 S. Shankar, 'Literatures of the World: An Inquiry', *PMLA,* 131.5 (2016), pp. 1405–13 (p. 1412); Michael Allan, *In the Shadow of World Literature: Sites of Reading in Colonial Egypt* (Princeton, NJ: Princeton University Press, 2016).

21 Brian Lennon, *In Babel's Shadow: Multilingual Literatures, Monolingual States* (Minneapolis: University of Minnesota Press, 2010). As cited by Rebecca Walkowitz, *Born Translated: The Contemporary Novel in an Age of World Literature* (New York: Columbia University Press, 2015), p. 32.

of *parole in libertà* — speech freed into the wild of untranslatability (pure linguicity) at the expense of market-friendly readability. I see the attraction of surfing the zone of untranslatability, but would insist on underscoring the political role played by Untranslatables in the history of anticolonialism, specifically, their dissolution of regimes of what Ann Laura Stoler calls 'lettered governance', glossed by Baidik Bhattacharya as 'literary sovereignty'.[22]

***

A concrete way of mobilizing nontranslation involves subtractive reading and resistant translation. As Benjamin Conisbee Baer has noted, Gayatri Chakravorty Spivak, in her foreword to her translation from Bengali into English of Mahasweta Devi's story collection *Breast Stories*, alludes to the challenge of distinguishing between tribal exclusion and caste functionalism in relation to the broad category of the 'untouchables'. She takes as an example a line in the short story 'Draupadi': 'The untouchables don't get water.' While the original draws an important distinction between the untouchables who tend funeral pyres and those who dig graves, Spivak does not try to express this distinction in English. Noting that the caste term *untouchables* is highly problematic in Indian languages (giving rise to Mahatma Gandhi's assimilation of untouchables to tribals through the name *Harijan*, 'God's people' (a mistranslation insofar as tribals should not be confused with untouchables), Spivak underscores Devi's decision to

22 Ann Laura Stoler, *Along the Archival Grain: Epistemic Anxieties and Colonial Common Sense* (Princeton, NJ: Princeton University Press, 2010), p. 1. I refer as well to Baidik Bhattacharya's current book project *The Literary Sovereign: Colonial Histories, Critical Idioms, and Cultural Differences* sample chapters of which he kindly shared with me.

follow 'the Bengali practice of calling each so-called untouchable caste by the name of its menial and unclean task within the rigid structural functionalism of institutionalized Hinduism'. She then declared bluntly: 'I have been unable to reproduce this in my translation.'[23] Spivak's affirmation of untranslatability implicitly challenges the reading posture of all-knowingness directed by western anglophone readers in relation to texts in Indian languages. By acknowledging her act of translation manqué, Spivak marks out non-comprehension and un-understandability in her rendering of Devi's tale and discloses the pressure exerted on other languages by global English to submit to laws of equivalency on its terms. The not-translated reads no longer as an admission that translation is difficult to the point of impossibility but instead as a tactic of withholding deployed against the predominance of global English, or Globish. Globish promotes frictionless communication in business, research, and technology, much like the algorithmic codes of big data. In this context, translation is both a facilitator of Globish (a tool of monolingualism) and the name of a practice that is obsolete and no longer necessary since Globish already prevails as the world's lingua franca. Nontranslation under these conditions is weaponized against the unequal playing field induced by Globish.

To introduce questions of equality and the uneven distribution of linguistic shares in world languages and literatures is to foreground the political in translation theory. Non-equivalence, the right not to translate, cultural incommensurability: these topics not only anchor the problem-

23 Gayatri Chakravorty Spivak, 'Translator's Foreword', in Mahasweta Devi, *Breast Stories: Draupadi, Breast-Giver, Choli ke Pichhe*, trans. and intro. by Gayatri Chakravorty Spivak (Calcutta: Seagull Books, 1997), p. 13.

atic of untranslatability in world literature (and comparative literature more generally), they also engender the broader question of what it means 'to relate to' literarily. Useful here is François Noudelmann's notion of 'disruptive kinship', which interrogates the grounds of elective affinity, the ways in which preference, proximity, and likeness (and their negative correlatives — recoil, difference, and incommensurability) are tallied to shore up foundational aesthetics.[24] Untranslatability in this context may be construed as a process of disruptive kinship, a mode of antigenealogical thinking that prompts a rethinking (if not a return to) Derrida's theories of linguistic iterability, singularity, and relations of non-relation, as well as Jean-François Lyotard's conception of the differend. Translation and nontranslation, plotted as antinomies within complex geographies of reading, reveal emergent solidarities among readers as well as philologies that ceaselessly interrogate the legal and political statutes defining what border exists — and where — in language, or how the barrier of a frontier or checkpoint is geoterritorially inscribed as a site of nontranslation, linguistic derivation, and differentiation.

***

24 François Noudelmann, *Les Airs de famille. Une philosophie des affinités* (Paris: Gallimard, 2012). Noudelmann argues that affinities have been taken philosophically as disruptors of kinship and genealogical connection; capable of interfering (by virtue of their open relationality) in the bloodlines of philological inheritance and signifying grammar. Kant's initial uneasiness toward affinities is traced by Noudelmann to his suspicion that they muddied the clarity of concepts. He then describes how Kant changed his view with the help of a dinner party experiment consisting of throwing out non-following topics of conversation and observing how his guests would reestablish colloquy and congeniality. Affinities were thereafter cast as a unifying force of heterogeneous elements, as conduits of social harmony and mutual understanding. See, chapter v, 'Philosophies des affinités', pp. 257–305.

Attridge makes a convincing case for casting translation as 'creative labour'. A galvanizing telos of that labour is the application of the language continua model to literary studies, and more specifically, to translational praxis within an institutional critique of World Literature.

Translation continua, as we have seen, can be variously construed: as dialectal dialectics (a vernacular materialism defined by spontaneous outbursts against normative grammar); as one long Heraclitan stream of expressionism; as porous language worlds that emerge from coparticipant speech communities or 'world semiosis'; and as a program to decolonize monolingualism. In this instance monolingualism is adduced as a gathering term for ethnocentric unities conducive to management by neoliberal language policy.

To decolonize translation, to invent a decolonial translation theory responsive to the imperatives of newly-energized indigenous and racial justice movements, one must grapple with the ethnonationalist assumptions of linguistic epistemology. One must recognize (as Derrida did in his classic essay 'What Is a "Relevant" Translation?'[25]) that the history of translation cannot be divorced from the history of proselytism and forced conversion. And one must reckon to the fullest with how 'language' in the singular *is army*, which is to say, constitutive of regimes of white sovereignty. On this last point Attridge's essay is crucial: it shows how Afrikaans, 'worryingly close to the language spoken by the people known as "Coloureds" — many of them the descendants of slave-women impregnated by their Dutch-speaking

25 Jacques Derrida, 'What Is a "Relevant" Translation?', trans. by Lawrence Venuti, *Critical Inquiry*, 27.2 (2001), pp. 174–200.

masters' — had 'to be instituted and safeguarded as a pure language spoken by white people'.[26] Attridge writes:

> The white version of Afrikaans [Standaardafrikaans] was promoted and regulated by the Afrikaner Nationalist government that came to power in 1948, and Afrikaans writers did much to create the norms of the language and give it richness and prestige. The speech of the Cape Coloured community, [most often referred to as Kaaps], lacking an army and a navy, could then be safely classified as a mere 'dialect' of Afrikaans.[27]

Here, the common adage that 'language is a dialect surrounded by an army' yields a racially specific reformulation, something like '*white sovereignty* is the hegemony within Language surrounded by an army'. Here, Language capital L becomes not only the default of a nationally denominated, vehicular tongue, it is the name of racist violence in linguistic form.

Attridge's 'South African example' stands in for innumerable examples of racist quarantining, apartheid, and ethnic cleansing. It points the way to a long and ongoing history of linguistic persecution in which dialects and vernaculars, pidgins and creoles, argots and secret codes were hunted, incarcerated, and consigned to extinction. As Martin Puchner shows in his consideration of Rotwelsch, a language of migrants and travellers, mixing German, Hebrew, and Yiddish and stigmatized by the Nazis as a language of thieves, the affirmation of Aryanism — impossible to disintricate from National Socialist language policy — provided an exemplum for the subjection of nonconforming dialects to the laws of apartheid and the rule of white

26 Derek Attridge, in this volume, p. 35.

27 Ibid., p. 36.

sovereignty.[28] For translation studies — a field that is all about administering systems of regulative judgment that separate 'good' from 'bad' language — decolonizing translation (and with it World Literature as a literary heuristic) means demonstrating that the attachment to standard language distinctions perpetuates the *staying white* of language worlds.

In my own ongoing project on justice and translation I experiment with notions of reparative translation as a poetics of repair in the spirit of Fred Moten's lines 'Wrapped in the radiated weave of sackcloth as prayercloth [...] we're all right here, outside your jurisdiction, criminal in the work and out of phase, at prayer, in preparation, of repair'.[29] Christina Sharpe's notion of 'wake work' as care work — a problem of thinking 'of and for Black non/being in the world' — is equally a guiding thread.[30] Crucial too is Gayatri Chakravorty Spivak's call to redress 'translation-as-violation'. Spivak uses the example of Rudyard Kipling's 'pidgin Hindusthani', a subclass of British pidgin guaranteed to sound 'barbaric to the native speaker, devoid of syntactic connections, always infelicitous, almost always incorrect' and above all an effect of 'the mark of perceiving a language as subordinate'.[31] Pressing further, we could say

28 See Puchner's fascinating, autobiographically inflected history of Rotwelsch as idiolect of travelers and system of *Zinken* (lookout pictographs used to alert hoboes to danger, food, or shelter), in his *The Language of Thieves*. For theoretically and aesthetically attuned analyses of outlaw tongues, see Daniel Heller-Roazen, *Dark Tongues: The Art of Rogues and Riddlers* (New York: Zone Books, 2013) and Daniel Tiffany, *Infidel Poetics: Riddles, Nightlife, Substance* (Chicago: Chicago University Press, 2009).

29 Fred Moten, 'Nobody, Everybody', in *Black and Blur* (Durham, NC: Duke University Press, 2017), pp. 168–69 (p. 169).

30 Christina Sharpe, *In the Wake: On Blackness and Being* (Durham, NC: Duke University Press, 2016), pp. 17 and 5 respectively.

31 Gayatri Chakravorty Spivak, *A Critique of Postcolonial Reason: Toward a History of the Vanishing Present* (Cambridge, MA: Harvard University Press, 1999), p. 162.

that reparative translation can be seen as wound-dressing (*soins, pansements*) for racism as a pre-existing condition detrimental to mental and physical health. A 'creative labour' of reparative translation seeks to redress modes of social harming in speech that include rape-speech, hate-speech, violations of sacred tongues, abrogated rights to language, and unfree talk. Miles Ogborn, examining the long history of slavery, qualifies unfreedoms of speech as 'bondage made through speech', communicative practices that define 'social relations [...] underpinned by violence', talk whose disciplinary boundary lines produce 'another geography of slavery'.[32] In a complementary vein Tiphaine Samoyault's *Traduction et violence* explores translation's curtailment of free speech, noting the unfree condition of what Salman Rushdie called 'translated men' in sites of colonial domination.[33] Samoyault poses the challenge of an ethics of translation that plots the lines of translation polit-

32 Miles Ogborn, *The Freedom of Speech: Talk and Slavery in the Anglo-Caribbean World* (Chicago: University of Chicago Press, 2019), pp. 4 and 5. Reviewing Ogborn's book Fara Dabhoiwala writes: 'Freedom of speech and the power to silence may have been preeminent markers of white liberty, Ogborn argues, but at the same time, slavery depended on dialogue: slaves could never be completely muted. Even in conditions of extreme violence and unfreedom, their words remained ubiquitous, ephemeral, irrepressible, and potentially transgressive. In that sense, even the speech of the unfree was always free. Talk was the most common way for enslaved men and women to subvert the rules of their bondage, to gain more agency than they were supposed to have. Moreover, Africans, too, came from societies in which oaths, orations, and invocations carried great potency, both between people and as a connection to the all-powerful spirit world.' 'Speech and Slavery in the West Indies', *The New York Review of Books*, 67.13 (20 August 2020), p. 23.

33 'Having been borne across the world, we are translated men. It is normally supposed that something always gets lost in translation; I cling, obstinately, to the notion that something can also be gained' (Salman Rushdie, 'Imaginary Homelands', *London Review of Books*, 4.18 (7 October 1982) <https://www.lrb.co.uk/the-paper/v04/n18/salman-rushdie/imaginary-homelands> [accessed 10 September 2020]).

ics along overlapping and sometimes historically divergent axes of post-imperialism and post-slavery.

These are axes that Attridge also traces in orienting the labour of translation towards the goals of anti-apartheid and racial justice movements. Theoretical co-ordinates would include (among others) P. Khalil Saucier and Tryon P. Woods's 'conceptual aphasia in black', Barnor Hesse's analysis of the 'so-called N-word' as preeminent 'state repetitive violence' against policed black bodies, or Ronald Judy's 'poïesis in black', with 'black' understood in all three uses to refer to processes of languaging outside a discrete or given tongue.[34] 'Black' in these instances is not a synonym for the kind of linguistic essentialism found in national language names, it is rather, a processual dialectics of language whose workings allow us to perceive the warp of white sovereignty on historicized language worlds. 'Black' correlates further to the routing of forms of conceptual apartheid embedded in sectorized institutional infrastructures, such as the ostensibly benign 'languages and literatures' rubric employed by departments and conference organizers (which contributes in no small way to the whitening of literary studies). It's time to recognize the racial violence built into the division of the faculties, and reproduced through pedagogies of World Literature and World Language that take linguistic singularization as pregiven.

This involves an approach to remediation and repair in language that exceeds familiar moves to denationalize the

34 *Conceptual Aphasia in Black: Displacing Racial Formation*, ed. by P. Khalil Saucier and Tryon P. Woods (Lenham: Lexington Books, 2016); Barnor Hesse, 'White Sovereignty (...), Black Life Politics: The N****r They Couldn't Kill', *The South Atlantic* Quarterly, 116.3 (2017), pp. 581–604 (p. 582); Ronald A. Judy, *Sentient Flesh: Thinking in Disorder, Poiesis in Black* (Durham, NC: Duke University Press, 2020).

humanities — evident in rubrics like 'Languages', 'Literature' (along the lines of the Lit major at Yale developed in the 1970s by literary comparatists grounded in structuralist linguistics, deconstructive poetics, and narratology) or 'Theory'. These rubrics can facilitate plurilingual heuristics but they do little to frame the political work of repair that translation affords, particularly when it focuses on the history of unfreedoms of speech; linguistic antagonisms in regions of geopolitical conflict and dissensus; protection against verbal violence and microaggression; incommensurate vocabularies of pardonnability and amends-making; and the painstaking labour of restorative justice applied to language politics. Reparative translation, and the literary praxes it indicates, goes beyond the calculative legal logic of indemnity, recompense, damages, and moral hazard used to make whole the subject of a wrong. It looks towards recovery: towards recovering the dynamics of languaging that happen in the interstices of Languages; towards the restitution of extinguished indigenous languages, idiolects, and creoles; and towards recuperation from the myriad forms of translational violence committed in the name of languages surrounded by an army.

References

Acosta, Alberto, 'Después del saqueo: Caminos hacia el posextractivismo', *Perspectivas, Análisis y Comentarios Políticos América Latina*, 1 (2015), pp. 12–15

Adorno, Theodor, *Aesthetic Theory*, ed. by Gretel Adorno and Rolf Tiedermann, trans. by Robert Hullot-Kentor (London: Continuum, 2004)

Agamben, Giorgio, 'Che cos'è un comando?', in his *Creazione e anarchia. L'opera nell'età della religione capitalista* (Vicenza: Neri Pozza, 2017), pp. 91–112

—— 'Notes on Gesture', in his *Means without End: Notes on Politics*, trans. by Vincenzo Binetti and Cesare Casarino (Minneapolis: University of Minnesota Press, 2000), pp. 49–61

Ahmed, Sara, *Strange Encounters: Embodied Others in Postcoloniality* (London: Routledge, 2000)

Allan, Michael, *In the Shadow of World Literature: Sites of Reading in Colonial Egypt* (Princeton, NJ: Princeton University Press, 2016) <https://doi.org/10.23943/princeton/9780691167824.001.0001>

Anand [P. Sachidanandan], 'What is sahit in sahitya?', *Indian Folklife*, 1.3 (2000), pp. 12–14

Anderson, Benedict, *Imagined Communities*, 2nd edn (London: Verso, 1991)

Antonelli, Roberto, 'Canzoniere Vaticano latino 3793', in *Letteratura italiana: Le Opere*, ed. by Alberto Asor Rosa, 4 vols (Turin: Einaudi, 1992–96), I: *Dalle Origini al Cinquecento* (1992), pp. 27–44

—— 'L'"invenzione" del sonetto', *Cultura neolatina*, 47 (1987), pp. 19–59

—— ed., *I poeti della scuola siciliana*, 3 vols (Milan: Mondadori, 2008), I: *Giacomo da Lentini*

Apter, Emily, *Against World Literature: On the Politics of Untranslatability* (London: Verso, 2013)

—— *The Translation Zone: A New Comparative Literature* (Princeton, NJ: Princeton University Press, 2006) <https://doi.org/10.1515/9781400841219>

Attridge, Derek, 'Contemporary Afrikaans Fiction and English Translation: Singularity and the Question of Minor Languages', in *Singularity and Transnational Poetics*, ed. by Birgit Mara Kaiser (New York: Routledge, 2014), pp. 61–78 <https://doi.org/10.4324/9781315773629-4>

—— 'Contemporary Afrikaans Fiction in the World: The Englishing of Marlene van Niekerk', *Journal of Commonwealth Studies*, 49.3 (2014), pp. 395–409 <https://doi.org/10.1177/0021989414531591>

—— *J. M. Coetzee and the Ethics of Reading: Literature in the Event* (Chicago: University of Chicago Press, 2004)

—— *Peculiar Language: Literature as Difference from the Renaissance to James Joyce* (Ithaca, NY: Cornell University Press, 1988)

—— *The Singularity of Literature* (London: Routledge, 2004) <https://doi.org/10.4324/9780203420447>

—— '"This Strange Institution Called Literature": An Interview with Jacques Derrida', trans. by Geoffrey Bennington and Rachel Bowlby, in Jacques Derrida, *Acts of Literature*, ed. by Derek Attridge (London: Routledge, 1993), pp. 33–75 <https://doi.org/10.4324/9780203873540-2>

—— *Well-Weighed Syllables: Elizabethan Verse in Classical Metres* (Cambridge: Cambridge University Press, 1974)

—— *The Work of Literature* (Oxford: Oxford University Press, 2015) <https://doi.org/10.1093/acprof:oso/9780198733195.001.0001>

Auerbach, Erich, 'Philology and *Weltliteratur*', trans. by Maire and Edward Said, *The Centennial Review*, 13.1 (1969), pp. 1–17

Austin, J. L., *How to Do Things with Words* (Cambridge, MA: Harvard University Press, 1975) <https://doi.org/10.1093/acprof:oso/9780198245537.001.0001>

Badiou, Alain, *Infinite Thought: Truth and the Return to Philosophy* (London: Continuum, 2003)

Barthes, Roland, *How to Live Together: Novelistic Simulations of Some Everyday Experience*, trans. by Kate Briggs (New York: Columbia University Press, 2012)

Behera, Hari Charan, 'Land, Property Rights and Management Issues in Tribal Areas of Jharkhand: An Overview', in *Shifting Perspectives in Tribal Studies*, ed. by Maguni Charan Behera (Singapore: Springer, 2019), pp. 251–71

Benjamin, Walter, *Selected Writings*, 4 vols (Cambridge, MA: Harvard University Press, 1996–2003)

—— 'Commentary on Poems by Brecht', trans. by Edmund Jephcott, in his *Selected Writings*, IV: *1938–1940*, ed. by Howard Eiland and Michael W. Jennings (2003), pp. 215–50

—— 'Notes from Svendborg, Summer 1934', trans. by Rodney Livingstone, in his *Selected Writings*, II.2: *1931–1934*, ed. by Michael W. Jennings, Howard Eiland, and Gary Smith (1999), pp. 783–91

—— 'What is Epic Theatre? (II)', trans. by Harry Zohn, in his *Selected Writings*, IV: *1938–1940*, ed. by Howard Eiland and Michael W. Jennings (2003), pp. 302–09

Bird, Emma, 'A Platform for Poetry: The PEN All-India Centre and a Bombay Poetry Scene', *Journal of Postcolonial Writing*, 53.1–2 (2017), pp. 207–20 <https://doi.org/10.1080/17449855.2017.1282927>

Bly, Robert, *The Fish in the Sea is Not Thirsty: Kabir Versions* (Northwood Narrows, NH: Lillabulero Press, 1971)

Bourdieu, Pierre, *The Field of Cultural Production: Essays on Art and Literature* (Cambridge: Polity Press, 1993)

Brennan, Timothy, 'Cosmopolitanism and World Literature', in *The Cambridge Companion to World Literature*, ed. by Ben Etherington and Jarad Zimbler (Cambridge: Cambridge University Press, 2018), pp. 23–36

Briggs, Kate, *This Little Art* (London: Fitzcarraldo Editions, 2017)

Brugnolo, Furio, 'I siciliani e l'arte dell'imitazione: Giacomo da Lentini, Rinaldo d'Aquino e Iacopo Mostacci 'traduttori' dal provenzale', *La parola del testo*, 3 (1999), pp. 45–74

Burns, Lorna, *Postcolonialism After World Literature: Relation, Equality, Dissent* (London: Bloomsbury 2019) <https://doi.org/10.5040/9781350053052>

Burns, Lorna, and Katie Muth, eds, *World Literature and Dissent* (London: Routledge, 2019) <https://doi.org/10.4324/9780203710302>

Carstens, Wannie A. M., and Edith H. Raidt, *Die Storie van Afrikaans: Uit Europa en van Afrika* (Pretoria: Protea Boekhuis, 2017)

Casanova, Pascale, *La Langue mondiale. Traduction et domination* (Paris: Seuil, 2015)

—— 'Literature as a World', *New Left Review*, 31 (2005), pp. 71–90

—— *The World Republic of Letters*, trans. by Malcolm B. DeBevoise (Cambridge, MA: Harvard University Press, 2004)

Cassin, Barbara, 'Philosophising in Languages', *Nottingham French Studies*, 49.2 (2012), pp. 17–28 <https://doi.org/10.3366/nfs.2010-2.003>

—— ed., *Dictionary of Untranslatables: A Philosophical Lexicon*, trans. by Steven Rendall and others (Princeton, NJ: Princeton University Press, 2014) <https://doi.org/10.1515/9781400849918>

Chakrabarty, Dipesh, *Provincializing Europe: Postcolonial Thought and Historical Difference* (Delhi: Oxford University Press, 2000)

Chambers, J. K., and Peter Trudgill, *Dialectology*, 2nd edn (Cambridge: Cambridge University Press, 1998) <https://doi.org/10.1017/CBO9780511805103>

Cheah, Pheng, *What Is a World? On Postcolonial Literature as World Literature* (Durham, NC: Duke University Press, 2016) <https://doi.org/10.1215/9780822374534>

—— 'What Is a World? On World Literature as World-Making Activity', *Dædalus*, 137.3 (Summer 2008), pp. 26–38 <https://doi.org/10.1162/daed.2008.137.3.26>

Coetzee, J. M., *The Childhood of Jesus* (London: Vintage, 2014)

—— Draft of *Burning the Books* (unrealized), 19 October 1973, Manuscript Collection MS-0842, Container 33.1, Handwritten notes, and unfinished draft, 19 October 1973–4 July 1974, J. M. Coetzee Papers, Harry Ransom Center, The University of Texas at Austin

—— 'Jerusalem Prize Acceptance Speech', in J. M. Coetzee, *Doubling the Point: Essays and Interviews*, ed. by David Attwell (Cambridge, MA: Harvard University Press, 1992), pp. 96–100

Craig, Martin P. A., Hayley Stevenson, and James Meadowcroft, 'Debating Nature's Value: Epistemic Strategy and Struggle in the Story of "Ecosystem Services"', *Journal of Environmental Policy & Planning*, 21.6 (2019), pp. 811–25

Critchley, Simon, *Infinitely Demanding: Ethics of Commitment, Politics of Resistance* (London: Verso, 2007)

Culler, Jonathan, 'Apostrophe,' in Jonathan Culler, *The Pursuit of Signs: Semiotics, Literature, Deconstruction*, 2nd edn (London: Routledge, 2001), pp. 149–71

—— *Theory of the Lyric* (Cambridge, MA: Harvard University Press, 2015) <https://doi.org/10.4159/9780674425781>

Dabhoiwala, Fara, 'Speech and Slavery in the West Indies', *The New York Review of Books*, 67.13 (20 August 2020)

Damrosch, David, *How to Read World Literature* (Chichester: Wiley-Blackwell, 2009) <https://doi.org/10.1002/9781444304596>

—— *What Is World Literature?* (Princeton, NJ: Princeton University Press, 2003) <https://doi.org/10.1515/9780691188645>

Damrosch, David, and Gayatri Chakravorty Spivak, 'Comparative Literature / World Literature: A Discussion', *Comparative Literature Studies*, 48.4 (2011), pp. 455–85 <https://doi.org/10.5325/complitstudies.48.4.0455>

Deckard, Sharae, 'Land, Water, Waste: Environment and Ecology in South Asian Fiction', in *The Oxford History of the Novel in English*, 11 vols (Oxford: Oxford University Press, 2010–19), x: *The Novel in South and South East Asia since 1945*, ed. by Alex Tickell (2019), pp. 172–86

Deleuze, Gilles, and Félix Guattari, *Kafka: Toward a Minor Literature*, trans. by Dana Polan (Minneapolis: University of Minnesota Press, 1986)

—— *A Thousand Plateaus: Capitalism and Schizophrenia*, trans. by Brian Massumi (London: Continuum, 2002)

Delle Donne, Fulvio, *La porta del sapere: Cultura alla corte di Federico II di Svevia* (Rome: Carocci, 2019)

de Man, Paul, 'Lyrical Voice in Contemporary Theory', in *Lyric Poetry: Beyond New Criticism*, ed. by Chaviva Hošek and Patricia Parker (Ithaca, NY: Cornell University Press, 1985), pp. 55–72

Derrida, Jacques, *The Gift of Death* (Second Edition) *& Literature in Secret*, trans. by David Wills (Chicago: University of

Chicago Press, 2008) <https://doi.org/10.7208/chicago/9780226571676.001.0001>
—— *Le Monolinguisme de l'autre* (Paris: Galilée, 1996)
—— '"This Strange Institution Called Literature": An Interview with Jacques Derrida', trans. by Geoffrey Bennington and Rachel Bowlby, in Jacques Derrida, *Acts of Literature*, ed. by Derek Attridge (London: Routledge, 1993), pp. 33–75 <https://doi.org/10.4324/9780203873540-2>
—— 'Two Words for Joyce', in *Post-structuralist Joyce: Essays from the French*, ed. by Derek Attridge and Daniel Ferrer (Cambridge: Cambridge University Press, 1984), pp. 145–59
—— 'What Is a "Relevant" Translation?', trans. by Lawrence Venuti, *Critical Inquiry*, 27.2 (2001), pp. 174–200 <https://doi.org/10.1086/449005>
—— 'Who or What Is Compared? The Concept of Comparative Literature and the Theoretical Problems of Translation', trans. by Eric Prenowitz, in *'Who?' or 'What?' — Jacques Derrida*, ed. by Dragan Kujundžić (= *Discourse* 30.1/2 (Winter/Spring 2008)), pp. 22–53
Derrida, Jacques, and Maurizio Ferraris, *A Taste for the Secret*, trans. by Giacomo Donis (Malden: Polity, 2001)
Dimock, Wai Chee, *Through Other Continents: American Literature Across Deep Time* (Princeton, NJ: Princeton University Press, 2006)
Dimock, Wai Chee, and Laurence Buell, eds, *Shades of the Planet: American Literature as World Literature* (Princeton, NJ: Princeton University Press, 2007) <https://doi.org/10.1515/9780691188256>
Doniger, Wendy, 'Preface', in Mehrotra, *Songs of Kabir*, pp. vi-xviii
Eskin, Michael, 'The Double "Turn" to Ethics and Literature?', *Poetics Today*, 25.4 (2005), pp. 557–72 <https://doi.org/10.1215/03335372-25-4-557>
Etherington, Ben, 'What Is Materialism's Material? Thoughts toward (Actually against) a Materialism for "World Literature"', *Journal of Postcolonial Writing*, 48.5 (2012), pp. 539–51 <https://doi.org/10.1080/17449855.2012.720801>
—— 'World Literature as a Speculative Literary Totality: Veselovsky, Auerbach, Said, and the Critical Humanist Tradition', *Modern Language Quarterly*, 82.2 (2021)

Etherington, Ben, and Jarad Zimbler, *The Cambridge Companion to World Literature* (Cambridge: Cambridge University Press, 2018) <https://doi.org/10.1017/9781108613354>

—— 'Field, Material, Technique: On Renewing Postcolonial Literary Criticism', *Journal of Commonwealth Literature*, 49.3 (2014), pp. 279–98 <https://doi.org/10.1177/0021989414538435>

—— 'Introduction', in *The Cambridge Companion to World Literature*, ed. by Ben Etherington and Jarad Zimbler (Cambridge: Cambridge University Press, 2018) <https://doi.org/10.1017/9781108613354.002>

Felski, Rita, *The Limits of Critique* (Chicago: University of Chicago Press, 2015) <https://doi.org/10.7208/chicago/9780226294179.001.0001>

Folchetto di Marsiglia, *Le poesie di Folchetto di Marsiglia*, ed. by Paolo Squillacioti (Pisa: Pacini, 1999)

Friedman, Susan Stanford, *Planetary Modernisms* (New York: Columbia University Press, 2015) <https://doi.org/10.7312/columbia/9780231170901.003.0002>

Gago, Verónica, and Sandro Mezzadra, 'A Critique of the Extractive Operations of Capital: Toward an Expanded Concept of Extractivism', trans. by Liz Mason-Deese, *Rethinking Marxism*, 29.4 (2017), pp. 574–91

Ghose, Kali Mohan, and Ezra Pound, 'Certain Poems of Kabir', *The Modern Review*, 13.6 (1913), pp. 611–13

Giusti, Francesco, 'Literature at Work: A Conversation with Derek Attridge', *Los Angeles Review of Books*, 11 June 2018 <https://lareviewofbooks.org/article/literature-at-work-a-conversation-with-derek-attridge/> [accessed 23 May 2020]

—— 'Reversion: Lyric Time(s) II', in *Re-: An Errant Glossary*, ed. by Christoph F. E. Holzhey and Arnd Wedemeyer (Berlin: ICI Berlin, 2019), pp. 151–61 <https://doi.org/10.25620/ci-15_19>

—— 'Temporalità liriche. Ripetizione e incompiutezza tra Dante e Caproni, Montale e Sanguineti', *California Italian Studies*, 8.1 (2018) <https://escholarship.org/uc/item/87x199p7> [accessed 23 May 2020]

Gómez-Barris, Macarena, *The Extractive Zone: Social Ecologies and Decolonial Perspectives* (Durham, NC: Duke University Press, 2017)

Grobbelaar, Peter, ed., *Reader's Digest Afrikaans–Engels Woordeboek/English–Afrikaans Dictionary* (Cape Town: Reader's Digest Association, 1987)

D'haen, Theo, David Damrosch, and Djelal Kadir, eds, *The Routledge Companion to World Literature* (London: Routledge, 2012) <https://doi.org/10.4324/9780203806494>

Hamilton, John T., *Security: Politics, Humanity, and the Philology of Care* (Princeton, NJ: Princeton University Press, 2013) <https://doi.org/10.23943/princeton/9780691157528.001.0001>

Harman, Graham, *Prince of Networks: Bruno Latour and Metaphysics* (Melbourne: re:press, 2009)

Harrison, Nicholas, 'World Literature: What Gets Lost in Translation?', *Journal of Commonwealth Literature*, 29 (2014), pp. 411–26 <https://doi.org/10.1177/0021989414535420>

Hartog, François, *Regimes of Historicity: Presentism and Experiences of Time*, trans. by Saskia Brown (New York: Columbia University Press, 2015) <https://doi.org/10.7312/columbia/9780231163767.001.0001>

Harvey, David, 'The New Imperialism: Accumulation as Dispossession', *The Socialist Register*, 40 (2009), pp. 63–87

Hayot, Eric, 'On Literary Worlds', *Modern Language Quarterly*, 72.2 (2011), pp. 133–34 <https://doi.org/10.1215/00267929-1161286>

—— 'World Literature and Globalization', in *The Routledge Companion to World Literature*, ed. by Theo D'haen, David Damrosch, and Djelal Kadir (London: Routledge, 2012), pp. 223–31 <https://doi.org/10.4324/9780203806494>

Heaney, Seamus, *District and Circle* (London: Faber, 2006)

Heath, Stephen, 'The Politics of Genre', in *Debating World Literature*, ed. by Christopher Prendergast (London: Verso, 2004), pp. 163–74

Helgesson, Stefan, 'Clarice Lispector, J. M. Coetzee and the Seriality of Translation', *Translation Studies*, 3 (2010), pp. 318–33 <https://doi.org/10.1080/14781700.2010.496929>

—— 'Translation and the Circuits of World Literature', in *The Cambridge Companion to World Literature*, ed. by Ben Etherington and Jarad Zimbler (Cambridge: Cambridge

University Press, 2018), pp. 85–99 <https://doi.org/10.1017/9781108613354.007>

Heller-Roazen, Daniel, *Dark Tongues: The Art of Rogues and Riddlers* (New York: Zone Books, 2013)

Herd, David, and Anna Pincus, eds, *Refugee Tales* (London: Comma Press, 2016)

—— eds, *Refugee Tales II* (London: Comma Press, 2017)

Hesse, Barnor, 'White Sovereignty (…), Black Life Politics: The N****r They Couldn't Kill', *The South Atlantic* Quarterly, 116.3 (2017), pp. 581–604 <https://doi.org/10.1215/00382876-3961494>

Horace, *Odes and Epodes*, ed. and trans. by Niall Rudd (Cambridge, MA: Harvard University Press, 2004) <https://doi.org/10.4159/DLCL.horace-odes.2004>

Huehls, Mitchum, *After Critique: Twenty-First Century Fiction in a Neoliberal Age* (Oxford: Oxford University Press, 2016) <https://doi.org/10.1093/acprof:oso/9780190456221.001.0001>

Huggan, Graham, *Interdisciplinary Measures: Literature and the Future of Postcolonial Studies* (Liverpool: Liverpool University Press, 2008) <https://doi.org/10.5949/UPO9781846313332>

Ives, Peter, *Gramsci's Politics of Language: Engaging the Bakhtin Circle and the Frankfurt School* (Toronto: University of Toronto Press, 2004) <https://doi.org/10.3138/9781442675490>

Jameson, Fredric, *Allegory and Ideology* (London: Verso, 2019)

—— *The Cultural Turn: Selected Writings on the Postmodern, 1983–1998* (London: Verso, 1998)

—— *The Political Unconscious: Narrative as a Socially Symbolic Act* (London: Methuen, 1982)

—— 'Third-World Literature in the Era of Multinational Capitalism', *Social Text*, 15 (Autumn, 1986), pp. 65–88

Joubert, Marlise, ed., *In a Burning Sea* (Pretoria: Protea House, 2014)

Judy, Ronald A., *Sentient Flesh: Thinking in Disorder, Poiesis in Black* (Durham, NC: Duke University Press, 2020) <https://doi.org/10.1215/9781478012559>

Jullien, François, *Entrer dans une pensée ou Des possibles de l'esprit* (Paris: Gallimard, 2012)

Kadir, Djelal, 'Comparative Literature in an Age of Terrorism', in *Comparative Literature in an Age of Globalization*, ed. by Haun Saussy (Baltimore, MD: Johns Hopkins University Press, 2006), pp. 68–77

Kamfer, Ronelda, *Hammie* (Cape Town: Kwela Books, 2016)

—— *Noudat slapende honed* (Cape Town: Kwela Books, 2008)

Kliger, Ilya, 'World Literature Beyond Hegemony in Yuri M. Lotman's Cultural Semiotics', *Comparative Critical Studies*, 7.2–3 (2010), pp. 257–74 <https://doi.org/10.3366/ccs.2010.0010>

Kohli, Suresh, and Nissim Ezekiel, 'Suresh Kohli Interviews Nissim Ezekiel: A Search for Limits', *Mahfil*, 8.4 (1972), pp. 7–10

Kohli, Suresh, and Pritish Nandy, 'Suresh Kohli Interviews Pritish Nandy: Tradition and the Individual Talent', *Mahfil*, 8.4 (1972), pp. 11–15

Latour, Bruno, *The Pasteurization of France*, trans. by Alan Sheridan and John Law, (Cambridge, MA: Harvard University Press, 1993)

—— *Reassembling the Social: An Introduction to Actor-Network Theory* (Oxford: Oxford University Press, 2007)

—— *We Have Never Been Modern*, trans. by Catherine Porter (Cambridge, MA: Harvard University Press, 1993)

Lazarus, Neil, *The Postcolonial Unconscious* (Cambridge: Cambridge University Press, 2011)

Lefevere, André, 'Composing the Other', in *Postcolonial Translation: Theory and Practice*, ed. by Susan Bassnett and Harish Trivedi (London: Routledge, 1999), pp. 79–94

—— 'Literary Theory and Translated Literature', *Dispositio*, 7.19/21 (1982), pp. 3–22

Lennon, Brian, *In Babel's Shadow: Multilingual Literatures, Monolingual States* (Minneapolis: University of Minnesota Press, 2010) <https://doi.org/10.5749/minnesota/9780816665013.001.0001>

Leonardi, Lino, ed., *I canzonieri della lirica italiana delle origini*, 4 vols (Florence: SISMEL-Edizioni del Galluzzo, 2000), I: *Il Canzoniere Vaticano*

Lotman, Yuri M., *Universe of the Mind: A Semiotic Theory of Culture*, trans. by Ann Shukman (Bloomington: Indiana University Press, 2000)

Louis, Prakash, 'Marginalisation of Tribals', *Economic and Political Weekly*, 35.47 (2000), pp. 4087–91

Lucretius, *On the Nature of Things*, trans., with introduction and notes by Martin Ferguson Smith (Indianapolis, IN: Hackett Publishing Company, 2001)

Luxemburg, Rosa, *The Accumulation of Capital*, trans. by Agnes Schwarzschild (London: Routledge and Kegan Paul Ltd, 1951)

Martinez-Alier, Joan, *The Environmentalism of the Poor: A Study of Ecological Conflicts and Valuation* (Cheltenham: Edward Elgar, 2003)

Maslov, Boris, 'Lyric Universality', in *The Cambridge Companion to World Literature*, ed. by Ben Etherington and Jarad Zimbler (Cambridge: Cambridge University Press, 2018), pp. 133–48 <https://doi.org/10.1017/9781108613354.010>

Mbembe, Achille, *Critique of Black Reason*, trans. by Laurent Dubois (Durham, NC: Duke University Press, 2017)

McDonald, Peter, *Artefacts of Writing: Ideas of the State and Communities of Letters from Matthew Arnold to Xu Bing* (Oxford: Oxford University Press, 2017) <https://doi.org/10.1093/oso/9780198725152.001.0001>

Mehrotra, Arvind Krishna, 'Arvind Krishna Mehrotra on his Translations of Kabir's Songs', online video recording of his interview with Souradeep Roy of *Guftugu Journal*, YouTube, 13 September 2018 <https://www.youtube.com/watch?v=y2FdL4OSgnY> [accessed 19 June 2020]

—— *Bharatmata: A Prayer* (Bombay: ezra-fakir press, 1966)

—— Editorial Note, *ezra: an imagiste magazine*, 1 (1967)

—— 'Introduction', in *A History of Indian Literature in English*, ed. by Arvind Krishna Mehrotra (New York: Columbia University Press, 2003), pp. 1–26

—— 'Recastings from Kabir', *Vrishchik*, 1.11–12 (1970), pp. 4–6

—— *Songs of Kabir* (New York: New York Review of Books, 2011)

—— 'statement', *damn you: a magazine of the arts*, 6 (1968), np

—— ed., *ezra: a magazine of neo imagiste poetry*, 3 (1968)

Mesthrie, Rajend, ed., *Language in South Africa* (Cambridge: Cambridge University Press, 2002) <https://doi.org/10.1017/CBO9780511486692>

Moretti, Franco, *Distant Reading* (London: Verso, 2013)

—— *Modern Epic: The World-System from Goethe to García Márquez* (London: Verso, 1996)
—— *The Way of the World: The Bildungsroman in European Culture* (London: Verso, 2000)
Moten, Fred, 'Nobody, Everybody', in *Black and Blur* (Durham, NC: Duke University Press, 2017), pp. 168–69 <https://doi.org/10.1215/9780822372226-012>
Mufti, Aamir R., *Forget English! Orientalisms and World Literatures* (Cambridge, MA: Harvard University Press, 2016) <https://doi.org/10.4159/9780674915404>
—— 'Orientalism and the Institution of World Literature', *Critical Inquiry*, 36 (2010), pp. 458–98 <https://doi.org/10.1086/653408>
Murray, David, 'Telling the Difference: Linguistic Differentiation and Identity in Guillem de Berguedà, Giacomo da Lentini and Bonifacio Calvo', *Zeitschrift für romanische Philologie*, 134.2 (2018), pp. 381–403 <https://doi.org/10.1515/zrp-2018-0024>
New York Review of Books, 'Arvind Krishna Mehrotra, *Selected Poems and Translations*', website page <https://www.nyrb.com/products/arvind-krishna-mehrotra> [accessed 8 November 2019]
Nietzsche, Friedrich, *The Anti-Christ, Ecce Homo, Twilight of the Idols, and Other Writings*, ed. by Aaron Ridly and Judith Norman (Cambridge: Cambridge University Press, 2005)
Nixon, Rob, *Slow Violence and the Environmentalism of the Poor* (Cambridge, MA: Harvard University Press, 2013)
Noudelmann, François, *Les Airs de famille. Une philosophie des affinités* (Paris: Gallimard, 2012)
'Othe [sic] Groups', *Waste Paper: A Hungry Generation Newsletter*, 1 (1967), p. 5
Ogborn, Miles, *The Freedom of Speech: Talk and Slavery in the Anglo-Caribbean World* (Chicago: University of Chicago Press, 2019) <https://doi.org/10.7208/chicago/9780226657714.001.0001>
Okoth, Christine, 'Extraction and Race, Then and Now: Ecology and the Literary Form of the Contemporary Black Atlantic', forthcoming in a special issue of *Textual Practice*
Ostler, Rosemarie, *Dewdroppers, Waldos, and Slackers: A Decade-by-Decade Guide to the Vanishing Vocabulary of the Twentieth Century* (Oxford: Oxford University Press, 2003)

Parry, Benita, *Postcolonial Studies: A Materialist Critique* (London: Routledge, 2004) <https://doi.org/10.4324/9780203420539>

Picone, Michelangelo, 'Aspetti della tradizione/traduzione nei poeti siciliani', in *Percorsi della lirica duecentesca. Dai siciliani alla 'Vita nova'* (Fiesole: Cadmo, 2003), pp. 17–31

Pinto, Jerry, 'Key Document: Eight Books, Seven Poets, One Clearing House', *Journal of Postcolonial Writing*, 53.1–2 (2017), pp. 233–46 <https://doi.org/10.1080/17449855.2017.1298507>

Pippin, Robert, 'What Does J. M. Coetzee's Novel *The Childhood of Jesus* Have to Do with the Childhood of Jesus?', in *J. M. Coetzee's 'The Childhood of Jesus': The Ethics of Ideas and Things*, ed. by Anthony Uhlmann and Jennifer Rutherford (London: Bloomsbury, 2017), pp. 9–32

Pollock, Sheldon, *The Language of the Gods in the World of Men: Sanskrit, Culture, and Power in Premodern India* (Berkeley and Los Angeles: University of California Press, 2009)

Puchner, Martin, *The Language of Thieves: My Family's Obsession with a Secret Code the Nazis Tried to Eliminate* (New York: Norton, 2020)

—— *The Written World: The Power of Stories to Shape People, History, and Civilization* (New York: Random House, 2017)

Puttnaik, Sudhir, 'Tribal Rights and Big Capital', in *Adivasi Rights and Exclusion in India*, ed. by V. Srinivasa Rao (Delhi: Routledge India, 2019), pp. 142–52

Ramazani, Jahan, *Poetry and its Others: News, Prayer, Song, and the Dialogue of Genres* (Chicago: University of Chicago Press, 2014) <https://doi.org/10.7208/chicago/9780226083421.001.0001>

—— *A Transnational Poetics* (Chicago: University of Chicago Press, 2009) <https://doi.org/10.7208/chicago/9780226703374.001.0001>

Rancière, Jacques, *Disagreement: Politics and Philosophy*, trans. by Julie Rose (Minneapolis: University of Minnesota Press, 1999)

—— *Dissensus: On Politics and Aesthetics*, trans. by Steven Corcoran (London: Continuum, 2010)

—— *On the Shores of Politics*, trans. by Liz Heron (London: Verso, 2007)

—— *The Politics of Aesthetics: The Distribution of the Sensible*, trans. with an introduction by Gabriel Rockhill, afterword by Slavoj Žižek (London: Continuum, 2004)

—— 'Ten Theses on Politics', trans. by Rachel Bowlby and Davide Panagia, *Theory & Event*, 5.3 (2001) <https://doi.org/10.1353/tae.2001.0028>

Reiser, Marius, *Bibelkritik und Auslegung der Heiligen Schrift: Beiträge zur Geschichte der biblischen Exegese und Hermeneutik* (Tübingen: Mohr Siebeck, 2007)

Rilke, Rainer Maria, *Werke*, ed. by Manfred Engel, Ulrich Fülleborn, Horst Nalewski, and August Stahl, 4 vols (Frankfurt a.M.: Insel, 1996), II: *Gedichte 1910 bis 1926*, ed. by Manfred Engel and Ulrich Fülleborn

Robbins, Bruce, 'Uses of World Literature', in *The Routledge Companion to World Literature*, ed. by Theo D'haen, David Damrosch, and Djelal Kadir (London: Routledge, 2012), pp. 383–92 <https://doi.org/10.4324/9780203806494>

Rushdie, Salman, 'Imaginary Homelands', *London Review of Books*, 4.18 (7 October 1982) <https://www.lrb.co.uk/the-paper/v04/n18/salman-rushdie/imaginary-homelands> [accessed 10 September 2020]

Said, Edward, *Reflections on Exile, and Other Literary and Cultural Essays* (London: Granta, 2001)

—— *The World, the Text, and the Critic* (Cambridge, MA: Harvard University Press, 1983)

Sakai, Noaki, 'How Do We Count a Language? Translation and Discontinuity', *Translation Studies*, 2 (2009), pp. 71–88 <https://doi.org/10.1080/14781700802496266>

Saucier, P. Khalil, and Tryon P. Woods, eds, *Conceptual Aphasia in Black: Displacing Racial Formation*, ed. by (Lenham: Lexington Books, 2016)

Scott, Clive, *Literary Translation and the Rediscovery of Reading* (Cambridge: Cambridge University Press, 2012)

—— *Translating the Perception of Text: Translation and Phenomenology* (Oxford: Legenda, 2012)

—— *The Work of Literary Translation* (Cambridge: Cambridge University Press, 2018) <https://doi.org/10.1017/9781108678162>

Shankar, S., 'Literatures of the World: An Inquiry', *PMLA*, 131.5 (2016), pp. 1405–13 <https://doi.org/10.1632/pmla.2016.131.5.1405>

Sharpe, Christina, *In the Wake: On Blackness and Being* (Durham, NC: Duke University Press, 2016) <https://doi.org/10.1215/9780822373452>

Shekhar, Hansda Sowvendra, *The Adivasi Will Not Dance* (New Delhi: Speaking Tiger, 2015)

Small, Adam, *Kitaar my Kruis* (Cape Town: Hollandsche Afrikaansche Uitgewers Maatschappij, 1973)

Smirnoff, Nicolay, 'Left-Wing Eurasianism and Postcolonial Theory', *e-flux journal*, 97 (2019) <https://www.e-flux.com/journal/97/252238/left-wing-eurasianism-and-postcolonial-theory/> [accessed 10 September 2020]

Smith, Ali, 'The Detainee's Tale as told to Ali Smith', in *Refugee Tales*, ed. by David Herd and Anna Pincus (London: Comma Press, 2016), pp. 49–62

—— 'Welcome from Ali Smith' <http://refugeetales.org> [accessed 22 September 2019]

Spivak, Gayatri Chakravorty, *A Critique of Postcolonial Reason: Toward a History of the Vanishing Present* (Cambridge, MA: Harvard University Press, 1999)

—— 'Can the Subaltern Speak?', in *Can the Subaltern Speak? Reflections on the History of an Idea*, ed. by Rosalind C. Morris (New York: Columbia University Press, 2010), pp. 21–78

—— *Death of a Discipline* (New York: Columbia University Press, 2003)

—— *Other Asias* (Oxford: Blackwell, 2008)

—— 'Terror: A Speech After 9-11', *boundary2*, 31.2 (2004), pp. 82–111 <https://doi.org/10.1215/01903659-31-2-81>

—— 'Translator's Foreword', in Mahasweta Devi, *Breast Stories: Draupadi, Breast-Giver, Choli ke Pichhe*, trans. and intro. by Gayatri Chakravorty Spivak (Calcutta: Seagull Books, 1997)

Staten, Henry, *Techne Theory: A New Language for Art* (London: Bloomsbury, 2019) <https://doi.org/10.5040/9781350101371>

Steiner, George, *After Babel: Aspects of Language and Translation*, 3rd edn (Oxford: Oxford University Press, 1998)

Stoler, Ann Laura, *Along the Archival Grain: Epistemic Anxieties and Colonial Common Sense* (Princeton, NJ: Princeton University Press, 2010)

Tagore, Rabindranath, *One Hundred Poems of Kabir* (London: Macmillan, 1915)

Thomsen, Mads Rosendahl, *Mapping World Literature: International Canonization and Transnational Literatures* (London: Continuum, 2008)

Thorne, Christian, 'The Sea Is Not a Place: or, Putting the World Back into World Literature', *boundary2*, 40.2 (2013), pp. 53–79 <https://doi.org/10.1215/01903659-2151803>

Tiffany, Daniel, *Infidel Poetics: Riddles, Nightlife, Substance* (Chicago: Chicago University Press, 2009) <https://doi.org/10.7208/chicago/9780226803111.001.0001>

—— 'Lyric Poetry and Poetics', in *Oxford Research Encyclopedia of Literature*, 30 April 2020, Oxford University Press <https://doi.org/10.1093/acrefore/9780190201098.013.1111>

—— *My Silver Planet: A Secret History of Poetry and Kitsch* (Baltimore: Johns Hopkins University Press, 2014)

Trantraal, Nathan, *Alles het niet kom wôd* (Cape Town: Kwela Books, 2017)

—— *Chokers en survivors* (Cape Town: Kwela Books, 2013)

—— *Oolog* (Cape Town: Kwela Books, 2020)

—— *Wit issie 'n colour nie* (Cape Town: Kwela Books, 2018)

Van Heerden, Menán, 'Afrikaans: The Language of Black and Coloured Dissent', *South African History Online* <https://www.sahistory.org.za/article/afrikaans-language-black-and-coloured-dissent> [accessed 27 August 2019]

Van Niekerk, Marlene, *Die Kortstondige raklewe van Anastasia W* (TEATERteater, 2010)

Varma, Rashmi, 'Beyond the Politics of Representation', in *New Subaltern Politics: Reconceptualising Hegemony and Resistance in Contemporary India*, ed. by Srila Roy and Alf Nilsen (Delhi: Oxford University Press, 2015)

—— 'Primitive Accumulation: The Political Economy of Indigenous Art in Postcolonial India', *Third Text*, 27.6 (2013), pp. 748–61

Vaudeville, Charlotte, 'Sant Mat: Santism as the Universal Path to Sanctity', in *The Sants: Studies in a Devotional Tradition*, ed. by Karine Schomer and W. H. McLeod (Delhi: Motilal Banarsidass, 1987), pp. 21–40

Venuti, Lawrence, *Theses on Translation: An Organon for the Current Moment*, FlugSchriften, 5 (Pittsburgh, PA: Flugschriften, 2019) <https://flugschriften.com/2019/09/15/thesis-on-translation/> [accessed 10 September 2020]

—— *The Translator's Invisibility: A History of Translation* (London: Routledge, 2008)

Walkowitz, Rebecca L., *Born Translated: The Contemporary Novel in an Age of World Literature* (New York: Columbia University Press, 2015) <https://doi.org/10.7312/walk16594>

Warwick Research Collective (WReC), *Combined and Uneven Development: Towards a New Theory of World-Literature* (Liverpool: Liverpool University Press, 2015)

Waters, William, *Poetry's Touch: On Lyric Address* (Ithaca: Cornell University Press, 2003) <https://doi.org/10.7591/9781501717062>

Weber, Samuel, *Benjamin's -abilities* (Cambridge, MA: Harvard University Press, 2008)

—— 'A Touch of Translation: On Walter Benjamin's "Task of the Translator"', in *Nation, Language, and the Ethics of Translation*, ed. by Sandra Bermann and Michael Wood (Princeton, NJ: Princeton University Press, 2005), pp. 65–78 <https://doi.org/10.1515/9781400826681.65>

White, Tom, 'Lives Suspended: An Essay on "Refugee Tales" and "Refugee Tales II", ed. by David Herd and Anna Pincus', *Glasgow Review of Books* (21 September 2017) <https://glasgowreviewofbooks.com/2017/09/21/lives-suspended-an-essay-on-refugee-tales-and-refugee-tales-ii-edited-by-david-herd-and-anna-pincus/> [accessed 22 September 2019]

Xaxa, Virginius, 'Isolation, Inclusion and Exclusion: The Case of Adivasis in India', *Adivasi Rights and Exclusion in India*, ed. by V. Srinivasa Rao (Delhi: Routledge India, 2019), pp. 27–40

Young, Robert J. C., 'That Which Is Casually Called a Language', *PMLA*, 131.5 (2016), pp. 1207–21 <https://doi.org/10.1632/pmla.2016.131.5.1207>

—— 'World Literature and Postcolonialism', in *The Routledge Companion to World Literature*, ed. by Theo D'haen, David

Damrosch, and Djelal Kadir (London: Routledge, 2012), pp. 213–22 <https://doi.org/10.4324/9780203806494>
Zecchini, Laetitia, *Arun Kolatkar and Literary Modernism in India: Moving Lines* (London: Bloomsbury, 2014)
—— '"We Were Like Cartographers, Mapping the City": An Interview with Arvind Krishna Mehrotra', *Journal of Postcolonial Writing*, 52.1–2 (2017), pp. 190–206

Notes on the Contributors

Emily Apter is Julius Silver Professor of French and Comparative Literature at New York University. Her books include: *The Translation Zone: A New Comparative Literature* (2006), *Against World Literature: On The Politics of Untranslatability* (2013), and *Unexceptional Politics: On Obstruction, Impasse, and the Impolitic* (2018). Apter is co-editor with Jacques Lezra and Michael Wood of the 2014 English edition of the *Vocabulaire européen des philosophies: Dictionnaire des intraduisibles*, edited by Barbara Cassin, and editor of the book series Translation/Transnation from Princeton University Press.

Derek Attridge is Emeritus Professor in the Department of English and Related Literatures at the University of York, UK. Among his books are *The Singularity of Literature* (2004; reissued 2017), *J. M. Coetzee and the Ethics of Reading* (2004), *The Work of Literature* (2015), and *The Experience of Poetry: From Homer's Listeners to Shakespeare's Readers* (2019). He co-edited *Writing South Africa: Literature, Apartheid, and Democracy 1970–1995* (1998), *Semicolonial Joyce* (2000), and *The Cambridge History of South African Literature* (2012).

Lorna Burns is Senior Lecturer in Postcolonial Literatures in the School of English at the University of St Andrews. Her most recent monograph is *Postcolonialism After World Literature: Relation, Equality, Dissent* (2019), and she is the author of *Contemporary Caribbean Writing and Deleuze: Literature between Postcolonialism and Post-continental Philosophy* (2012). She is co-editor of the collection *World Literature and Dissent* (2019), *Postcolonial Literatures and Deleuze* (2012), and a special issue of the *Journal of Postcolonial Writing* on the author Wilson Harris.

Francesco Giusti teaches Comparative Literature at Bard College Berlin. Previously he held fellowships at the University of York, the Goethe-Universität Frankfurt am Main, and the

ICI Berlin Institute for Cultural Inquiry. He has published two books devoted respectively to the ethics of mourning and to creative desire in lyric poetry, *Canzonieri in morte: Per un'etica poetica del lutto* (2015) and *Il desiderio della lirica: Poesia, creazione, conoscenza* (2016), and co-edited, with Christine Ott and Damiano Frasca, the volume *Poesia e nuovi media* (2018).

Benjamin Lewis Robinson is University Assistant in the Department of German at the University of Vienna. He is the author of *Bureaucratic Fanatics: Modern Literature and the Passions of Rationalization* (2019) and is currently engaged in a project on biopolitics and literature titled *States of Need / States of Emergency*. Ben is also preparing a book on J. M. Coetzee's fiction. 'Passions for Justice: Kleist's Michael Kohlhaas and Coetzee's Michael K' appeared in *Comparative Literature* (2018).

Rashmi Varma teaches postcolonial and world literature and transnational feminism at the University of Warwick. She is the author of *The Postcolonial City and its Subjects* (2011) and co-editor of *Marxism, Postcolonial Theory and the Future of Critique: Critical Reflections on Benita Parry* (2019). She is a member of the Warwick Research Collective (WReC) and a founding editorial collective member of the journal *Feminist Dissent*.

Dirk Wiemann is Professor of English Literature at the University of Potsdam. He is spokesperson of the DFG-funded research training group *Minor Cosmopolitanisms*. His research interests and publications range from postcolonial theory with a special focus on South Asia to theatre and politics in the English Republic and genre transformations in contemporary world literature. He is co-author of *Postcolonial Literatures in English: An Introduction* (2019).

Jarad Zimbler is Senior Lecturer at the University of Birmingham. He is author of *J. M. Coetzee and the Politics of Style* (2014), as well as editor of *The Cambridge Companion to J. M. Coetzee* (2020), and, with Ben Etherington, of *The Cambridge Companion to World Literature* (2018). His current research project, *Literary Communities and Literary Worlds*, addresses the nature of and relationship between literary community, literary labour and literary belonging.

Index

Cultural Inquiry

EDITED BY CHRISTOPH F. E. HOLZHEY
AND MANUELE GRAGNOLATI

VOL. 1 TENSION/SPANNUNG
Edited by Christoph F. E. Holzhey

VOL. 2 METAMORPHOSING DANTE
Appropriations, Manipulations, and Rewritings in the Twentieth and Twenty-First Centuries
Edited by Manuele Gragnolati, Fabio Camilletti, and Fabian Lampart

VOL. 3 PHANTASMATA
Techniken des Unheimlichen
Edited by Fabio Camilletti, Martin Doll, and Rupert Gaderer

VOL. 4 Boris Groys / Vittorio Hösle
DIE VERNUNFT AN DIE MACHT
Edited by Luca Di Blasi and Marc Jongen

VOL. 5 SARA FORTUNA
WITTGENSTEINS PHILOSOPHIE DES KIPPBILDS
Aspektwechsel, Ethik, Sprache

VOL. 6 THE SCANDAL OF SELF-CONTRADICTION
Pasolini's Multistable Subjectivities, Geographies, Traditions
Edited by Luca Di Blasi, Manuele Gragnolati, and Christoph F. E. Holzhey

VOL. 7 SITUIERTES WISSEN UND REGIONALE EPISTEMOLOGIE
Zur Aktualität Georges Canguilhems und Donna J. Haraways
Edited by Astrid Deuber-Mankowsky and Christoph F. E. Holzhey

Vol. 8 MULTISTABLE FIGURES
On the Critical Potentials of Ir/Reversible Aspect-Seeing
Edited by Christoph F. E. Holzhey

Vol. 9 Wendy Brown / Rainer Forst
THE POWER OF TOLERANCE
Edited by Luca Di Blasi and Christoph F. E. Holzhey

Vol. 10 DENKWEISEN DES SPIELS
Medienphilosophische Annäherungen
Edited by Astrid Deuber-Mankowsky and Reinhold Görling

Vol. 11 DE/CONSTITUTING WHOLES
Towards Partiality Without Parts
Edited by Manuele Gragnolati and Christoph F.E. Holzhey

Vol. 12 CONATUS UND LEBENSNOT
Schlüsselbegriffe der Medienanthropologie
Edited by Astrid Deuber-Mankowsky and Anna Tuschling

Vol. 13 AURA UND EXPERIMENT
Naturwissenschaft und Technik bei Walter Benjamin
Edited by Kyung-Ho Cha

Vol. 14 LUCA DI BLASI
DEZENTRIERUNGEN
Beiträge zur Religion der Philosophie im 20. Jahrhundert

Vol. 15 RE-
An Errant Glossary
Edited by Christoph F. E. Holzhey and Arnd Wedemeyer

Vol. 16 CLAUDE LEFORT
DANTE'S MODERNITY
An Introduction to the Monarchia

With an Essay by Judith Revel
Translated from the French by Jennifer Rushworth
Edited by Christiane Frey, Manuele Gragnolati, Christoph F. E. Holzhey, and Arnd Wedemeyer

Vol. 17 WEATHERING
Ecologies of Exposure
Edited by Christoph F. E. Holzhey and Arnd Wedemeyer

Vol. 18 MANUELE GRAGNOLATI AND FRANCESCA SOUTHERDEN
POSSIBILITIES OF LYRIC
Reading Petrarch in Dialogue

Vol. 19 THE WORK OF WORLD LITERATURE
Edited by Francesco Giusti and Benjamin Lewis Robinson

Vol. 20 MATERIALISM AND POLITICS
Edited by Bernardo Bianchi, Emilie Filion-Donato, Marlon Miguel, and Ayşe Yuva

Lightning Source UK Ltd.
Milton Keynes UK
UKHW022038060521
383282UK00009B/752/J

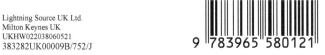